BLOOD WARS

100 Warrior Triptychs By Yoshitoshi

Publishing: Shinbaku
Date: 2020
Place: Gardena, CA
ISBN 978-1-84068-336-3
Editing: Ringo Yoshida
Editorial assistance: Kanako Wakamatsu @ Kobayashi Foundation
Japanese-English translation: Outer Rim Sensation, Osaka
Concept: Fabbrica Sodoma
Design: Fever Claw

BLOOD WARS

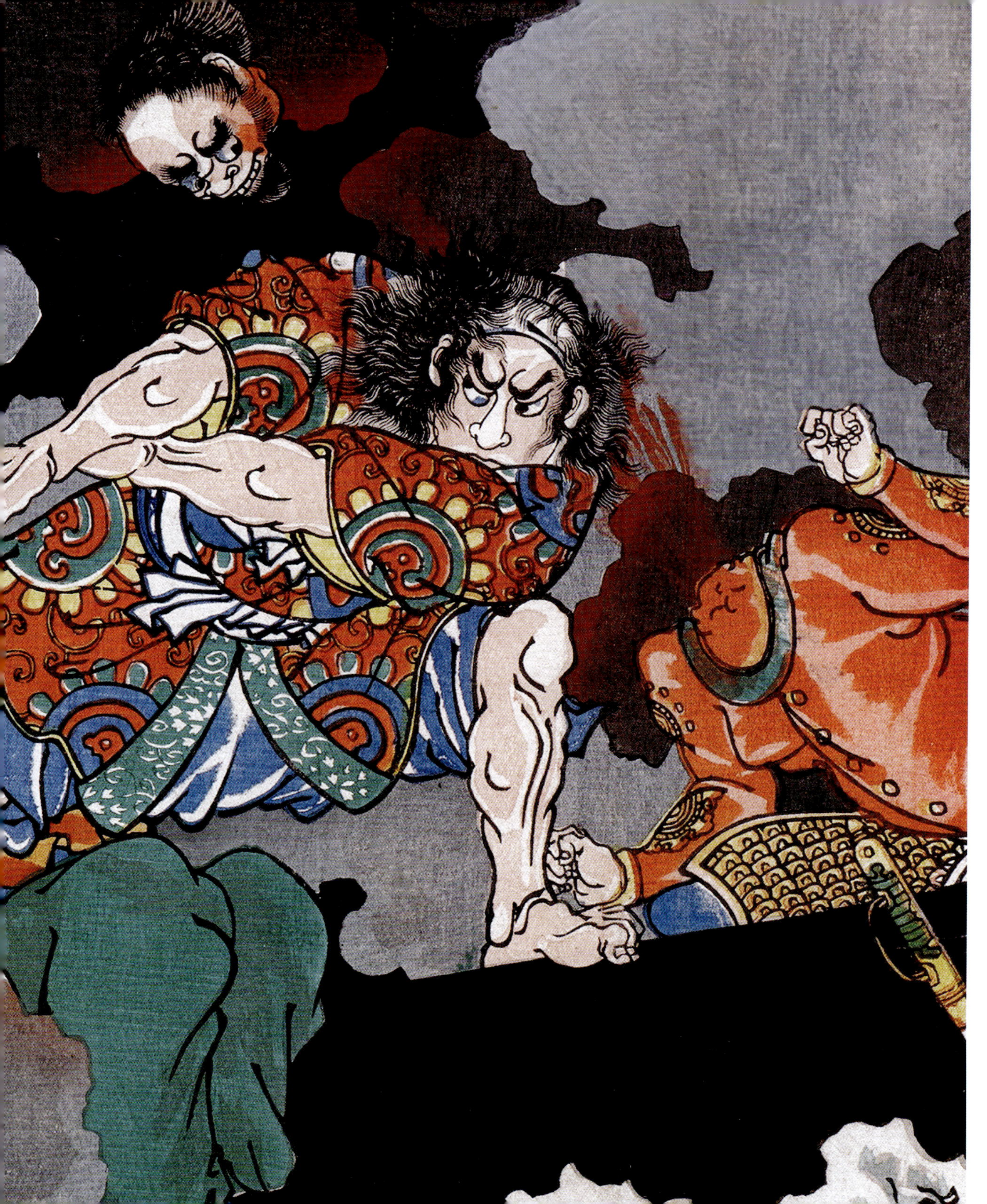

MASAKIYO SANKAN TAIJI
(1864)
Detail (full triptych – page 26).

Introduction

Ukiyo-e

"Pictures of the floating world." The floating world – a transient realm of pleasures, horrors, and dreams. *Ukiyo-e*, depictions of this shadowy projection of the human mind, formed the mainstay of Japanese paintings and woodblock prints produced between the 17th and 20th centuries.

Musha-e

"Pictures of warriors". This sub-division of *ukiyo-e* was dedicated to illustrating the heroic actions of *samurai* from Japan's martial history, in particular scenes from famous battles and scenes from popular mythology.

Yoshitoshi Tsukioka

Owariya Yonejiro was born in Edo, in 1839. He had an early interest in art, and at the age of eleven was apprenticed to the great *ukiyo-e* master, Kuniyoshi, who re-named him Yoshitoshi. His first published work came three years later, in 1853, when he was 14 or 15 years of age; **Bunji Gannen Heike No Ichimon Horobi Kaichu Ochiiru** ("In The First Year Of Bunji, The Heike Clan Plunged To Destruction In The Ocean"), published by Kasusaya Iwazu, is a classic *musha-e* subject – the suicide of Taira-no-Tomomori who, at the battle of Dan-no-Ura in 1185, tied himself to an anchor and descended to the ocean depths to join his drowned and defeated comrades, who we see hover there as bloody ghosts. Relatively few other prints by Yoshitoshi are known from this early period up to 1860, but a few of those – such as the triptychs **Ichiharano Kidomaru** ("Kidomaru On Ichihara Moor", 1859) or **Kusunoki Tamonmaru Kori Taiji** ("Kusunoki Tamonmaru Exterminates The Badger-Demon", 1860) – combine *musha-e* subjects with mythological elements, a mix which would reoccur in Yoshitoshi's output throughout the 1860s, a period when he identified himself as Yoshitoshi Tsukioka.

It was early in the decade when Yoshitoshi began to incoporate images of violence and decapitation into his work, as may be seen in his highly significant 1861 war triptych **Shizugamine Okassen** ("The Great Battle Of Shizugamine"), a depiction of *samurai* displaying the bloody severed heads of their enemies after battle (a design which boasts no fewer than twenty-one heads). Notable both for its subject matter and gruesome content, **Shizugamine Okassen** pointed the way forward for the artist, who would produce scores more dynamic and violent battle triptychs and portraits[1] during the course of the decade, underpinning a rise to popular status as his vivid *musha-e* quickly grabbed the public's imagination. The content of these works was invariably drawn from Japanese military history, mostly from the 12th to 16th centuries, although often imbued with an underlying layer of more

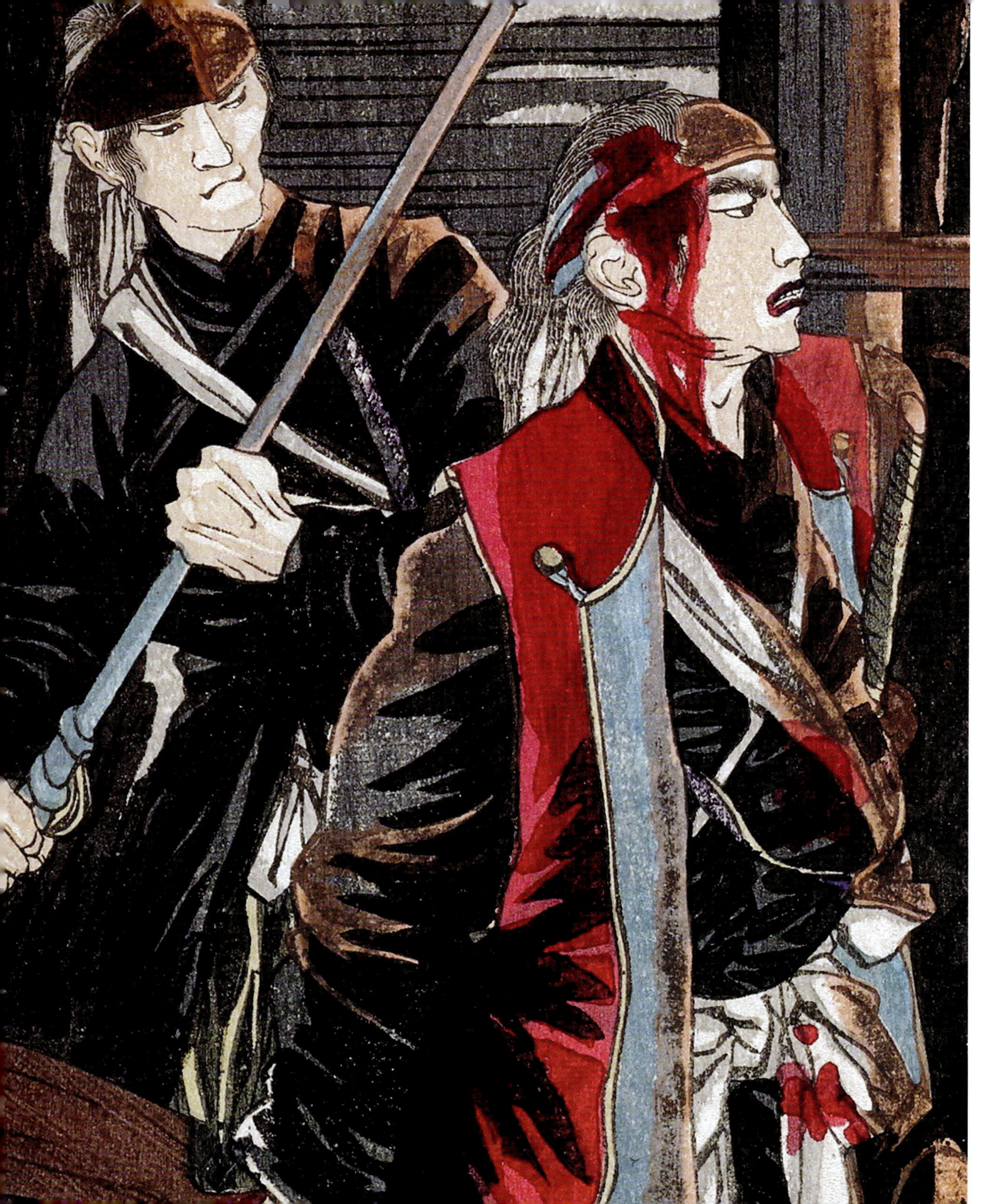

JOSHU FUSHIMI SHIMATOBA KASSEN
(1874)
Detail (full triptych – page 79).

contemporary meaning which could not be overtly expressed due to political censorship issues.

In 1868 Yoshitoshi was a first-hand witness to the Battle of Ueno, a desperately violent and gore-drenched Boshin War[2] showdown between the *Shogitai*, under Shibusawa Seiichirô and Amano Hachiro, and imperialist forces under the general command of Omura Masujiro, that brought death to many valiant *samurai*. Inspired and disturbed by this cataclysmic clash, Yoshitoshi at once set about producing a dynamic new *musha-e* portrait series, **Kaidai Hyaku Senso** ("100 Thrusting War Portraits"), that pulled no punches in glorifying heroic bloodshed, decapitation, and suicide by evisceration. His 1868 triptych **Zennojo Hadaka Seme** ("Zennojo's Unarmed Attack", 1868), featuring three warriors (one holding a severed head) was rendered in the same style as this series, and is his last great triple war image of the decade.

The period from 1869 to 1872 saw a marked decline in Yoshitoshi's output; this lack of commissions led to financial problems which, when combined with health and other personal issues, eventually led to the artist suffering some kind of mental and physical breakdown; by 1872 it looked as if Yoshitoshi's career might be prematurely at an end.

Yoshitoshi Taiso

And yet in 1873 Yoshitoshi miraculously returned, complete with the auspicious new appellation Taiso, meaning "great resurrection", and a new artistic vision. Now, Yoshitoshi's fascination with the ongoing civil strife in Japan during the birth throes of the Meiji period was given free reign, led him to document current events in a large series of triptychs and portrait sets, predominantly showcasing images of war.

A number of Yoshitoshi's war triptychs of the latter 1860s had seen him experiment with a new, flatter style, and he adopted this more journalistic format for both his *senso-e* ("war pictures") and news prints[3] of the early to mid-1870s. This signals the artist's first major stylistic move away from the tropes established by his tutor, the great Kuniyoshi, towards a more individual signature. Notable among Yoshitoshi's portrait series of modern events were **Keisei Suikoden** ("Biographies Of Valiant Outlaws", 1874) and **Meiyo Shindan** ("New Tales Of Honour", 1874); these, and his many striking and bloody triptychs of contemporary conflict, such as **Todai Sannozan Senso** ("Warfare At Sannozan-Todai", 1874), bear witness to the emergence of Yoshitoshi's own, definitive style, which was becoming increasingly painterly.

By 1877, Yoshitoshi's style had evolved to a new level – reputedly influenced by the painter Kikuchi Yosai – and a long series of stunning triptychs from that year documenting the Satsuma Rebellion point the way to his work in the following decade, including the incorporation of Western elements. Yoshitoshi was particularly interested in the figure of Saigo Takamori, a general in the Meiji restoration war who retired to Kagoshima with an army of some 15,000 rebels when his views clashed with those of the government. The ensuing battles at Kagoshima are documented by Yoshitoshi in a series of vivid triptychs, culminating in a phanstastic allegorical subject showing Takamori leading an oceanic attack on the legendary Dragon Palace.[4] In 1879, Yoshitoshi commenced work on the historical

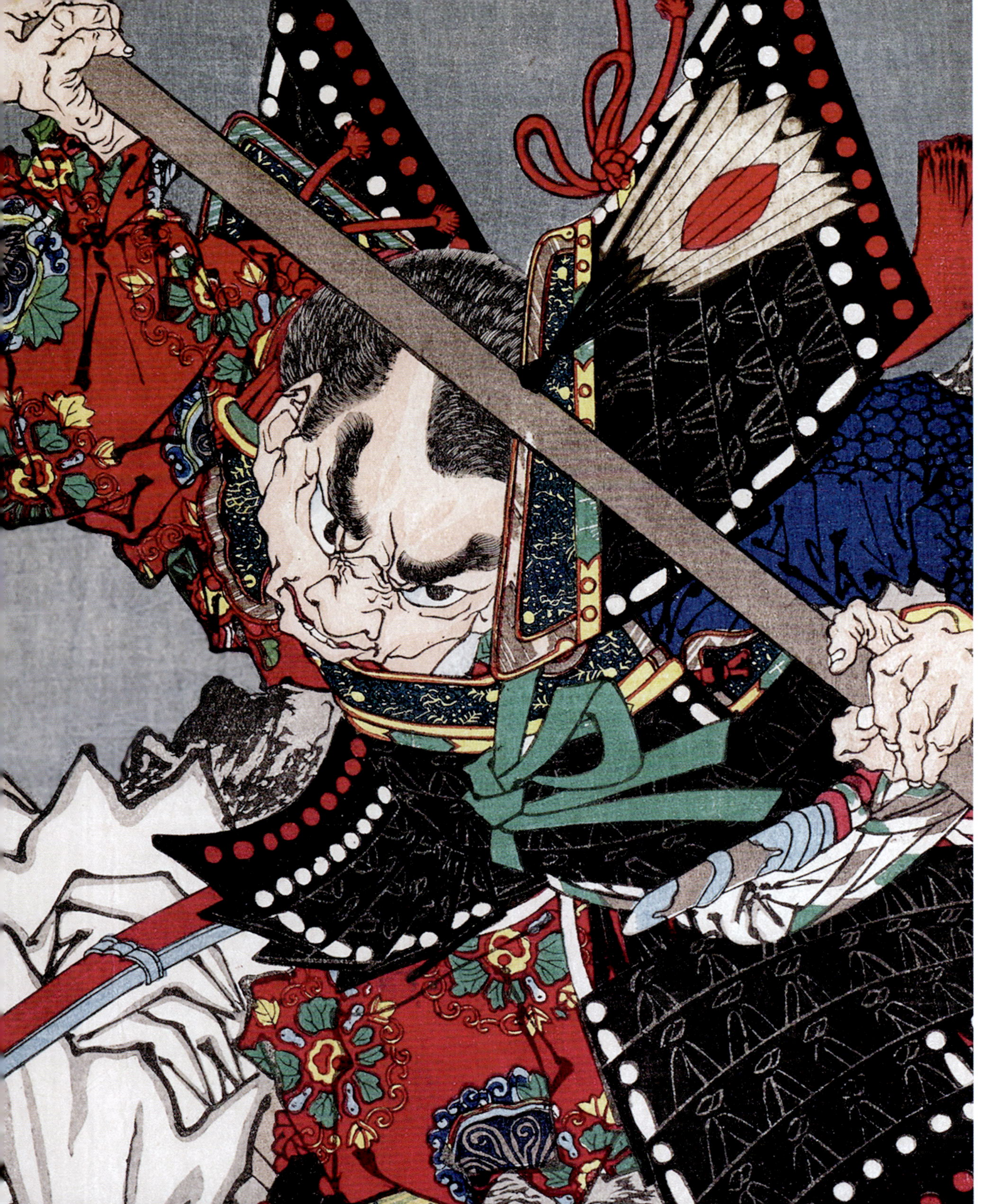

GIKEIKI GOJO-BASHI
(1881)
Detail (full triptych – page 101).

triptych series **Dai Nihon Shiryaku Zue** ("A Short Illustrated History Of Great Japan"), which he completed in 1880. Featuring figures ranging from the Shinto deity Ame no Uzume no Mikoto to Sutoku, the seventy-fifth emperor of the 12th century, this series indicated that Yoshitoshi was once again ready to engage with his country's great wealth of history, myth and legend.

Yoshitoshi produced several portrait print series which included *musha-e* subjects throughout the 1880s, the first being **Kokoku Nijushiko** ("24 Accomplishments Of Imperial Japan", 1881-87), which highlighted key incidents from Japanese history. His key *musha-e* portrait series of that decade was **Yoshitoshi Musha Burui** ("Yoshitoshi's Courageous Warriors"), which he began in 1883 and completed in 1886. His amount of triptych work significantly declined during this period, but includes a number of striking warrior illustrations which once more refer back to Japan's martial history of earlier centuries. Many of these are included in the present volume, completing a beautifully-crafted catalogue of carnage and heroism by one of the most renowned, revered, and revolutionary of all *ukiyo-e* artists.

In 1891 Yoshitoshi began to decline both mentally and physically; the following year he was dead from a cerebral haemorrhage, aged just fifty-three.

NOTES

1. Yoshitoshi's first *musha-e* portrait series of note was **Honcho Hyakuyu-Den** ("100 Brave Japanese Warriors", 1862), although it is unclear how many prints out of the proposed one hundred were actually completed. In 1865 he produced **Yumei Bujutsu No Homare** ("Brave Masters Of Warfare") and **Eimei Kumiuchi Zoroi** ("Famous Warriors In Combat"), a series of at least ten prints depicting historical one-on-one clashes. Other portrait series by Yoshitoshi from that decade which feature notable *musha-e* designs include **Azuma No Nishiki Ukiyo Kodan** "Tales From The Floating World On Eastern Brocade", 1867-68) and **Seichu Gishinden** ("Tales Of True Loyalty", 1868), one of several renderings by the artist of the 47 Ronin legend. But it was one portrait series in particular, drawn in collaboration with fellow *ukiyo-e* artist Ochiai Yoshiiku between 1866 and 1868, that would seal Yoshitoshi's immortal reputation in blood – **Eimei Nijuhasshuku** ("28 Famous Murders ").

2. The Boshin War was a ferocious civil war, fought from 1868 to 1869 between forces of the ruling Tokugawa shogunate and those seeking to return political power to the imperial court.

3. In 1875 Yoshitoshi started drawing news *nishiki-e* for the *Yubin Hochi Shinbun*, following in the footsteps of Yoshiiku. The garish illustrated broadsheets that featured news *nishiki-e* were highly popular between 1874 and 1877, before slowly waning until their eventual demise in the 1880s. Among the main imprints under which they appeared were the *Tokyo Nichinichi Shinbun*, the *Yubin Hochi Shinbun*, for which Yoshitoshi was main illustrator, and the *Osaka Nichinichi Shinbun*. These were the tabloids of their day, serving up picture-led bizarre or lurid stories for instant mass consumption. Bloody murder, suicide or accidental death was a staple feature of these publications. Yoshitoshi also did artwork for the *Kanayomi Shinbun* around 1879, and for the later *Yamato Shinbun* (1884-1886), and for its supplementary *Kinsei Jinbutsu Shi* ("Accounts Of Contemporary Personalities) series.

4. Takamori was killed in September 1877, but still featured in works by Yoshitoshi such as **Kagoshima Chintei Kubijikken** ("Identifying Severed Heads After The Suppression Of Kagoshima", 1877) and the haunting portrait **Saigo Takamori Rei Yumei Hosho** ("The Weird Ghost Of Saigo Takamori Bearing A Letter", 1878).

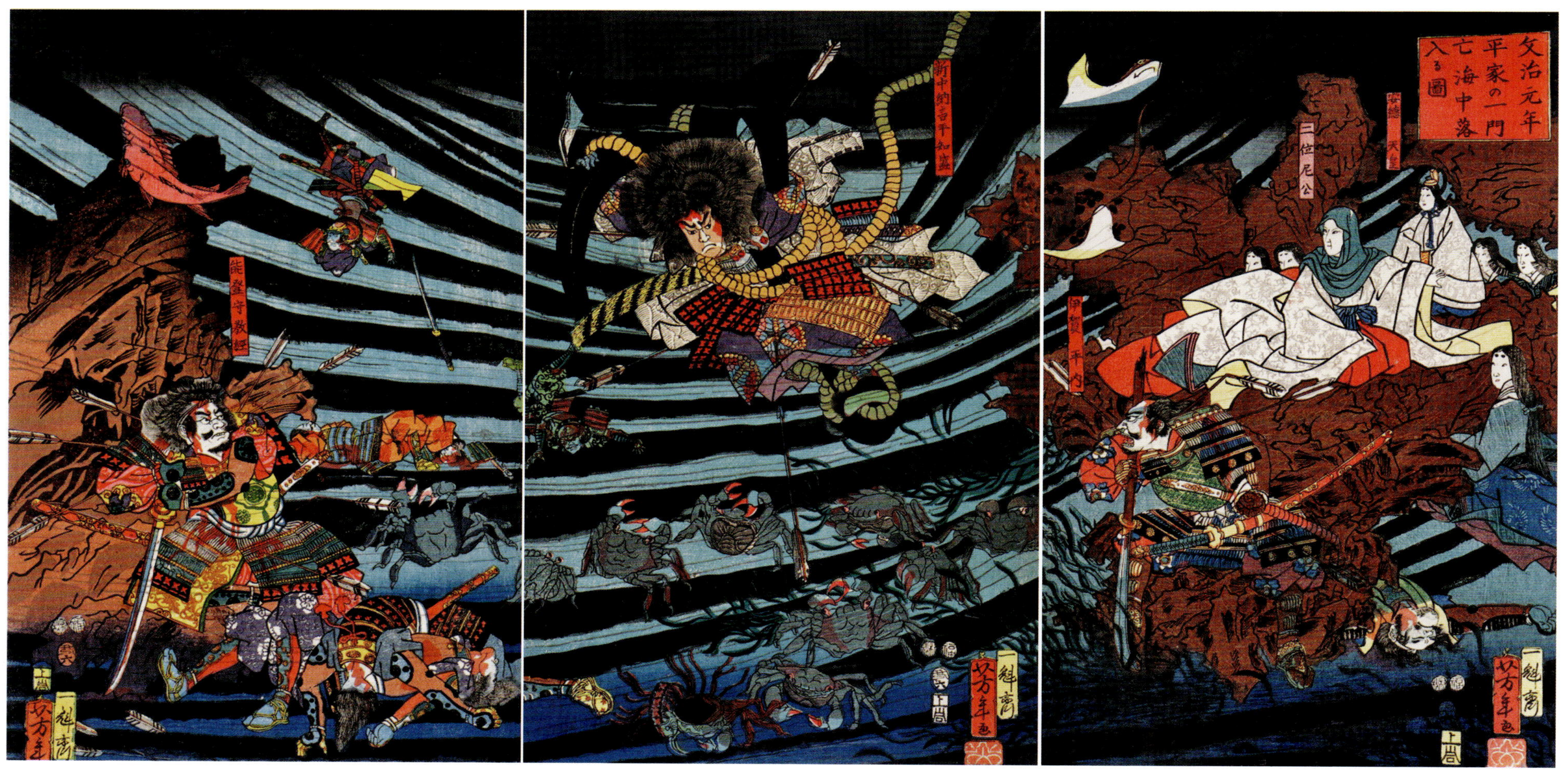

BUNJI GANNEN HEIKE NO ICHIMON HOROBI KAICHU NI OCHIIRU

"In The First Year Of Bunji, The Heike Clan Plunged To Destruction In The Ocean"; 1853
Yoshitoshi's first published print, a warrior triptych which audaciously reworks a mythological scene already depicted by Kuniyoshi in 1851. Following the battle of Dan-no-Ura, the corpse-ghosts of self-drowned Heike warriors are said to have possessed the huge crabs since known as *heikegani*. The central figure of the illustration is Heike commander Taira-no-Tomomori, who tied himself to a ship's anchor before plunging to his doom.

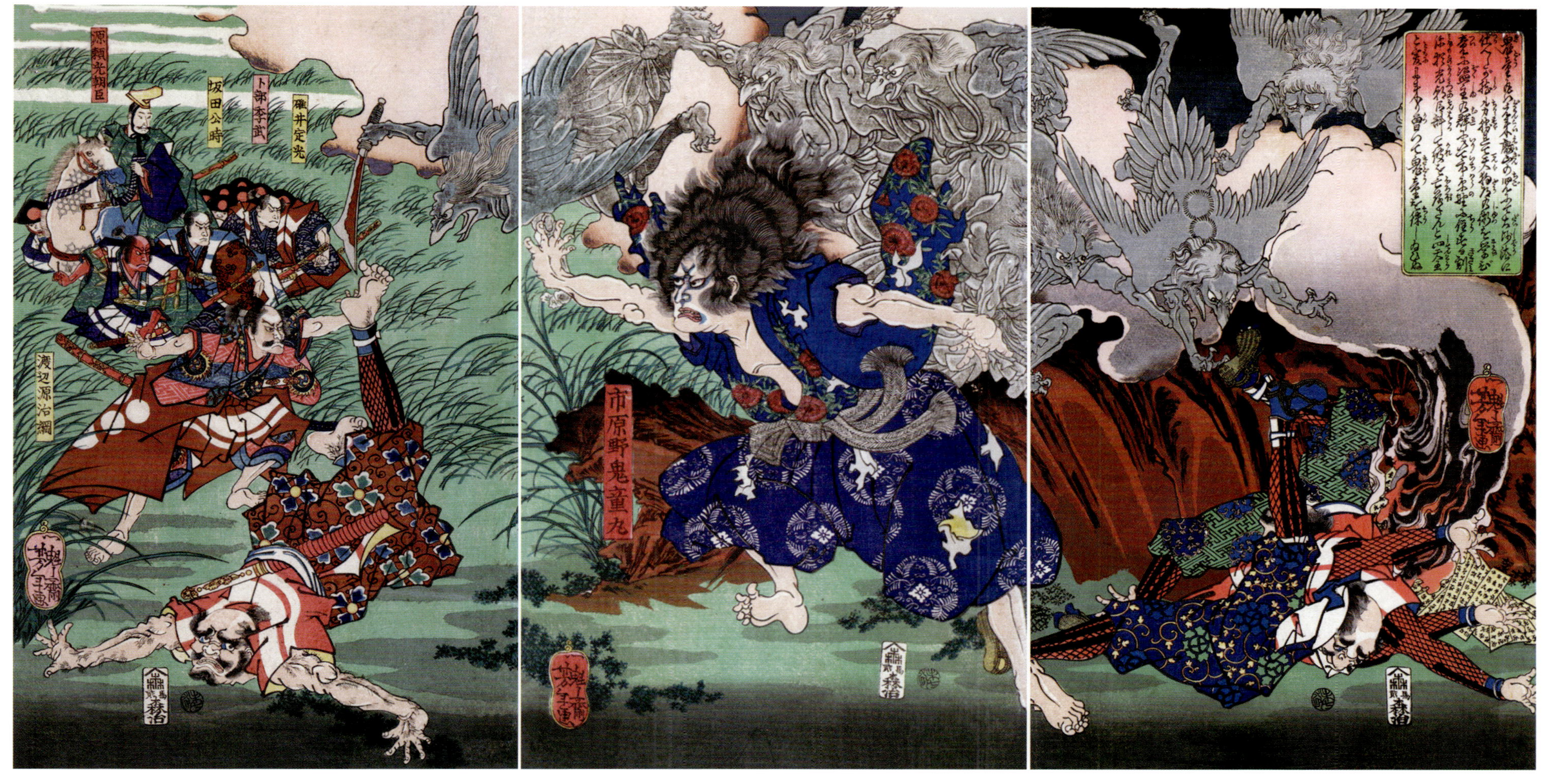

ICHIHARANO KIDOMARU

"Kidomaru On Ichihara Moor"; 1859

Kidomaru was a notorious 10th century bandit who preyed upon thsoe who wandered Ichihara moor; legend tells that he used black magic to ensnare his victims, which he was taught by *tengu* (winged mountain goblins, also shown in Yoshitoshi's illustration). Kidomaru was eventually overpowered and killed by the demon-hunter Raiko and his four knights of holy terror.

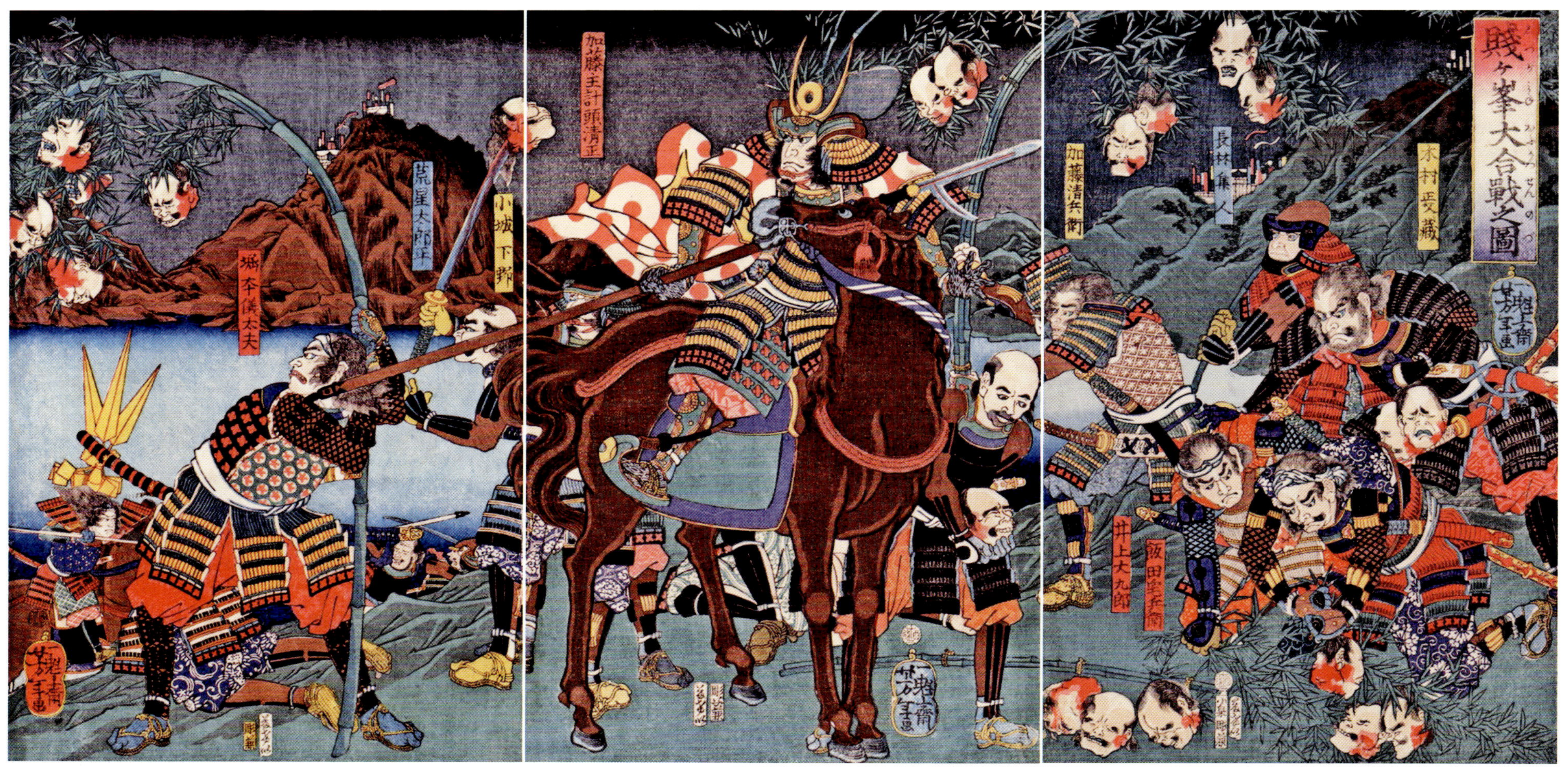

SHIZUGAMINE OKASSEN

"The Great Battle Of Shizugamine"; 1861

A scene from the battle of Shizugamine (Shizugatake) in 1583, where Toyotomi Hideyoshi defeated Shibata Katsuie during the long-running internecine conflicts of Japan's Sengoku period. The central figure of the triptych is most likely Kiyomasa Kato, one of the "Seven Spears" of Shizugatake. The bloody severed heads on display are an early indicator of Yoshitoshi's predilection for images of violence and carnage.

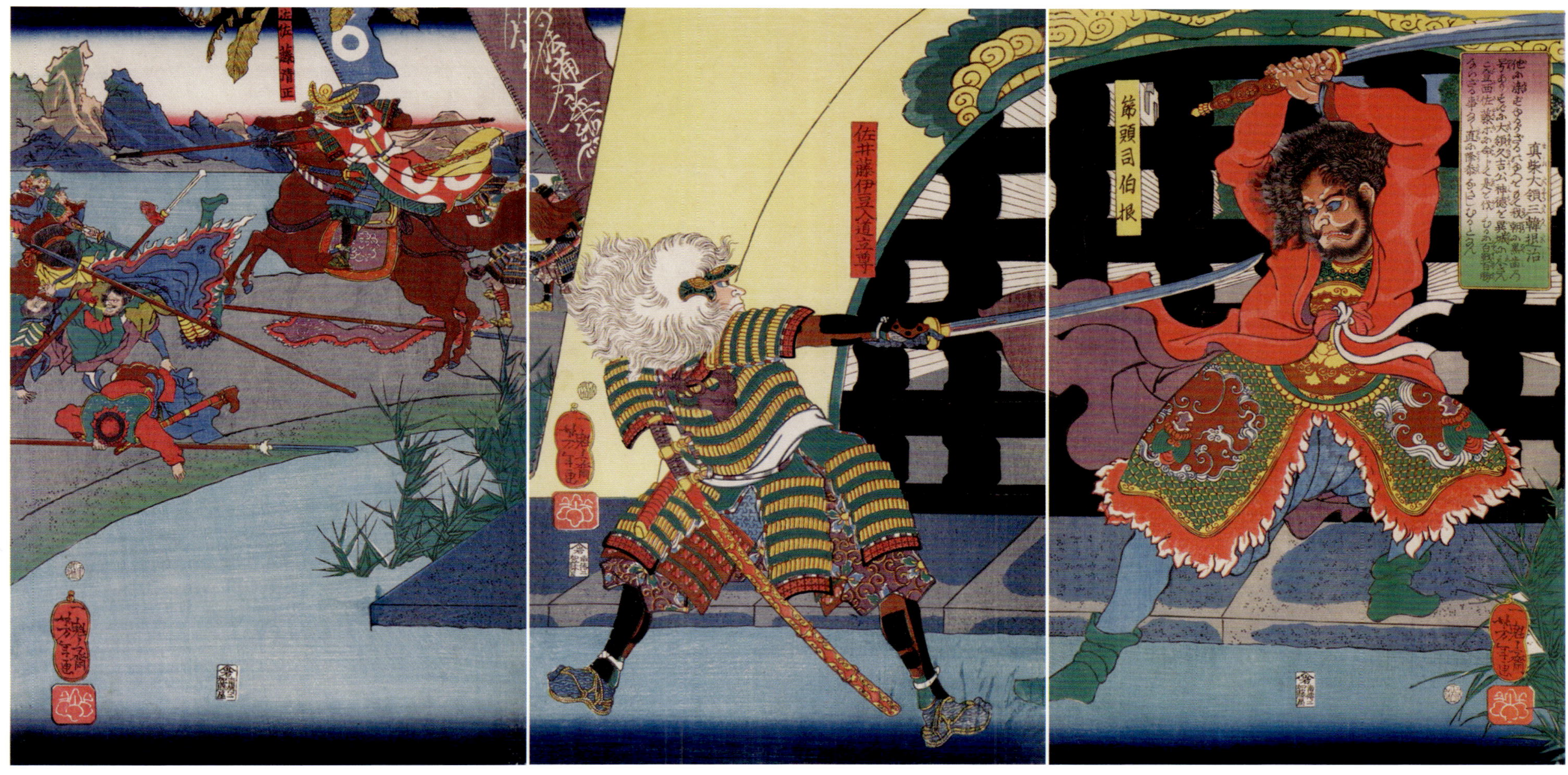

MASHIBA TAIRYO SANKAN TAIJI

"The Overlord Mashiba Exterminating Koreans"; 1862
This illustration refers to Japan's invasion of Korea in 1592 at the behest of the shogun Toyokomi Hideyoshi, formerly known as Hashiba. Japan's intent was to hack through Korea before invading China, but overwhelming resistance forced them to withdraw in 1598. Yoshitoshi's slight name-changing was due to an old Tokugawa law forbidding explicit depictions of the *shogun*.

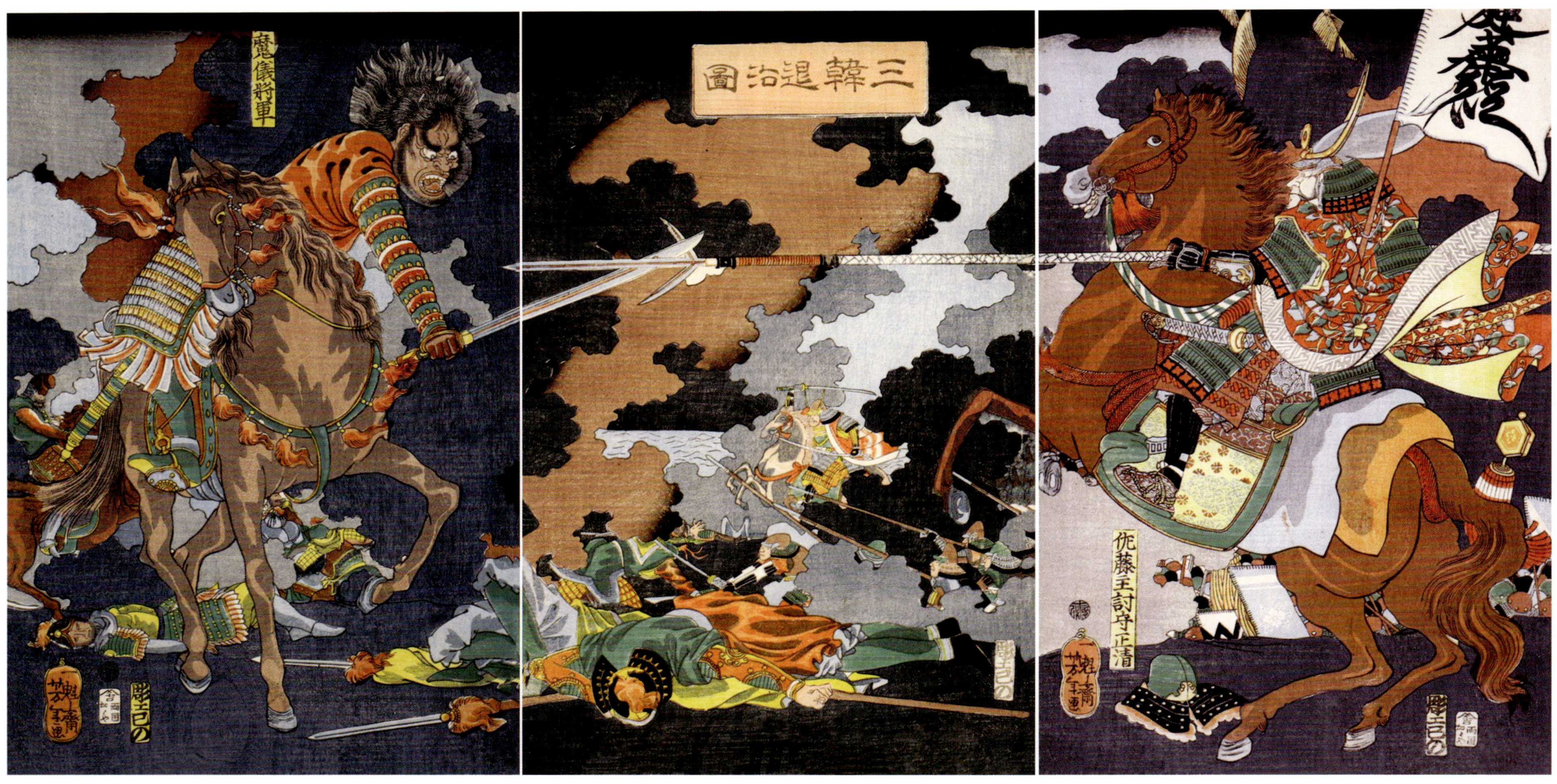

SANKAN TAIJI
"Exterminating Koreans"; 1863
Another depiction of Japan's 1592-98 invasions of Korea. As before, the Korean warrior is caricatured as a wild savage.

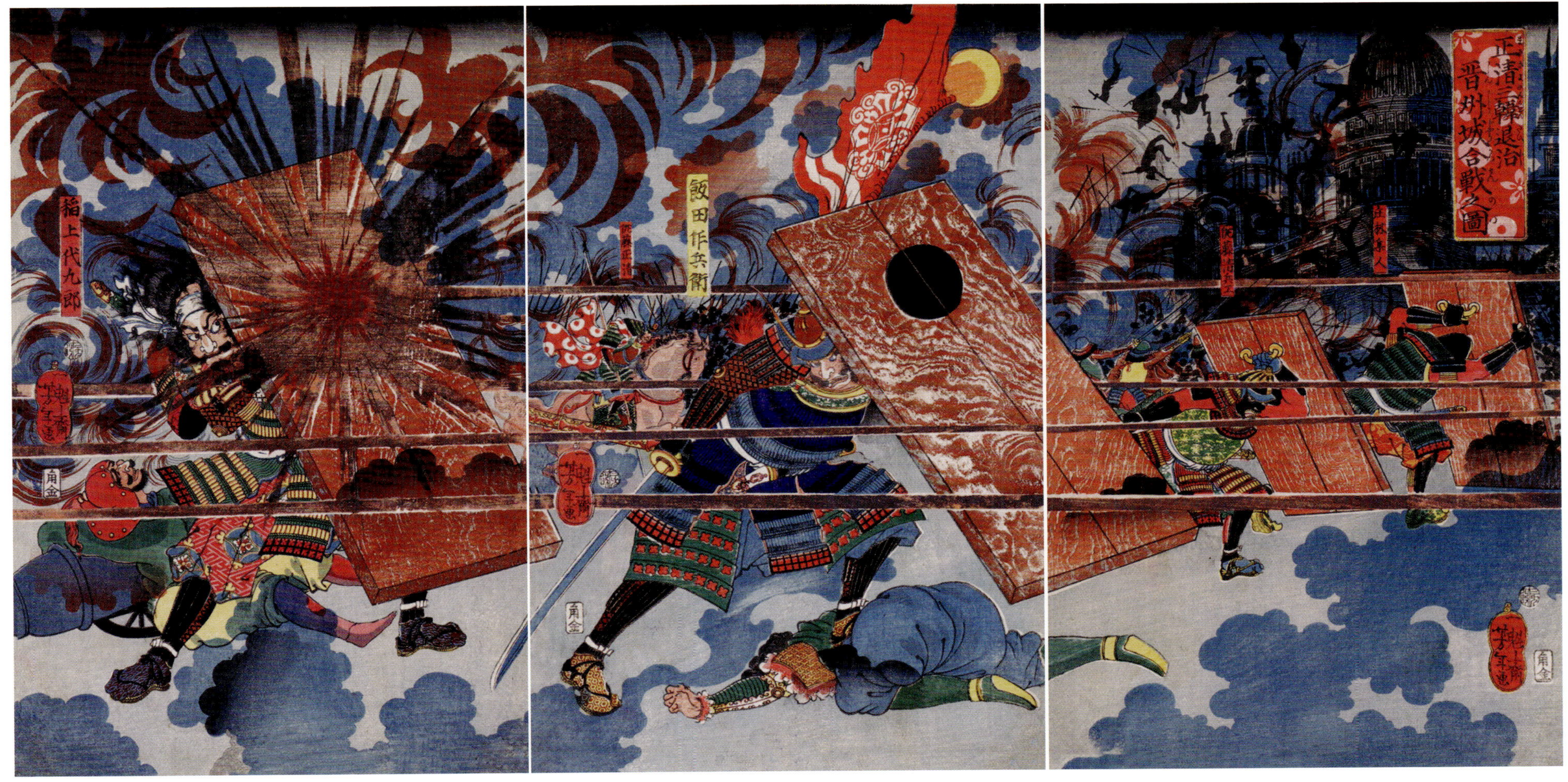

MASAKIYO SANKAN TAIJI SHINSHU-JO KASSEN

"Masakiyo Exterminating Koreans At The Battle Of Shinshu Castle"; 1863
Masakiyo is a thinly-veiled reference to Kiyomasa Kato, one of three warlords who led the forces of Toyotomi during the Korean invasion. Although the illustration refers to Shinshu castle, it most likely depicts the siege in 1598 of Ulsan castle, a fortress built by Kiyomasa in Korea; the background image of St. Paul's Cathedral may also refer to more a contemporary naval battle with the English at Kagoshima.

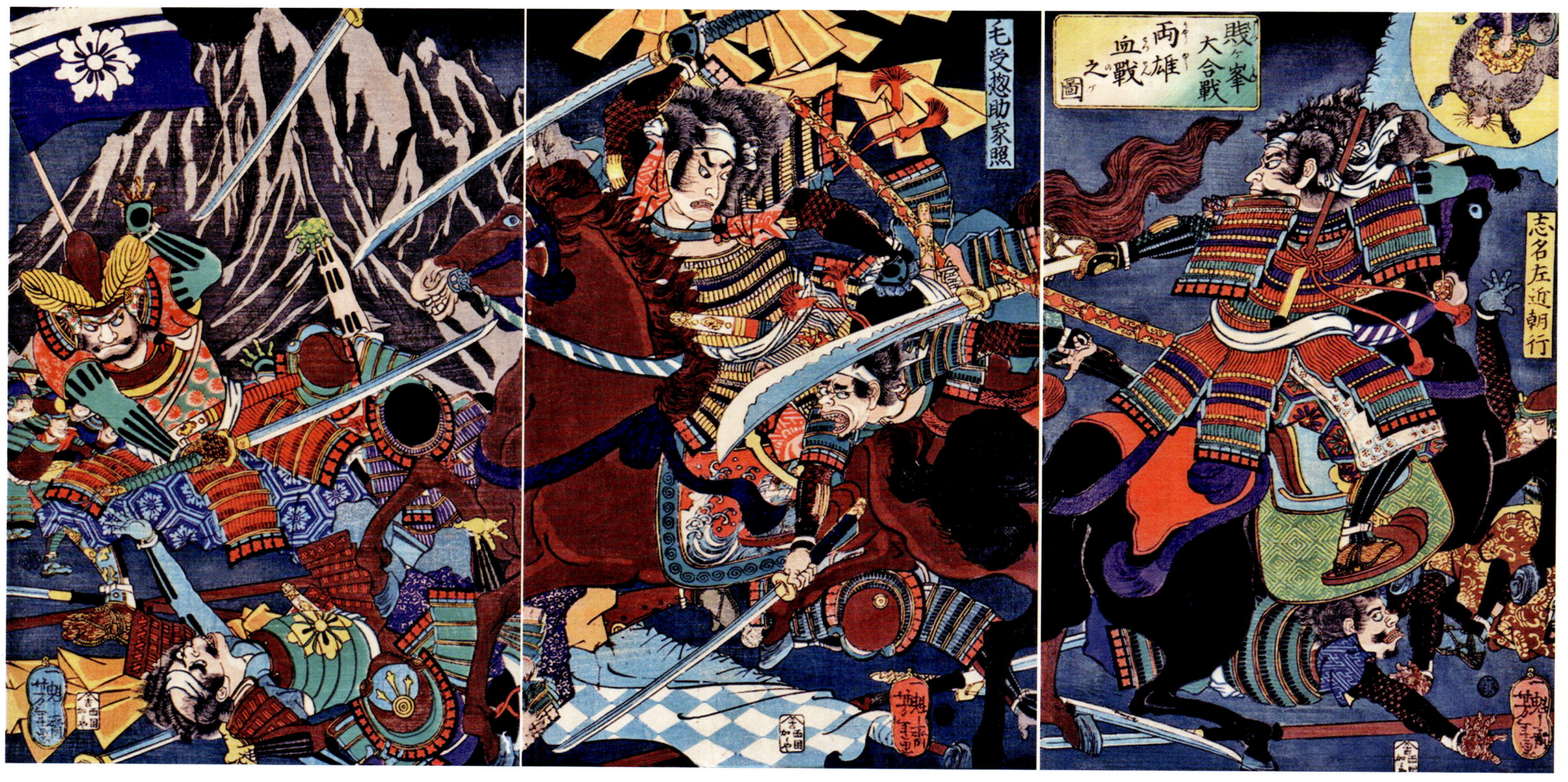

SHIZUGATAKE OKASSEN RYOYU KESSEN

"Bloody Fight Of Two Rival Warriors At The Great Battle Of Shizugatake"; 1863
Another depiction of events during the decisive 1583 battle, in this case a personal struggle between two great *samurai*.

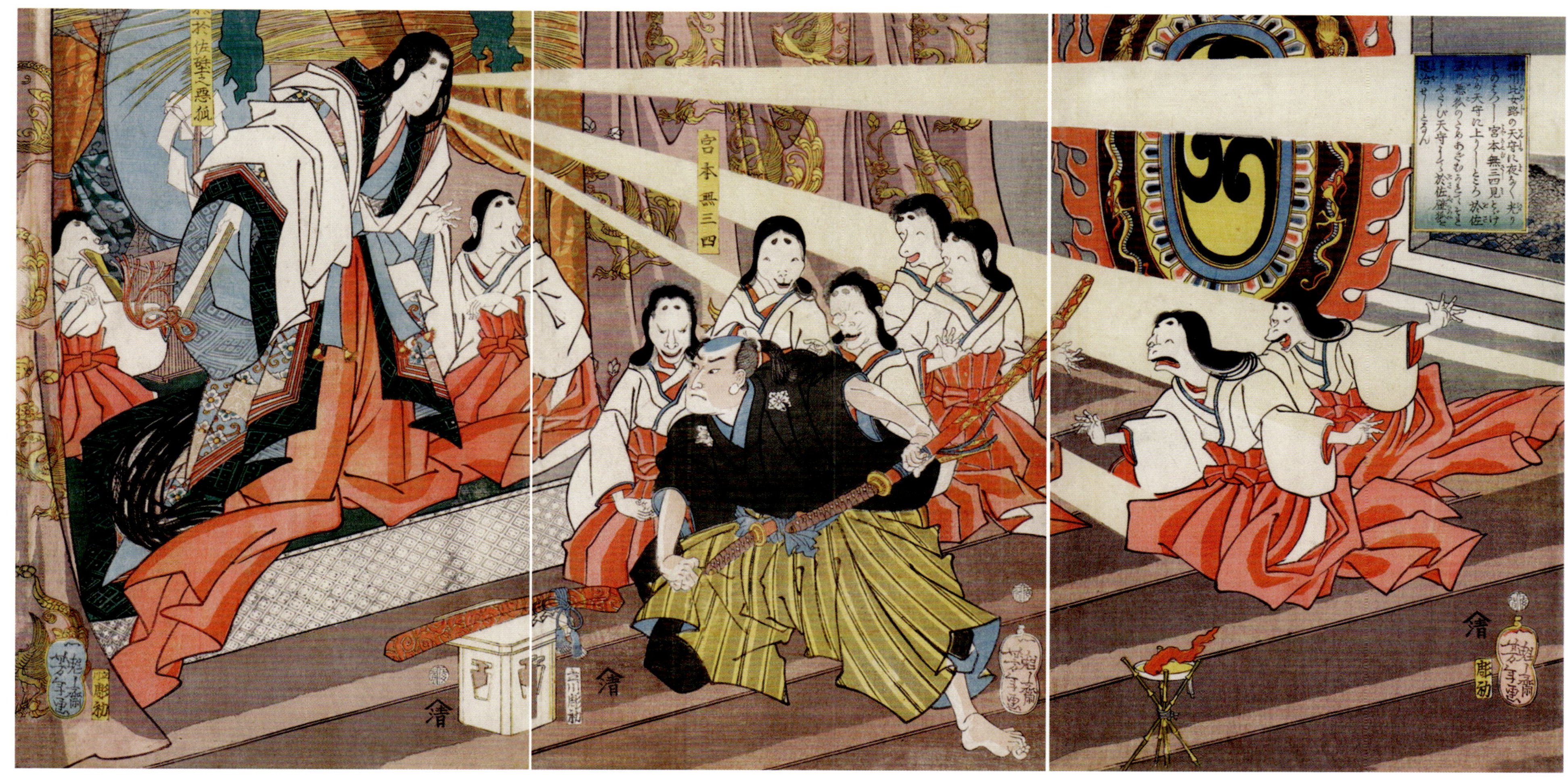

MIYAMOTO MUSASHI KITSUNE TAIJI

"Miyamoto Musashi Exterminates The Fox-Demon"; 1863

A depiction of the warrior Miyamoto Musashi at Himeji castle, exorcising Osakabe-hime, a vampiric princess who was possessed by the malign spirit of an ancient *kitsune*, or fox-demon. Miyamoto, a *ronin* born around 1584, was renowned in Japanese myth as a notable slayer of demons and monsters and may be seen in a number of popular prints. He was also the proponent of *nitenichi*, a two-sword combat technique.

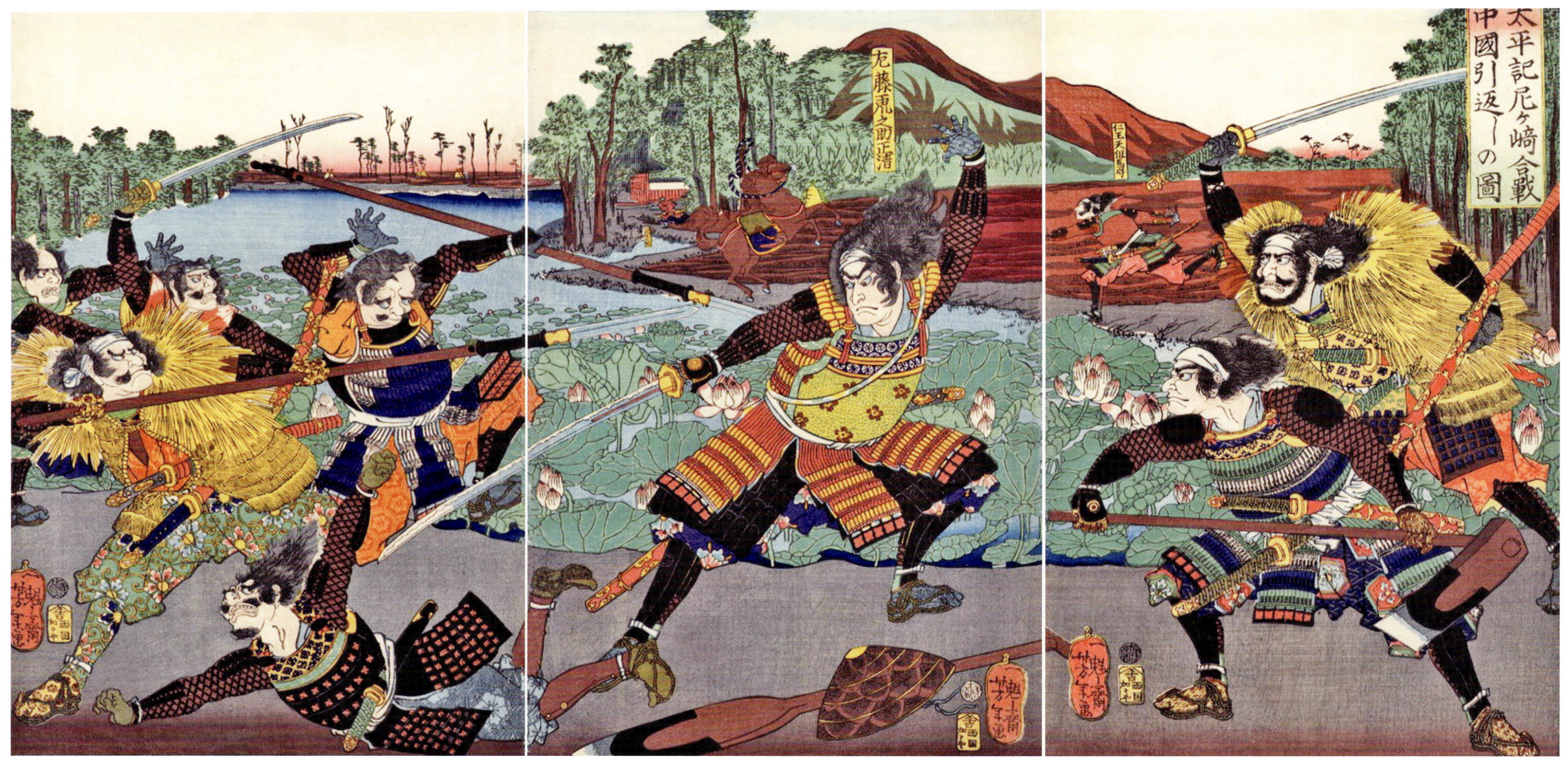

TAIHEIKI: AMAGASAKI KASSEN CHUGOKU HIKKAESU

"Scene From *Taiheiki*: Fighting At Amagasaki, Withdrawing To Chugoku Province"; 1863
Ostensibly a scene from the *Taiheiki* ("Chronicle Of The Great Peace"), a mythic text based on Japanese history from the period 1319 to 1367 during which a great war was fought between the Northern Court of Ashikaga Takauji in Kyoto, and the Southern Court of Emperor Go-Daigo in Yoshino; but Yoshitoshi often used *Taiheiki* as code for *Taikoki*, a 17th century biography of Toyotomi Hideyoshi.

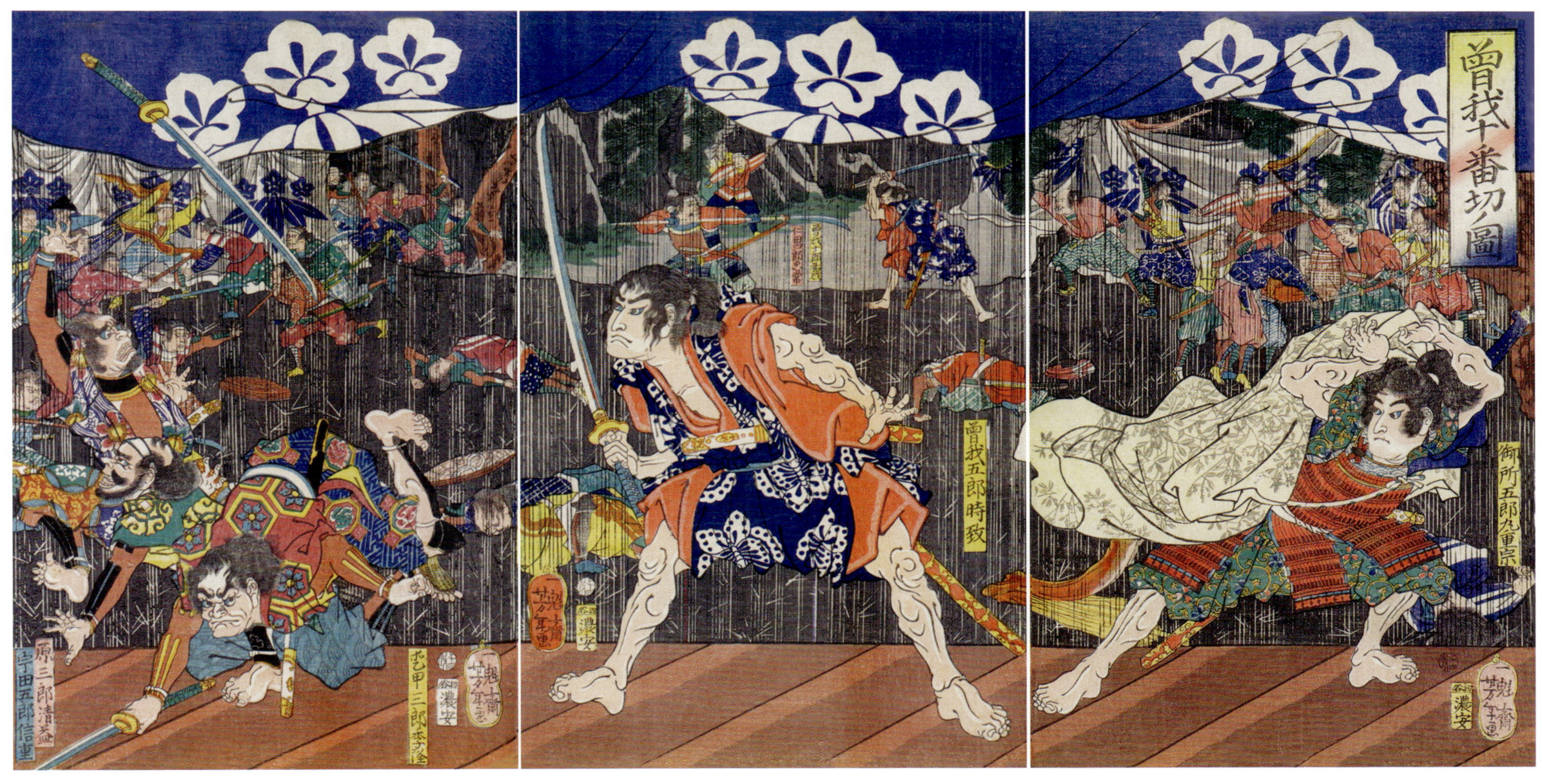

SOGA JUBANGIRI

"Soga Brothers Kill Ten Men"; 1864

A scene from historical legend of the 12th century, depicting the revenge slaughter rampage of Soga Juro and Soga Goro, whose father was murdered when they were infants. In most versions of the legend, the man responsible for this crime is a shogun's retainer named Kudo Kuketsune, who is butchered by the brothers.

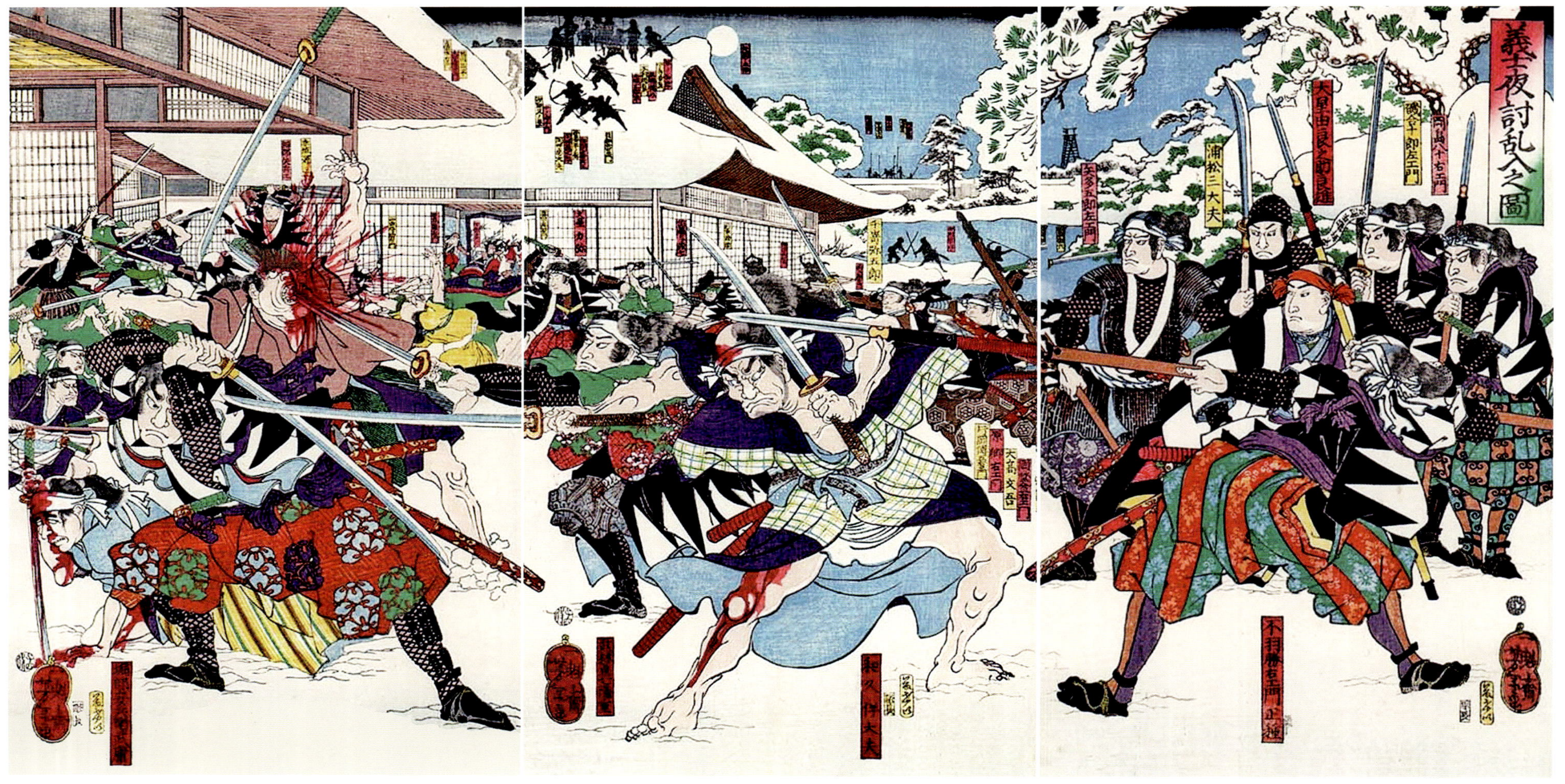

GISHI YOUCHI RANNYU

"Night Attack: Loyal Retainers' Violent Invasion"; 1864
Yoshitoshi's bloody depiction of the infamous revenge attack by 47 *ronin* on the house of Yoshinaka Kira, who had forced the *seppuku* (ritual suicide by beheading and disembowelment) of their master Asano. Kira was in turn decapitated by the *ronin* who then offered up his head to Asano's grave.

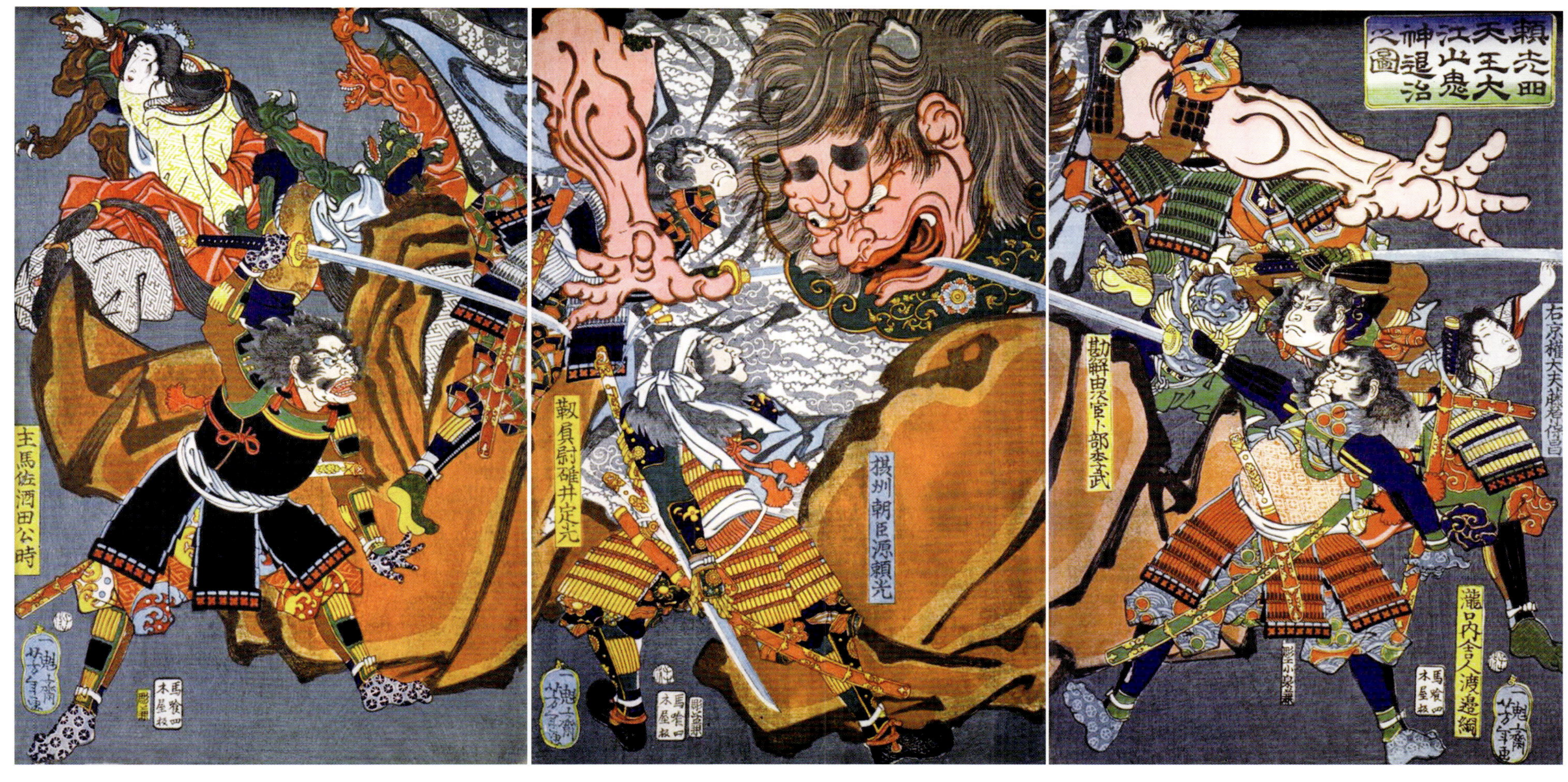

RAIKO SHITENNO OEYAMA KIJIN TAIJI
"Raiko And His Holy Knights: Monster Extermination On Mount Oe"; 1864
Yoshitoshi's depiction from the mythology of Raiko (Minamoto no Yorimitsu) the demon-slayer and his four knights; this illustration of Raiko's battle with the cannibal ogre Shutendoji shows the monster waking up as the five warriors attack him, moments before chopping off his head.

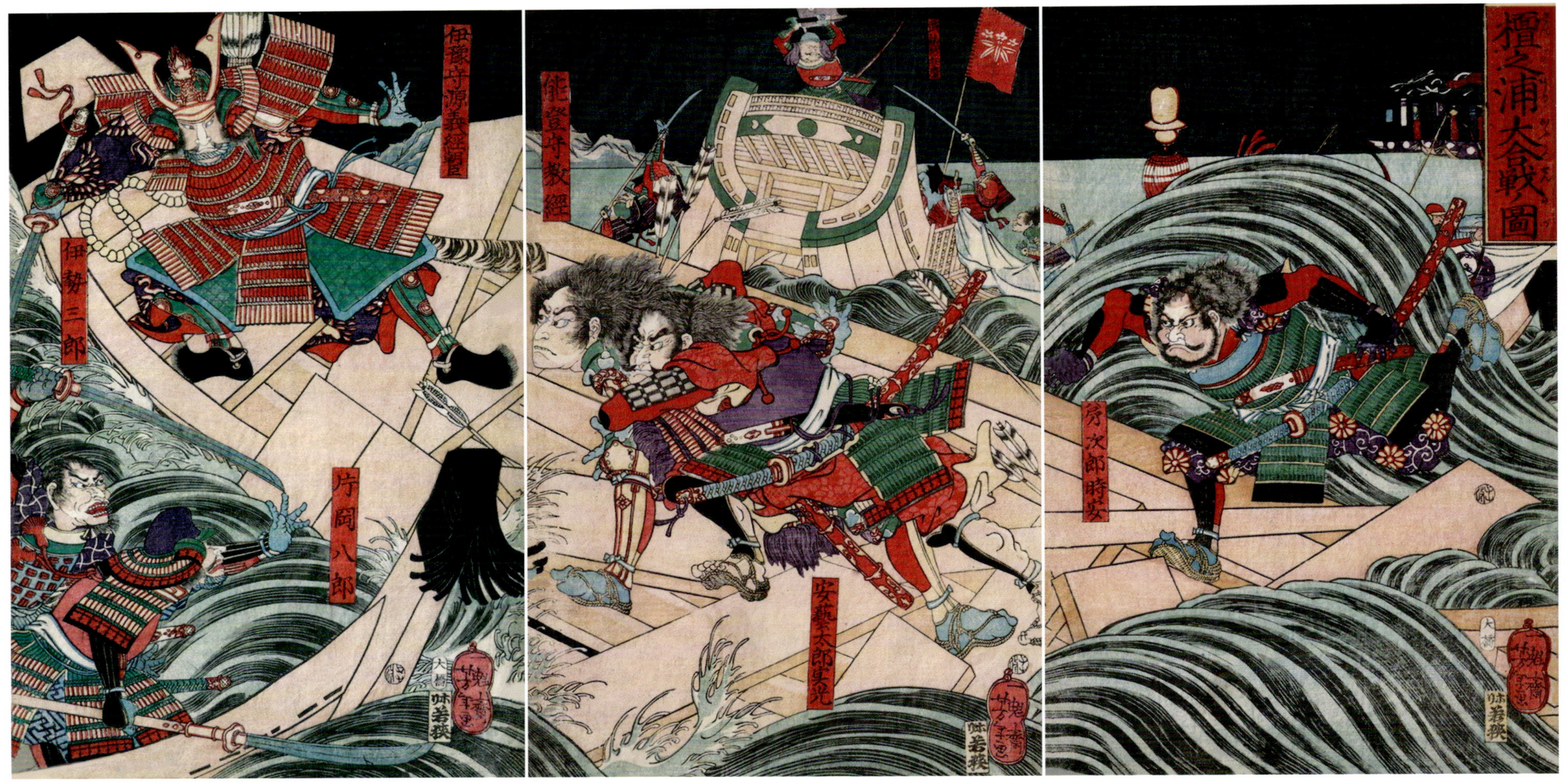

DAN-NO-URA DAIKASSEN / YASHIMA DAIKASSEN
"The Great Battle Of Dan-No-Ura" / "The Great Battle Of Yashima" (hexaptych); 1864
One of Yoshitoshi's earliest known double triptych or hexaptych designs, composed of six continuous sheets. The great Genpei sea battles at Yashima and Dan-no-Ura in 1185, when the Minamoto clan won a decisive victory over the Taira or Heike clan, were a subject which the artist would revisit many times in his career.

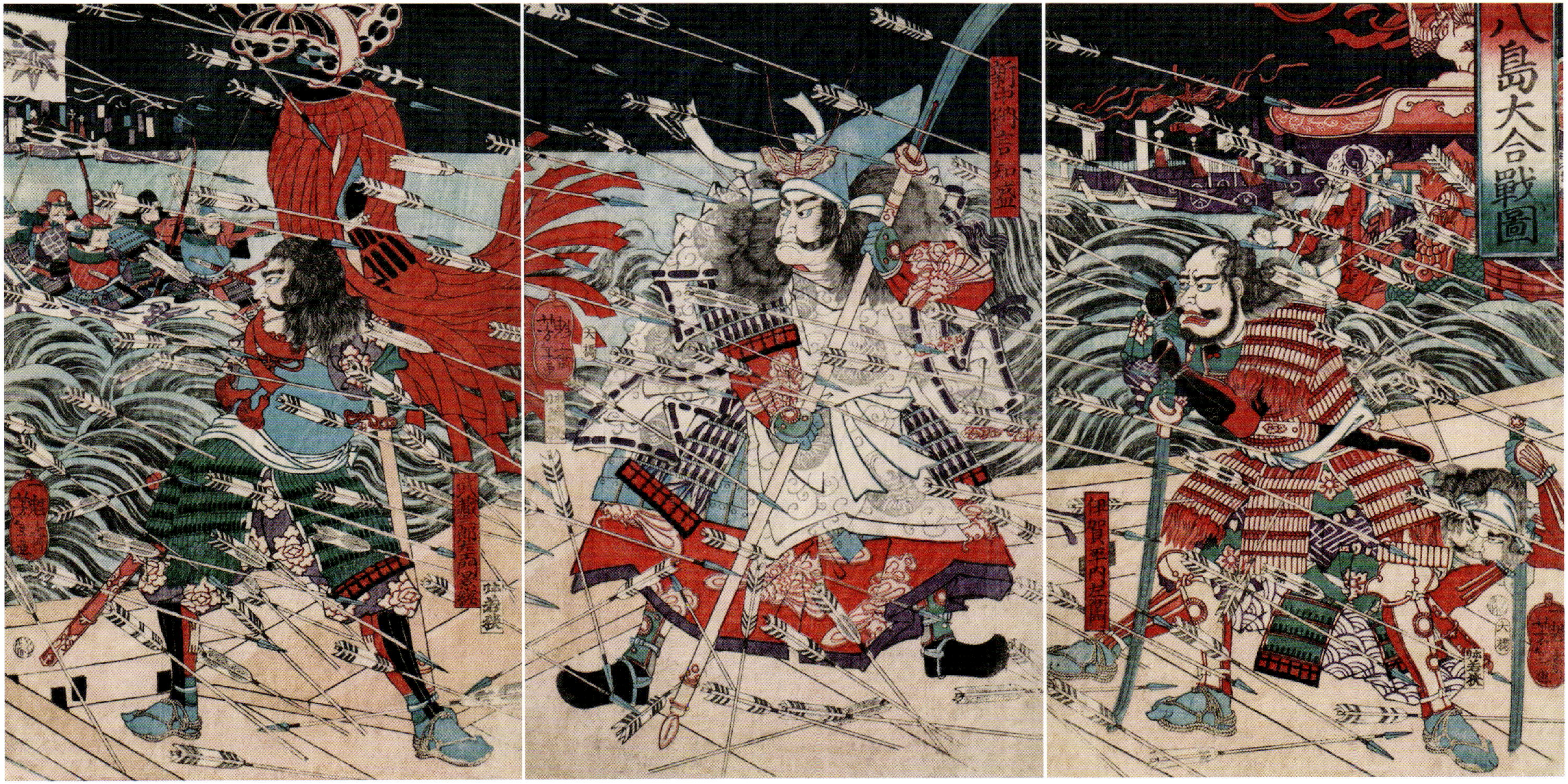

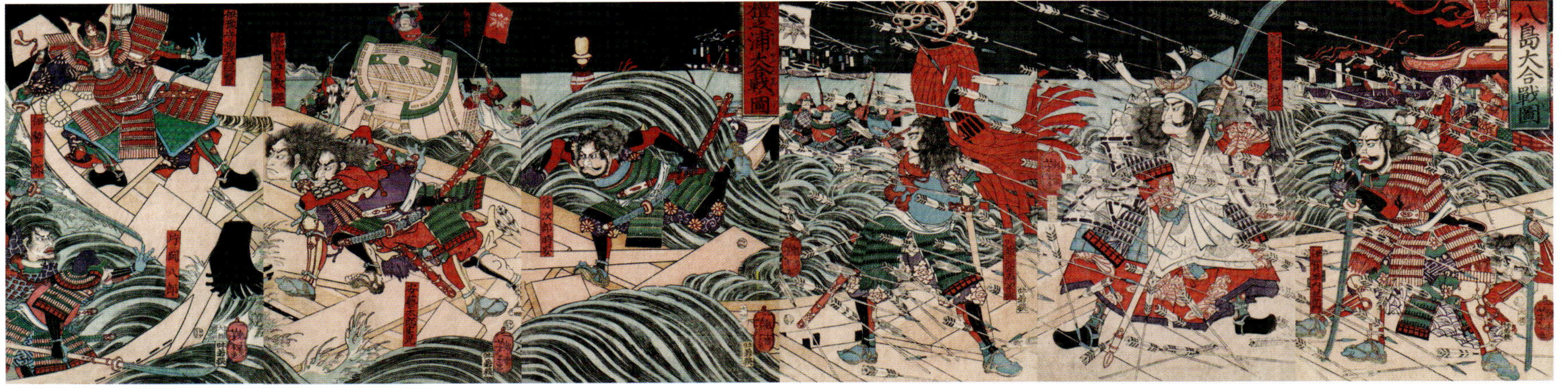
八島大合戦圖

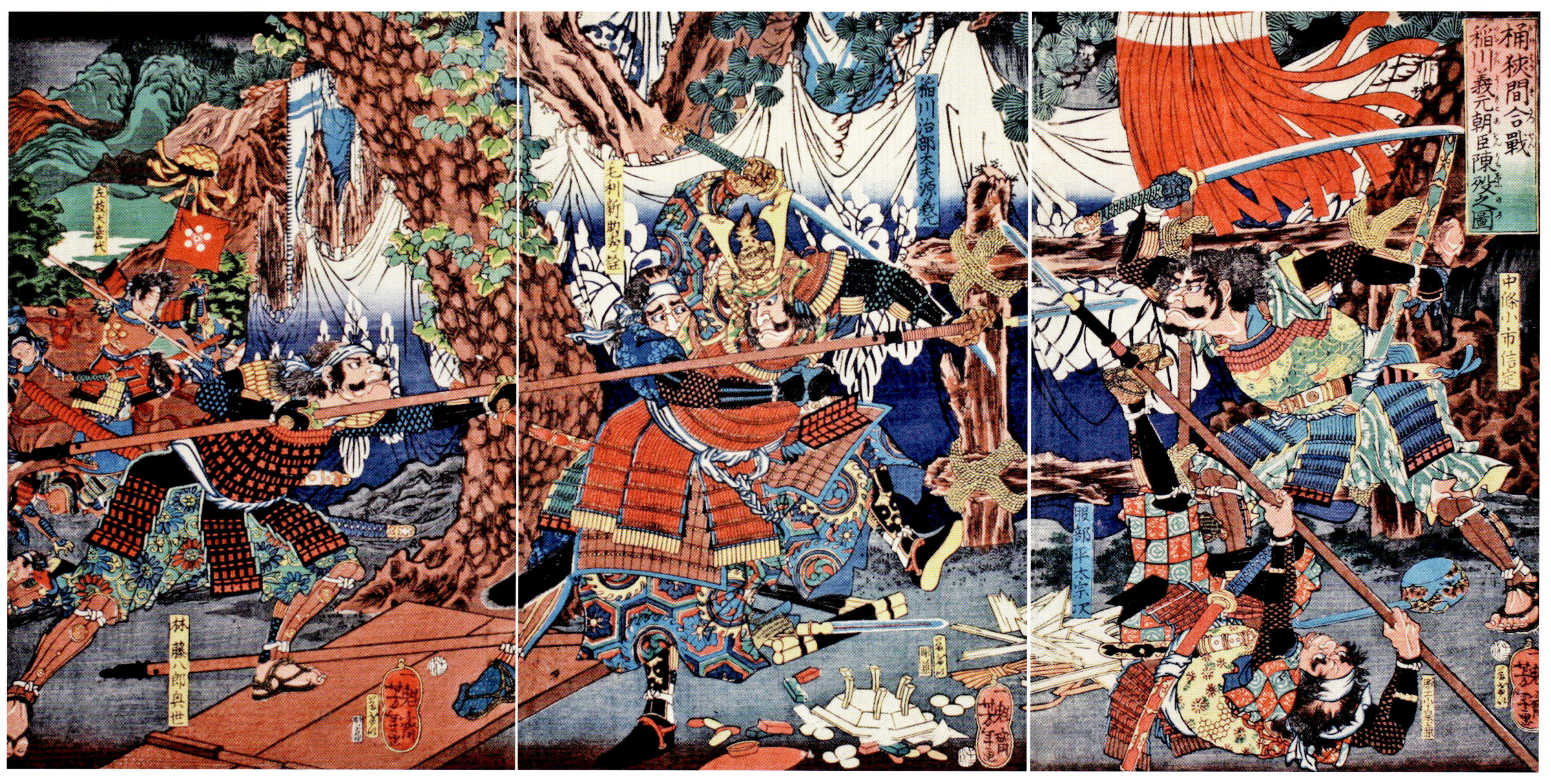

OKEHAZAMA KASSEN INAGAWA YOSHIMOTO ASON CHINBOTSU

"The Battle Of Okehazama: Death Of *Ason* Inagawa Yoshimoto"; 1864

A scene from the battle of Okehazama in 1560, in which the forces of Inagawa Yoshimoto were defeated by those of Oda Nobunaga. Yoshimoto's bloody death came at the hands of two *samurai*, Mori Shinsuke and Hattori Koheita.

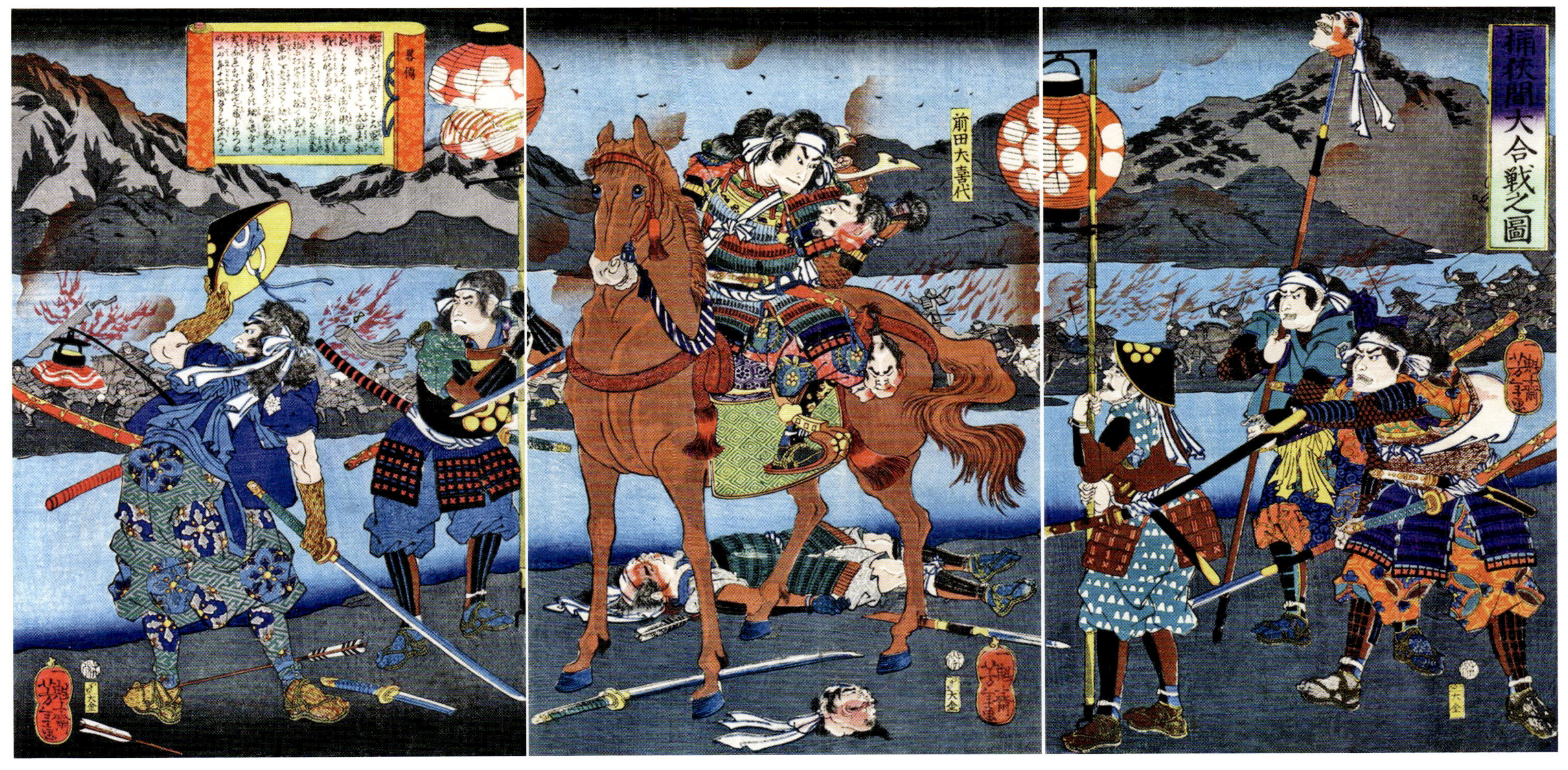

OKEHAZAMA OKASSEN
"The Great Battle Of Okehazama"; 1864
Another scene from Okehazama, with *samurai* and the severed heads of enemies.

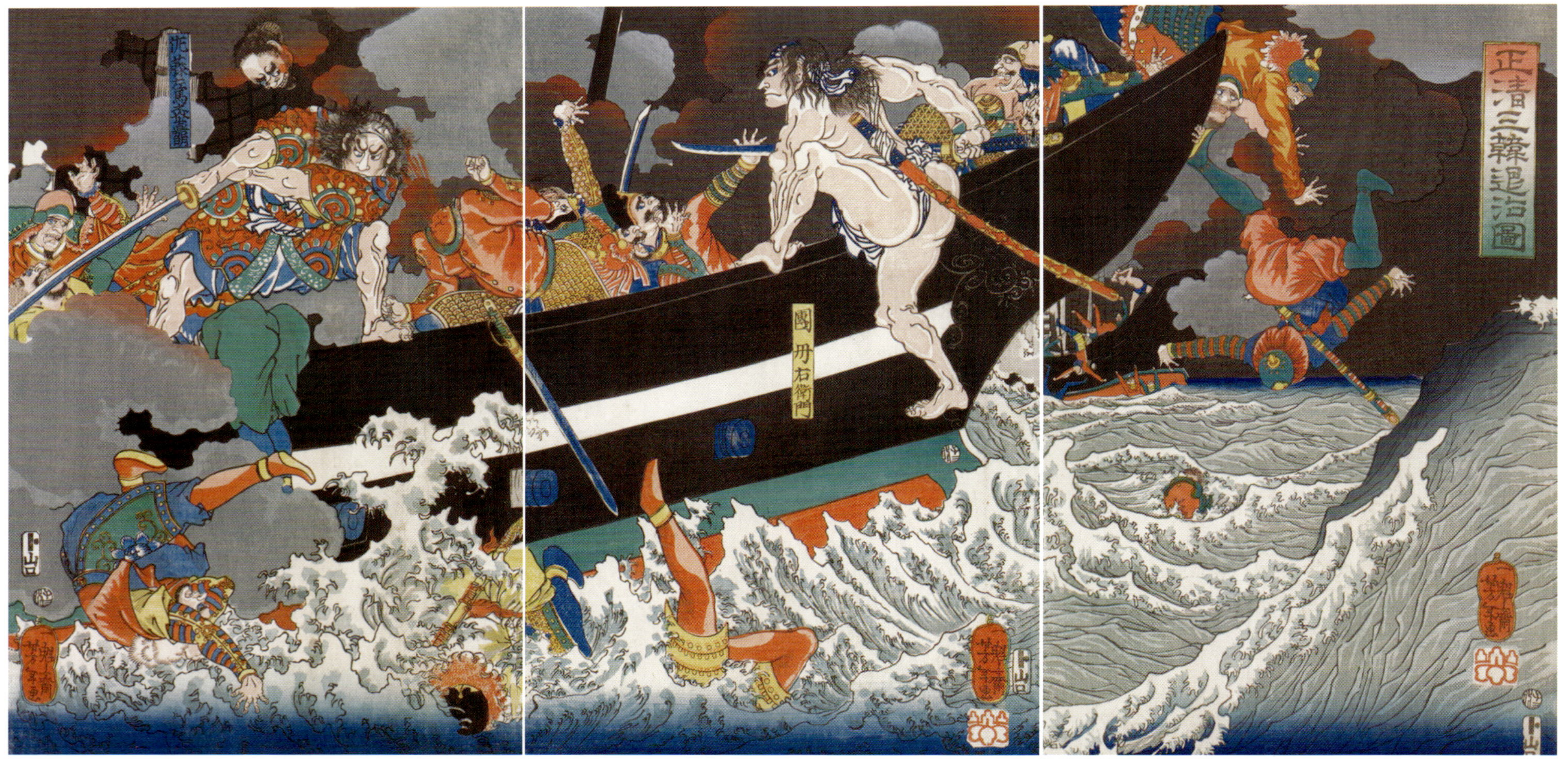

MASAKIYO SANKAN TAIJI
"Masakiyo Exterminating Koreans"; 1864
One of two illustrations by Yoshitoshi from 1864 which refer back to Kiyomasa Kato's exploits in the attempted subjugation of Korea. This image shows the bloody decapitation of a Korean mariner during a naval raid.

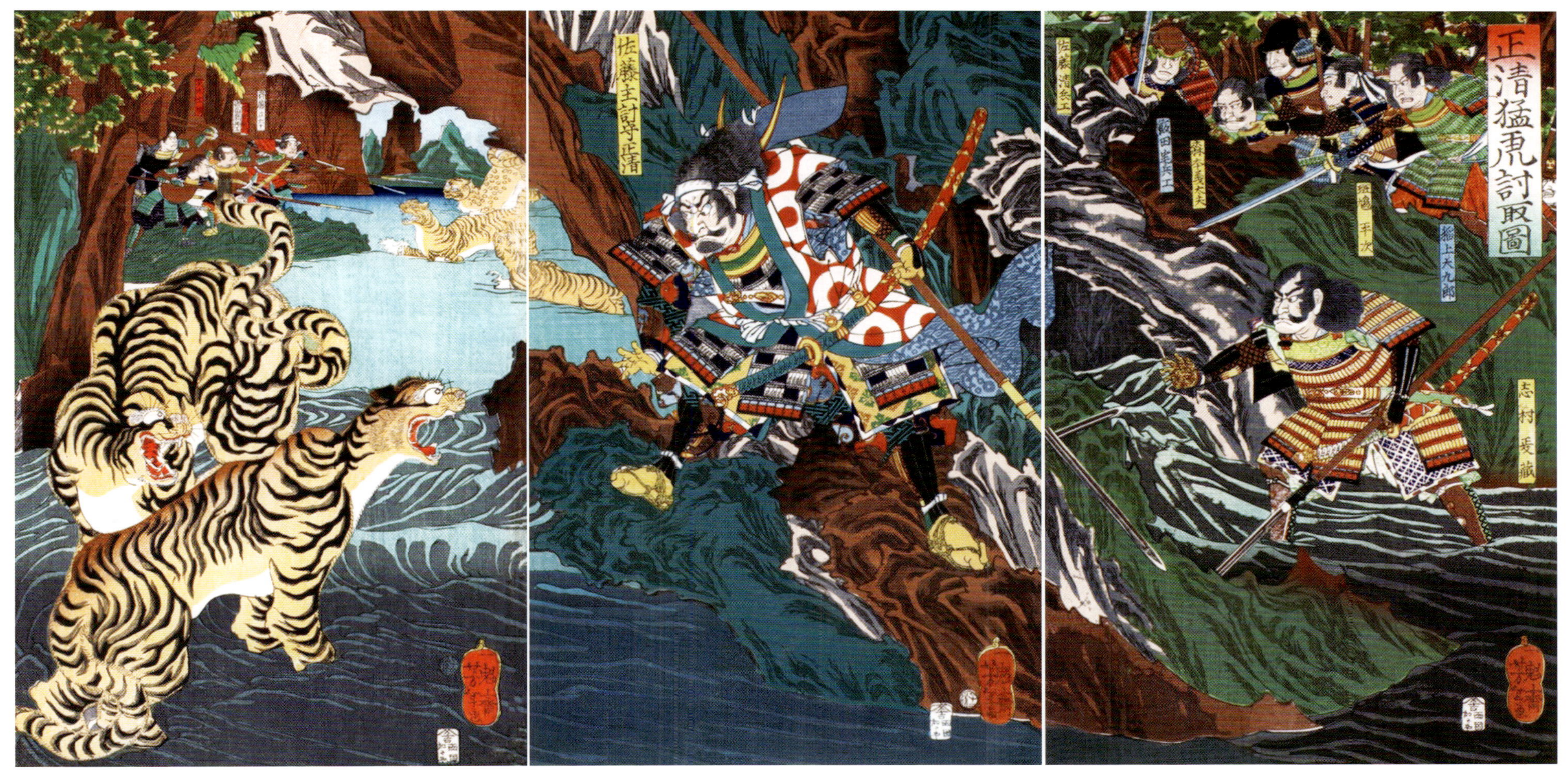

MASAKIYO MOKO UCHITORI

"Masakiyo Slaughtering Ferocious Tigers"; 1864

Whilst in Korea, Kiyomasa (known in his youth as Toranosuke, or "young tiger") became renowned as a hunter and killer of wild tigers. This illustration shows Kiyomasa ready to strike his quarry.

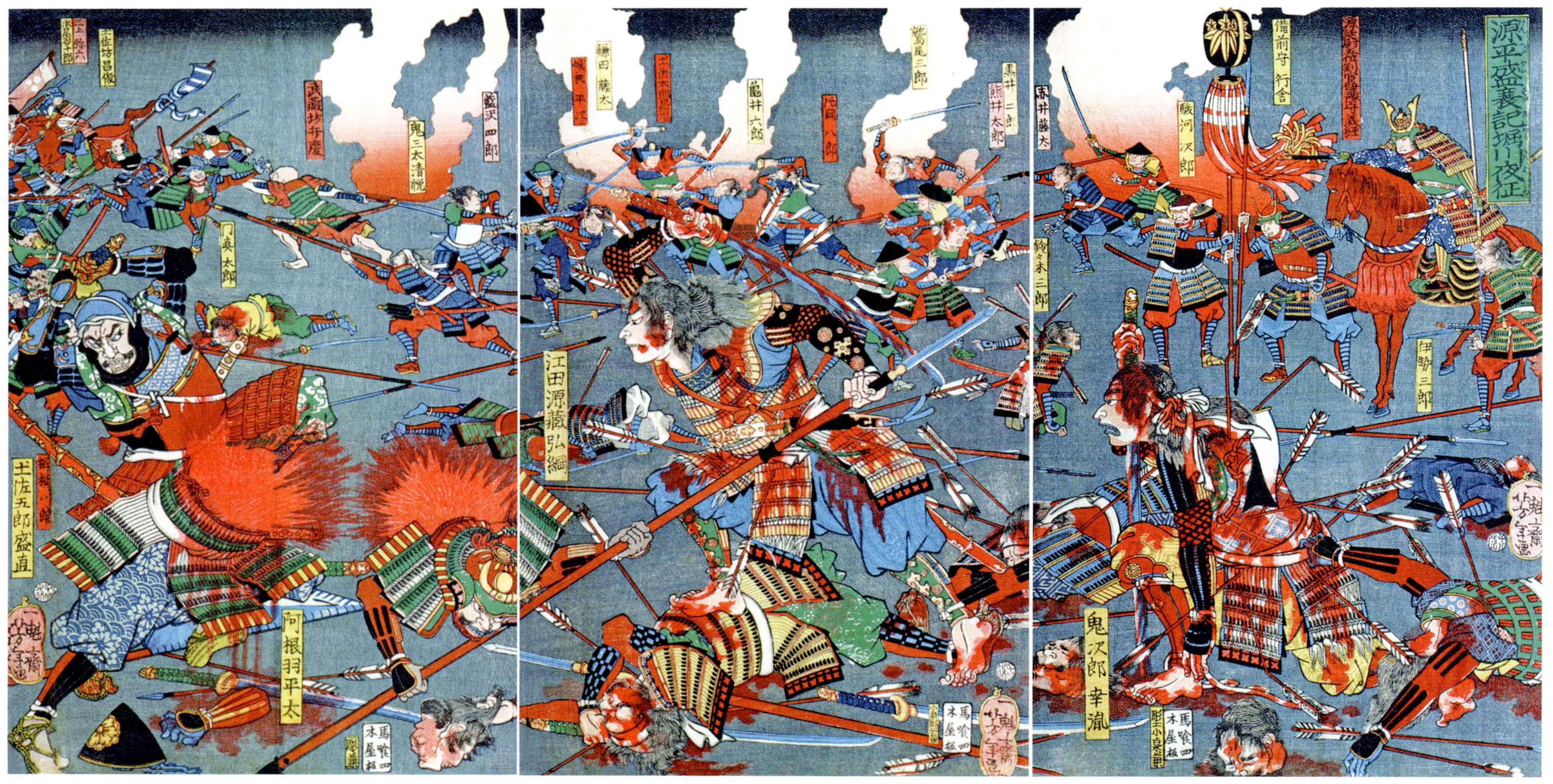

GENPEI SEISUIKI HORIKAWA YOUCHI

"Scene From The *Genpei Seisuiki*: Night Attack At Horikawa"; 1864
An illustration from the *Genpei Seisuiki*, a version of the *Heike Monogatari* which details the Genpei Wars of the late 12th century fought between the Taira clan and the Minamoto clan. The scene depicts a famous incident from 1185 when the *shogun* Minamoto Yoritomo launched a nocturnal attack on his younger brother Yoshitsune's mansion in the Horikawa district of Kyoto. The left-panel image of a *samurai* being cut in half through the waist with an explosion of blood makes this Yoshitoshi's most explicitly violent triptych.

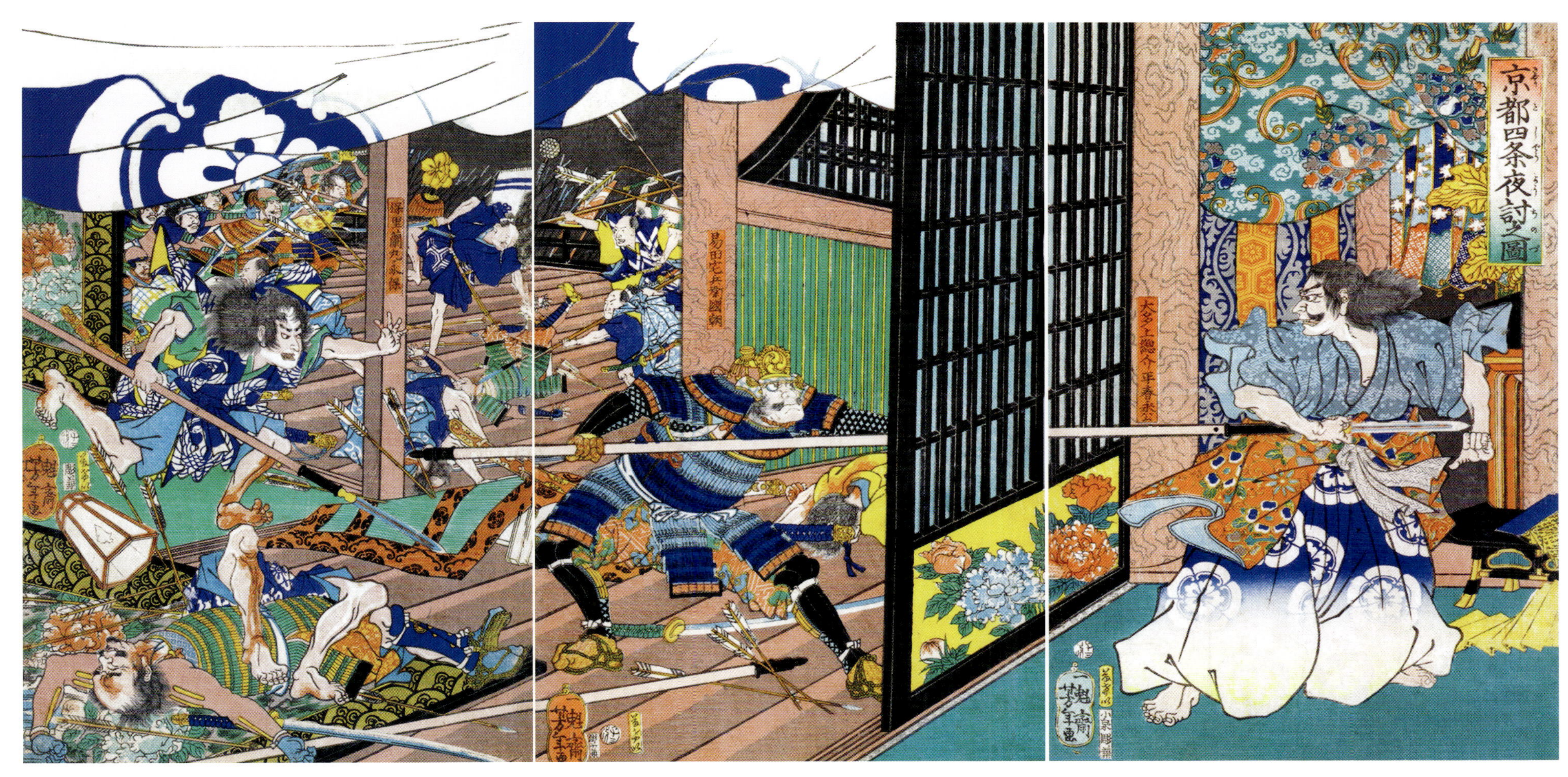

KYOTO SHIJO YOUCHI

"Night Attack At Shijo In Kyoto"; 1864

This illustration refers to the siege of Kyoto's Sanjo Palace in 1160 during the Heiji Rebellion, a civil war between rival subjects of the Emperor Go-Shirakawa, who duly abdicated. A night attack on Sanjo was launched by Fujiwara no Nobuyori and Minamoto no Yoshitomo who kidnapped both the former emperor and his successor, Nijo.

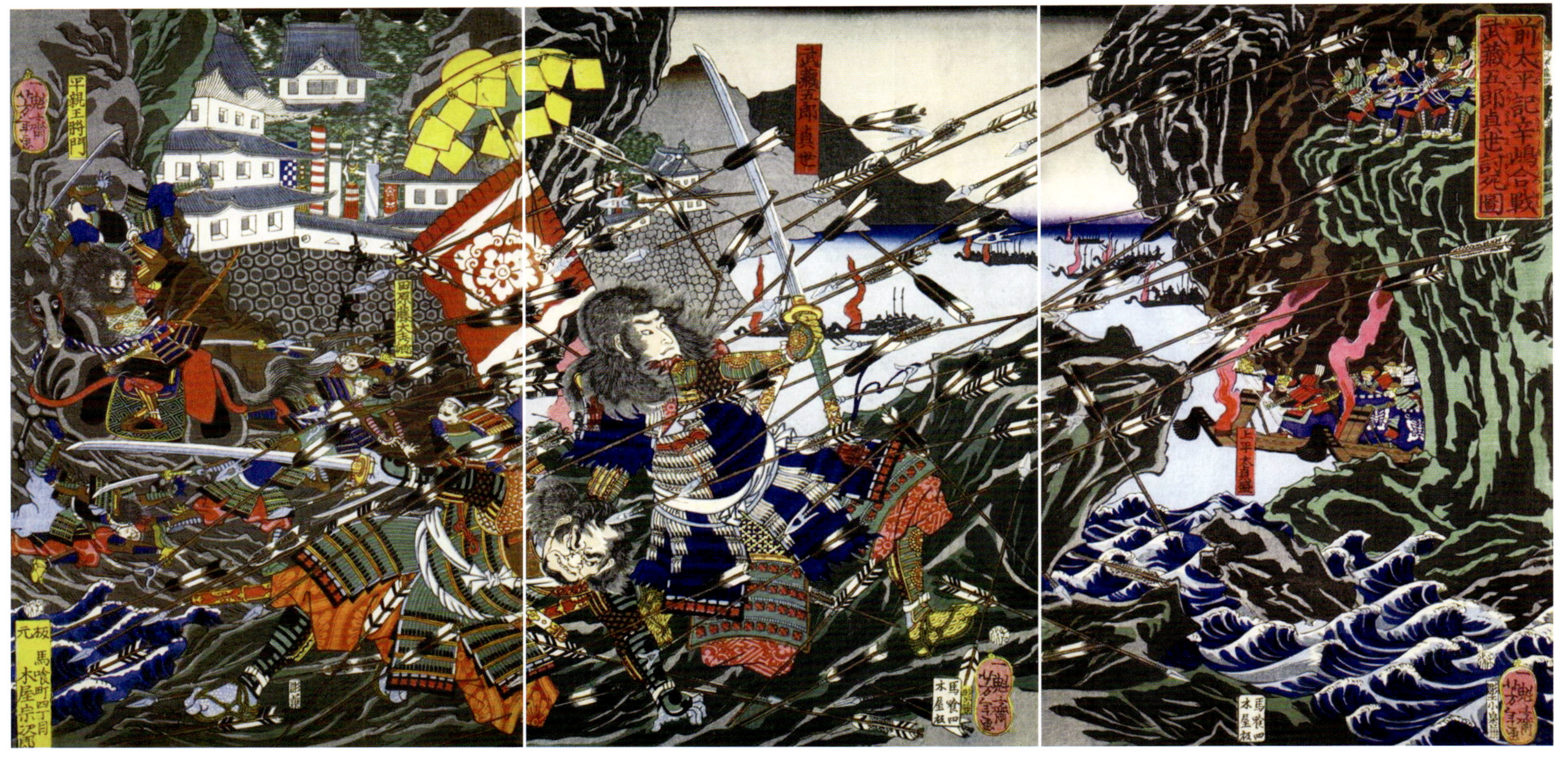

ZEN TAIHEIKI MUSASHI GORO SADAYO UCHIJINI
"From The *Zen Taiheiki*: Musashi Goro Sadayo Killed In Battle"; 1864
Samurai Sadayo was a 15-year-old retainer of Taira-no-Masakado, and died alongside his master in 940, at the battle of Shiroyama (depicted here as Karashima).

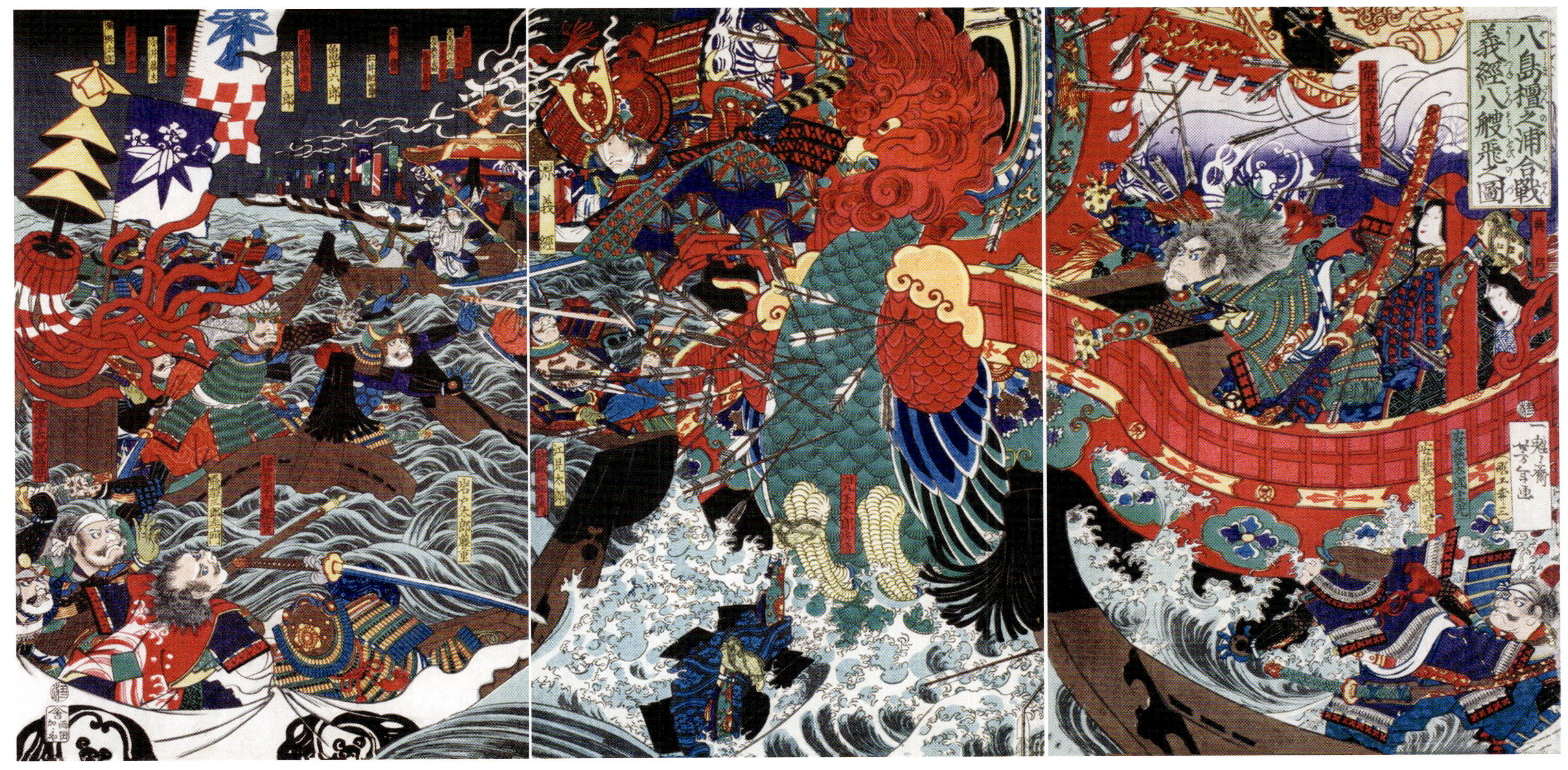

YASHIMA DANNOURA KASSEN YOSHITSUNE HASSO-TOBI

"At The Battle Of Yashima And Dan-No-Ura, Yoshitsune Leaps Over Eight Boats"; 1865

One of the most famous mythic incidents recorded about the battle of Dan-no-Ura is the prodigious, superhuman leap made by Minamoto-no-Yoshitsune to escape an attack by the enemy general Taira-no-Noritsune; exaggerated in each subsequent telling, Yoshitsune's original jump eventually became immortalised as clearing a whole eight boat-lengths. Yoshitoshi's illustration of the incident is one of many in *ukiyo-e*, and amplifies Kuniyoshi's design of 1845.

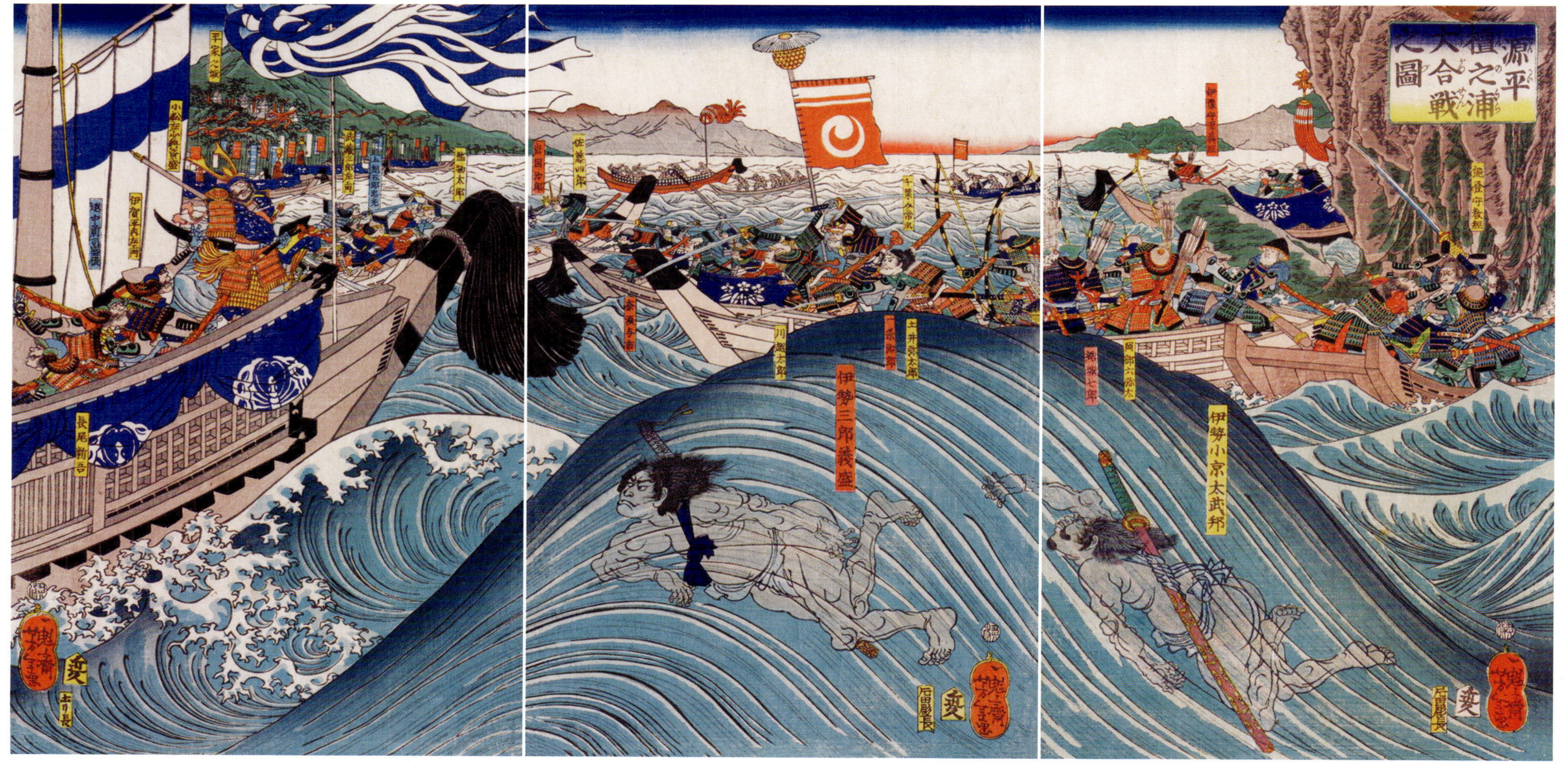

GENPEI DAN-NO-URA OKASSEN

"Genpei Wars: Great Battle At Dannoura"; 1865

The sea battle at Dan-no-Ura in 1185 was a decisive one in the Genpei Wars between the Minamoto and Taira clans; the Taira were defeated, enabling Minamoto no Yoritomo to become Japan's first *shogun*.

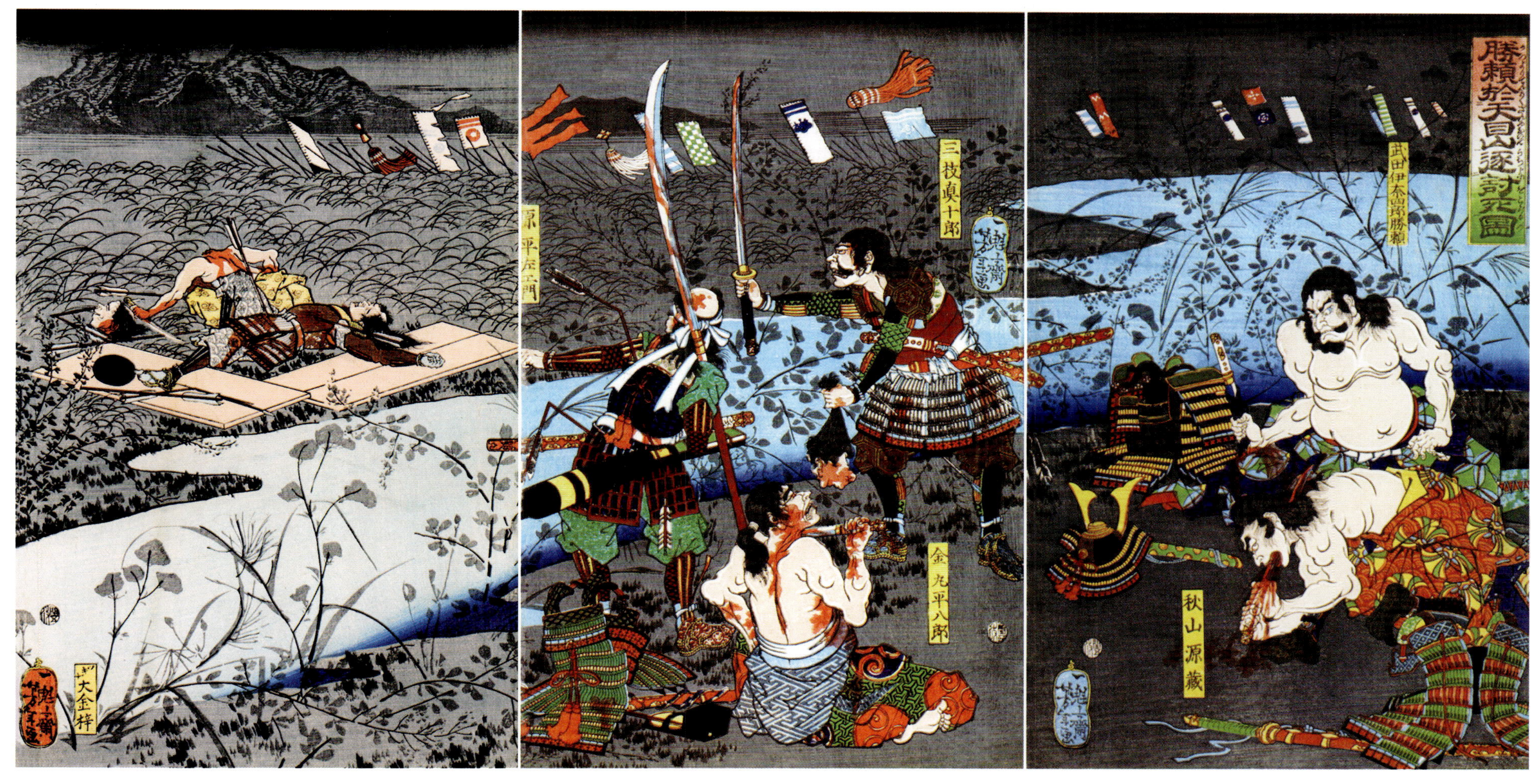

KATSUYORI O TENMOKUZAN SUI UCHIJINI
"Suicide Death Of Katsuyori On Mount Tenmoku"; 1865
The last stand of the Takeda clan was on Mount Tenmoku in 1582; unable to resist the combined forces of Tokugawa Ieyasu and Oda Nobunaga, Takeda Katsuyori committed bloody suicide by sword, along with his last remaining warriors.

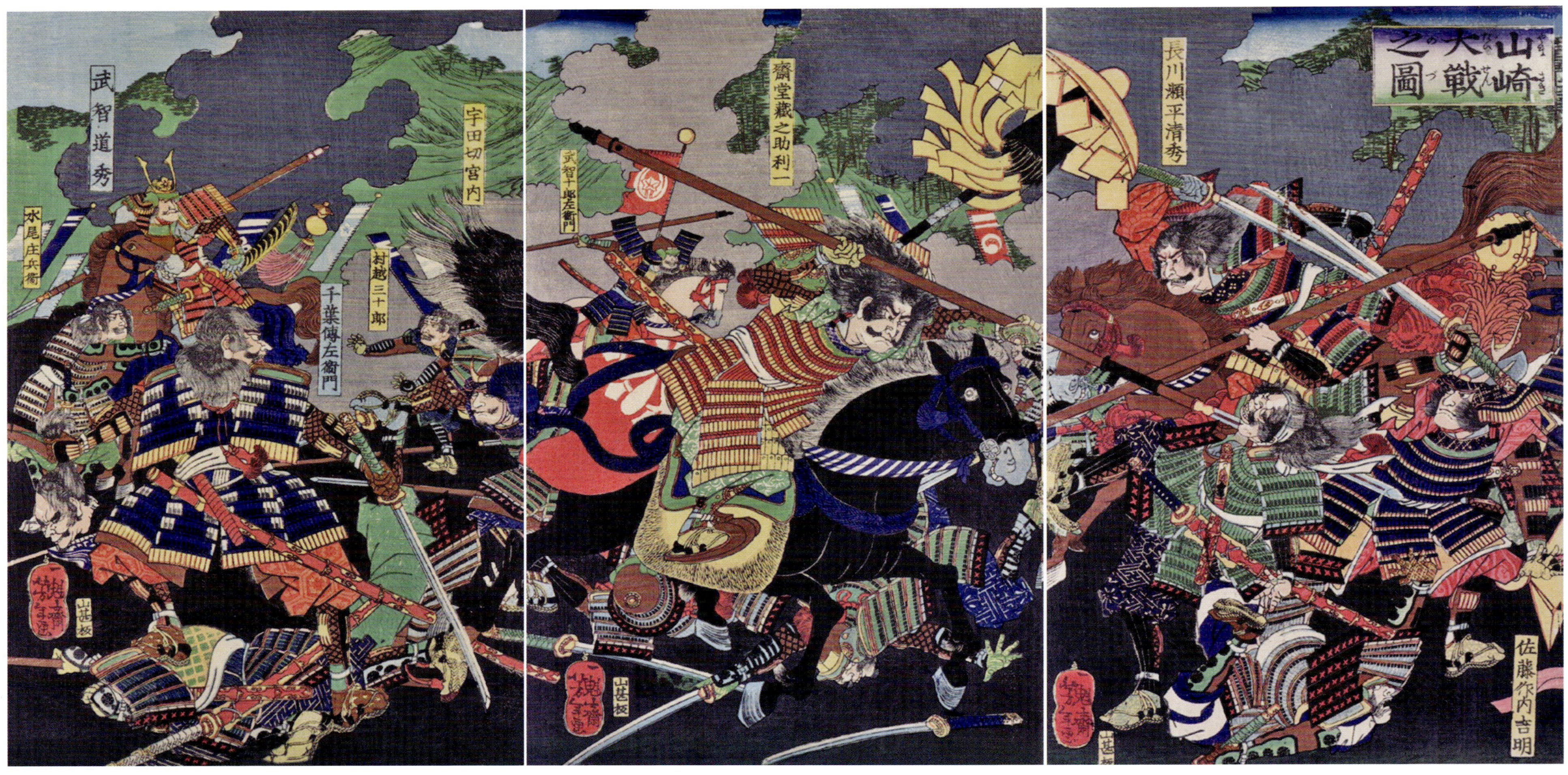

YAMAZAKI OKASSEN

"The Great Battle Of Yamazaki" (hexaptych); 1865
A double triptych illustrating the battle of Yamazaki of 1582, in which Toyotomi Hideyoshi defeated Akechi Mitsuhide who several days earlier had forced the ritual suicide of *daimyo* Oda Nobunaga at Honno temple in Kyoto.

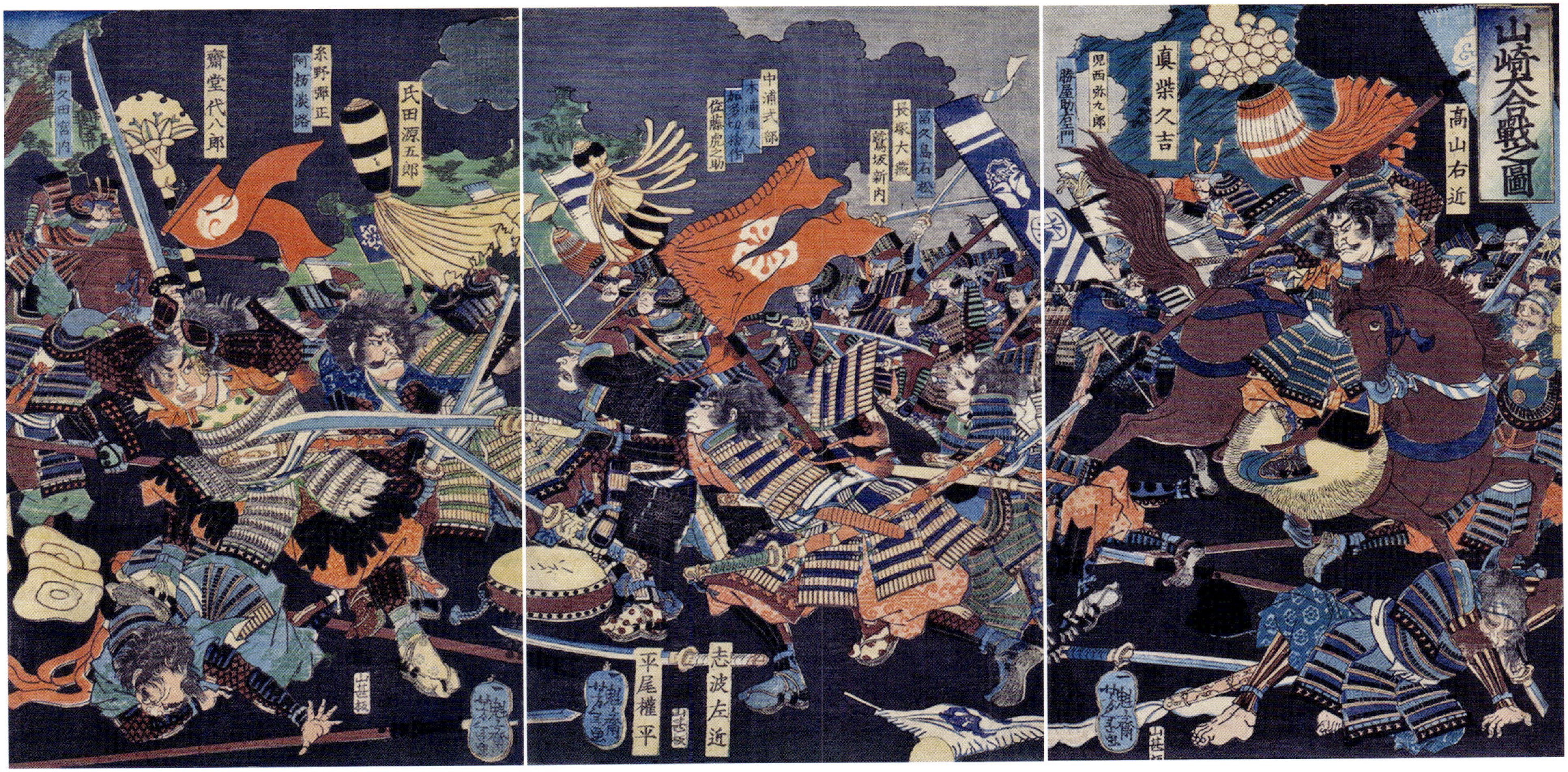

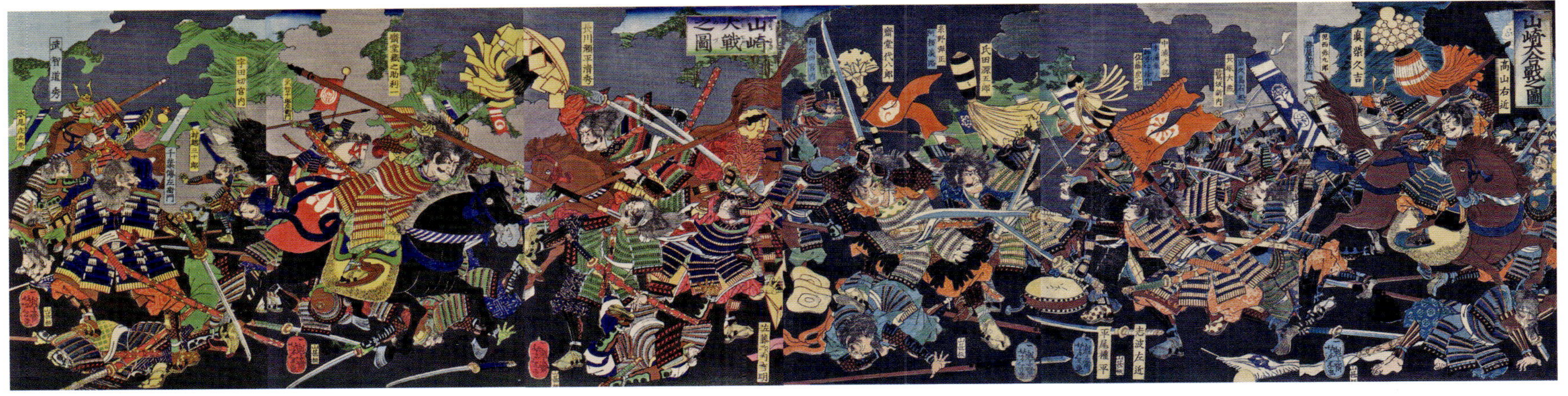
山崎大合戰之圖

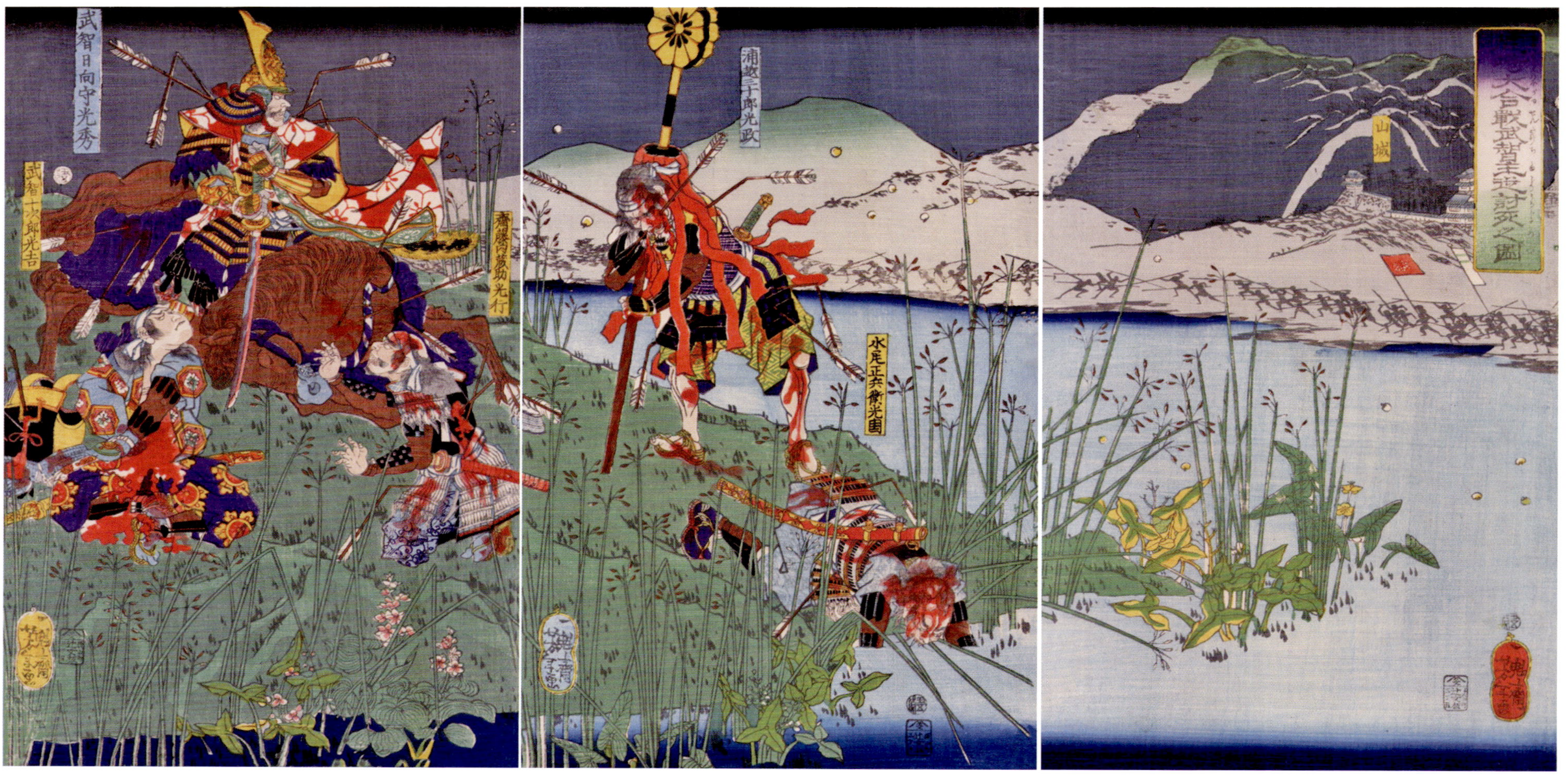

AMAGASAKI DAIKASSEN TAKECHI SHUJU UCHIJINI

"The Great Battle Of Amagasaki: Death Of Takechi's Close Retainers"; 1865

Another image relating to the battle of Yamazaki, showing the imminent suicide or death from war-wounds of Akechi Mitsuhide's principal followers.

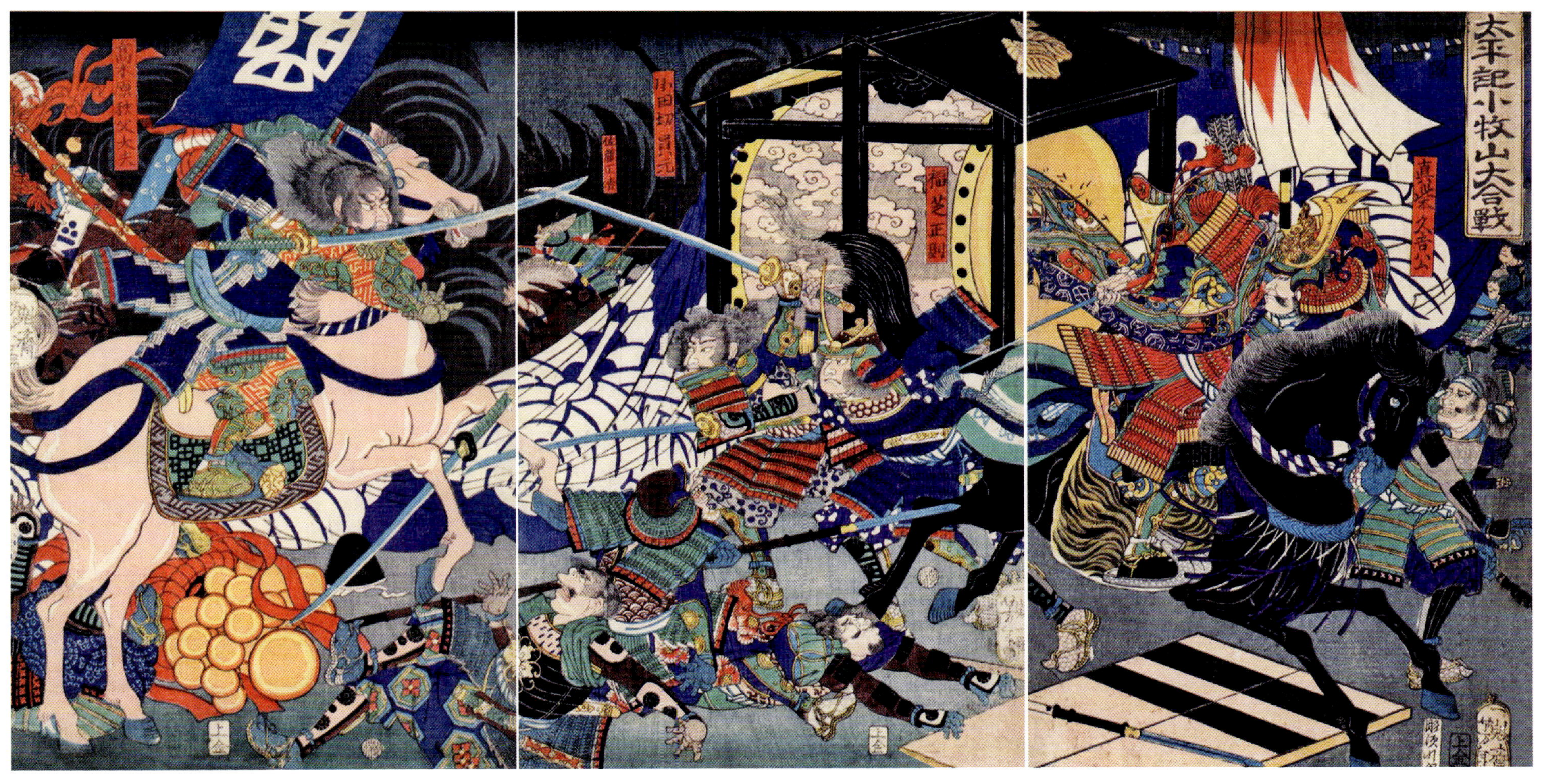

TAIHEIKI KOMAKIYAMA OKASSEN

"Scene From *Taiheiki*: Great Battle On Komakiyama"; 1865
This illustration refers to a battle fought on Mount Komaki in 1584, between the forces of Hashiba Hideyoshi and forces led by Oda Nobukatsu and Tokugawa Ieyasu. Five more battles in this conflict ensued, collectively known as the Battle of Komaki. *Taiheiki* is used by Yoshitoshi as code for *Taikoki*.

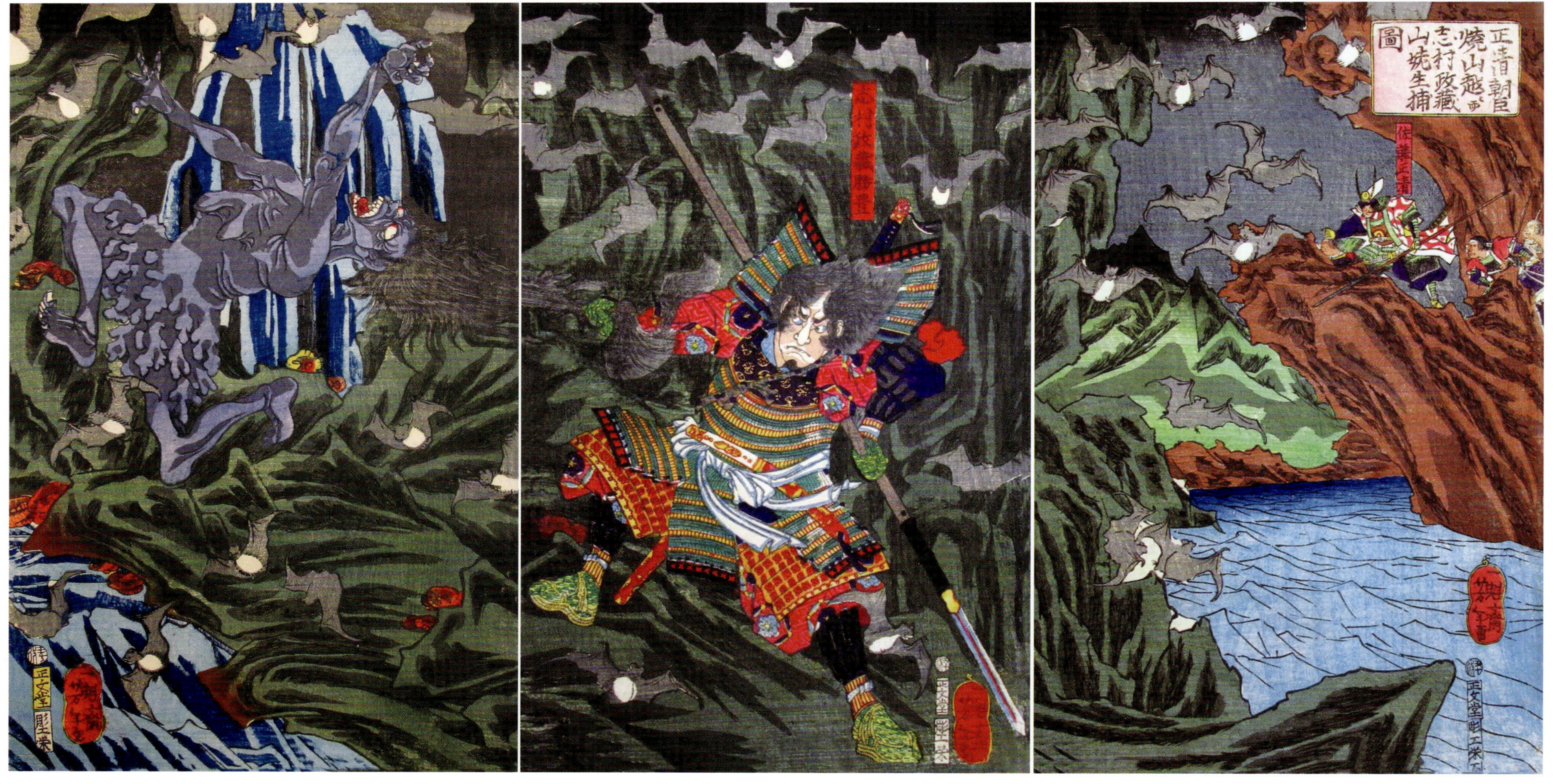

MASAKIYO ASON YAKEYAMA-GOE O SHIMURA MASAZO YAMAUBA IKEDORU

"*Ason* Masakiyo: Shimura Masazo Captures The Mountain Witch Alive At Yakeyama Pass"; 1865
On Yakeyama, the peak area of Mount Fuji said to represent the realm of death, the warrior Shimura captures *yamauba*, the mythic hell-hag. Masakiyo – Yoshitoshi's code for Kiyomasa Kato – is also shown, and the underlying meaning of this illustration remains obscure.

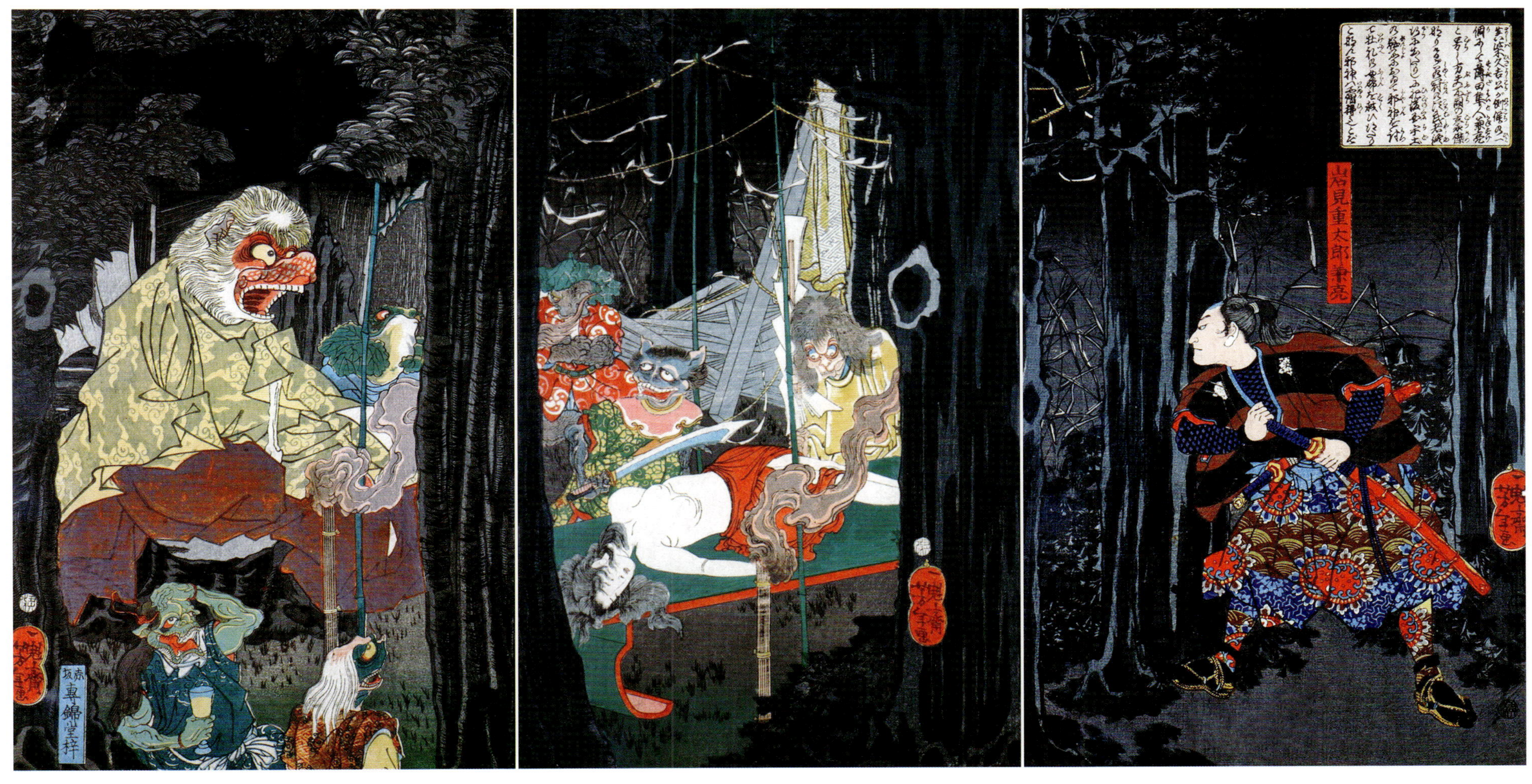

IWAMI JUTARO KAI UKAGAU

"Iwami Jutaro Spies On A Monster"; 1865

Iwami Jutaro, a legendary 16th century *samurai*, was renowned in myth as a slayer of bizarre beasts and monsters. In this depiction he watches secretly a midnight convocation of *yokai* from Hell, who are about to consecrate the blood sacrifice of a half-naked virgin.

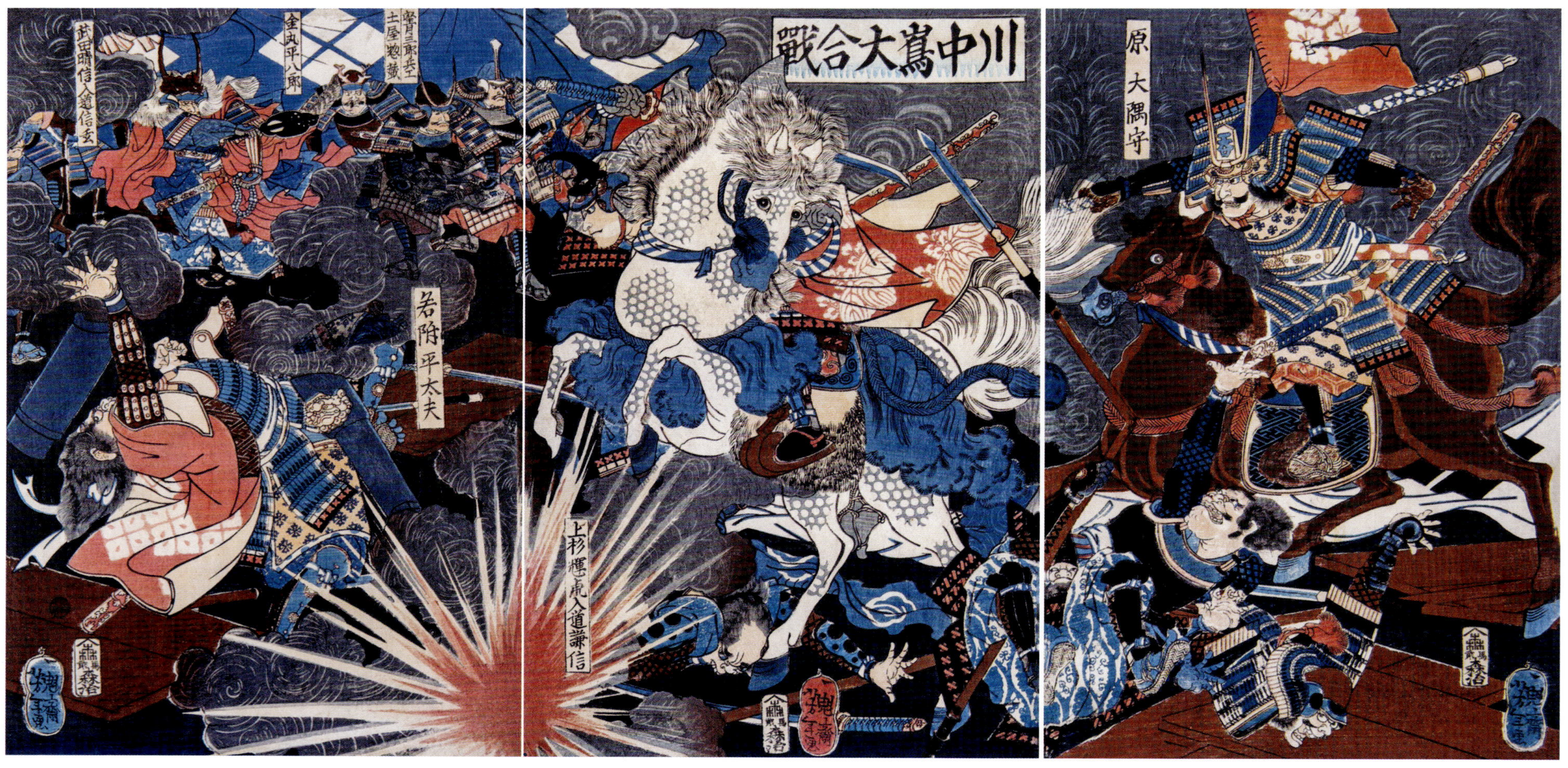

KAWANAKAJIMA OKASSEN

"The Great Battle Of Kawanakajima"; 1866

From 1553 to 1564 a series of five battles was fought at Kawanakajima between Takeda Shingen and Uesugi Kenshin. The battles were Fuse (1553), Saigawa (1555), Uenohara (1557), Hachimanbara (1561), and Shiozaki (1564). Hachimanbara was the only full-scale clash with mass casualties. This illustration is one of several created by Yoshitoshi in reference to Kawanajima, and one of three with identical titles.

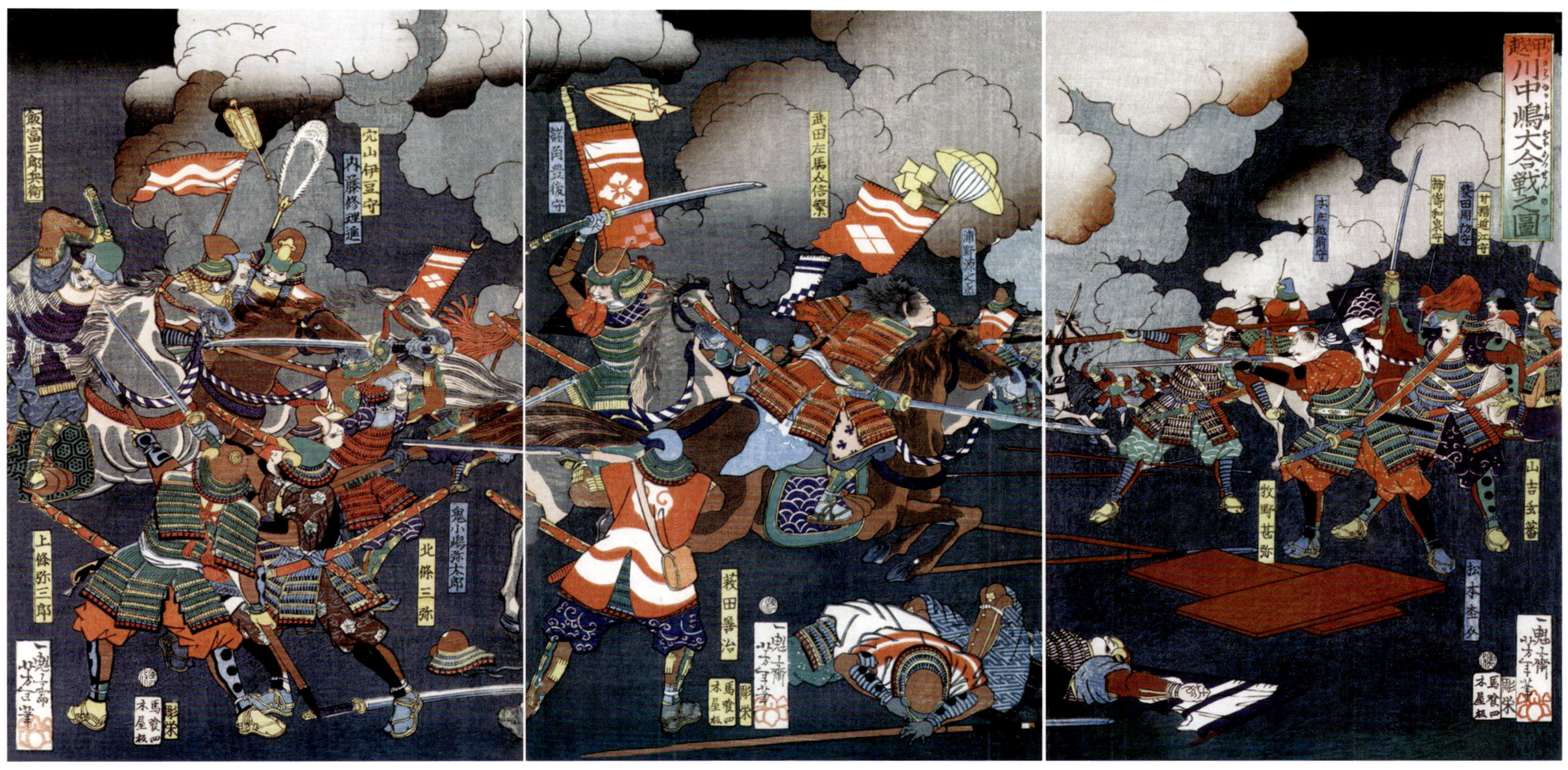

KOETSU KAWANAKAJIMA DAIKASSEN
"Kai And Echigo: The Great Battle Of Kawanakajima"; 1866
Another illustration of fighting at Kawanakajima, where Kai Province was represented by Takeda Shingen and Echigo Province by Uesugi Kenshin. Guns were first used in Japanese warfare from around 1560, which makes this illustration most likely to be a representation of Hachimanbara in 1561.

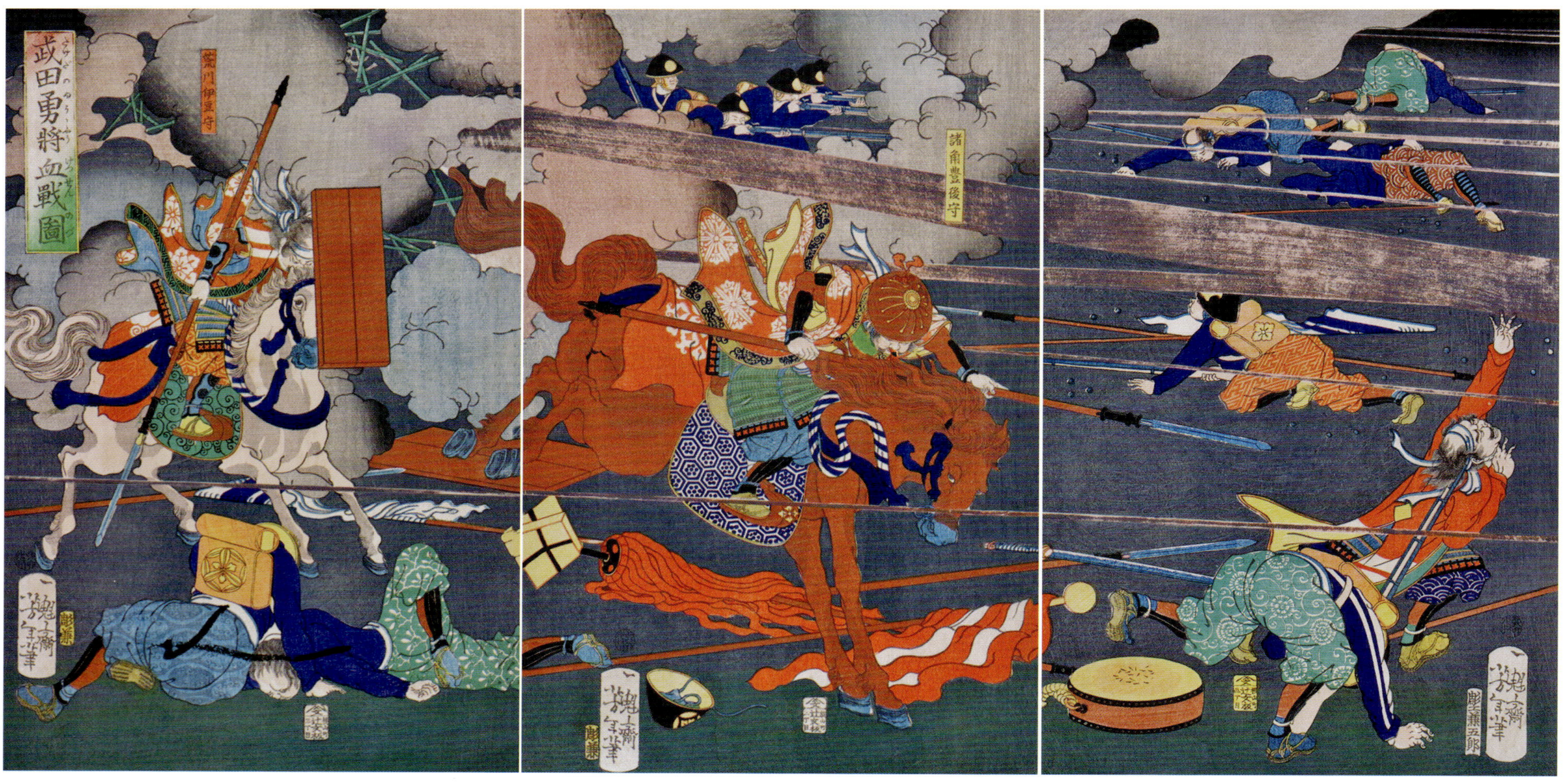

KAWANAKAJIMA OKASSEN / TAKEDA YUSHO KESSEN

"The Great Battle Of Kawanakajima" / "Bloody Fighting By The Brave Takeda Generals" (hexaptych); 1866-67

A double triptych of fighting scenes from one of the five battles, again with guns and also cannon-fire; most likely another representation of Hachimanbara. The right-hand triptych, "The Great Battle Of Kawanakajima", was published in 1866 while the left-hand triptych, "Bloody Fighting By The Brave Takeda Generals", was published some six months later in 1867; this gap may explain the discrepancy in perspective between the two illustrations. As was often the case, this historical depiction also serves as covert commentary on issues of the day – possibly the *shogun*'s war against radical rebels in Choshu Province.

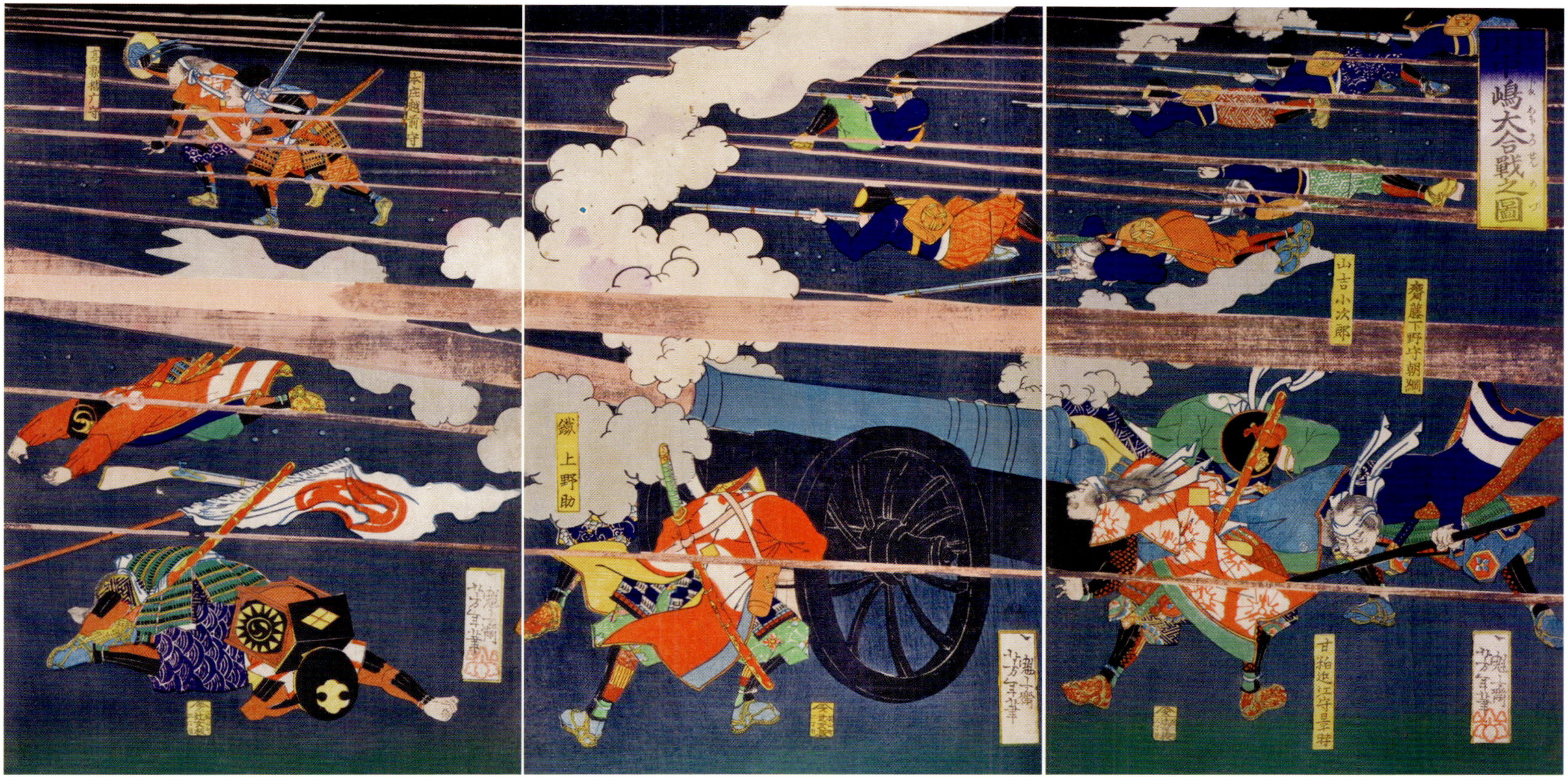

嶋大合戦之圖
山吉小次郎
鐵上野助
芳年筆

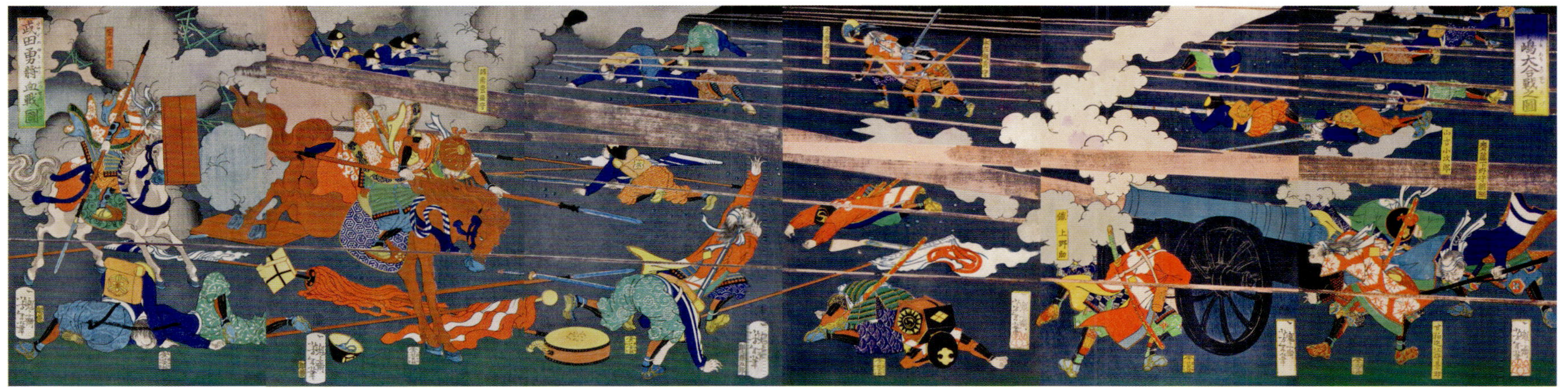

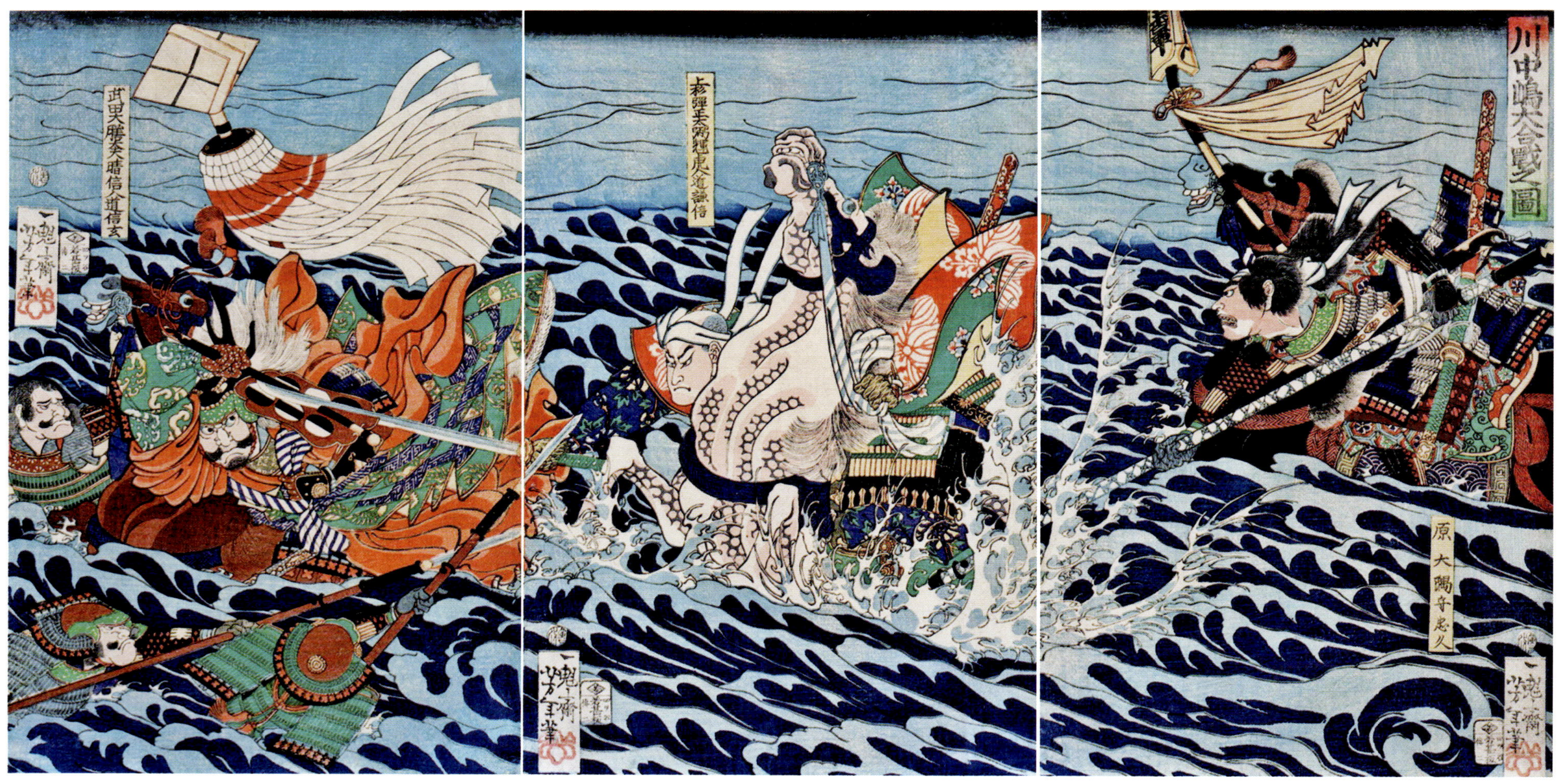

KAWANAKAJIMA OKASSEN
"The Great Battle Of Kawanakajima"; 1866
Kawanakajima means "island between two rivers", and much of the fighting was inevitably carried out in water.

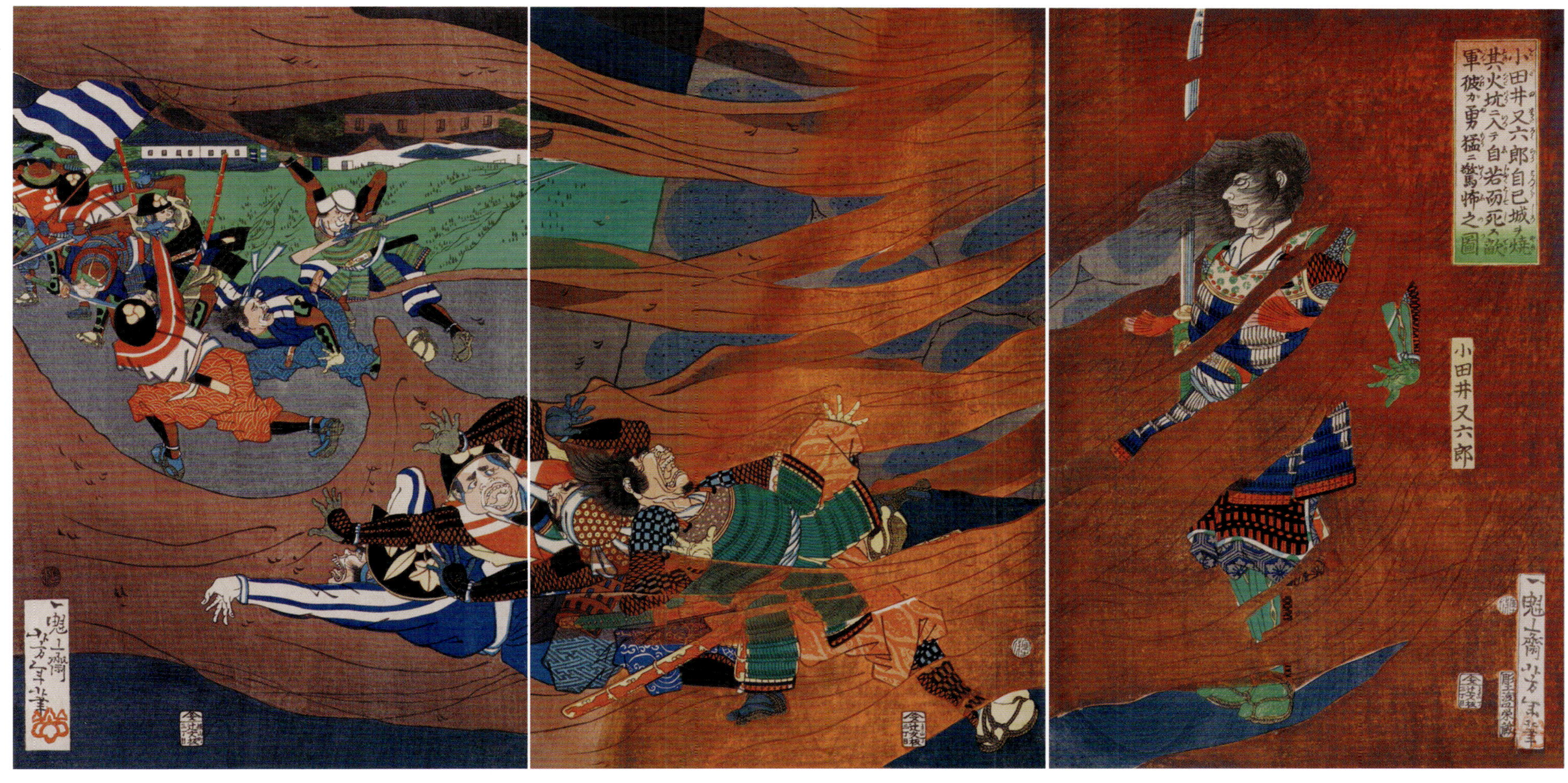

ODAI MATAROKURO MIZUKARA SHIRO O YAKI

"Osai Matarokuro Burns Down His Own Castle"; 1866

Odai Matarokuro Horisada was a *daimyo* who in 1170 came into conflict with Takeda Shingen; after he was defeated by Takeda follwing a prolonged siege, he staged a remarkable suicide by setting fire to his castle and burning alive in the flames. The full text accompanying this illustration translates as follows: "Odai Matarokuro burns down his own castle, calmly perishing in the fiery pit; enemy troops are stupefied by his courage".

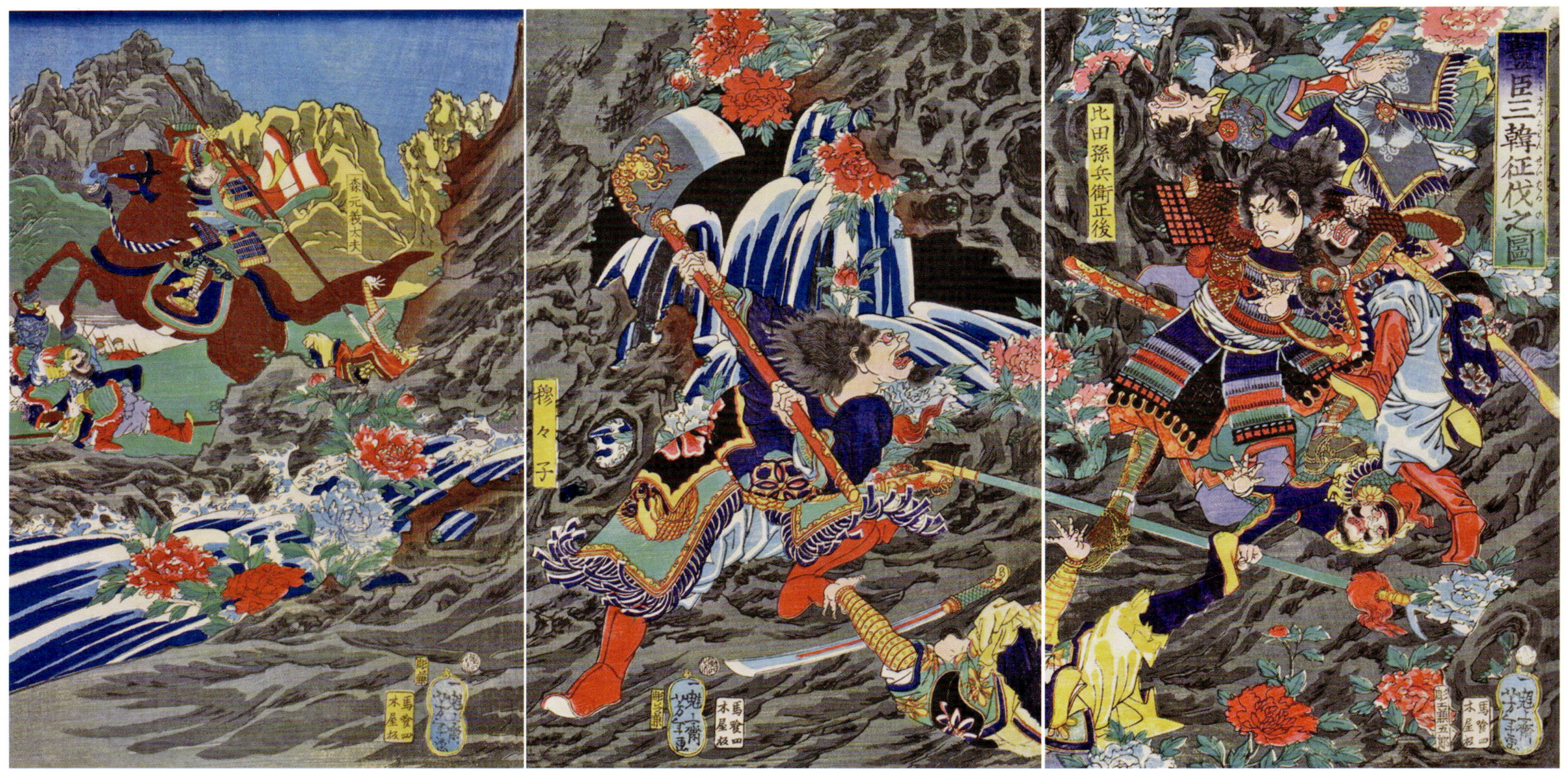

TOYOTOMI SANKAN SEIBATSU

"Toyotomi's Subjugation Of Korea"; 1866

Yoshitoshi returns to one of his favourite subjects, the exploits of Toyotomi Hideyoshi's forces in occupied Korea. The unkempt and rabid Korean warrior, armed with a huge axe, is contrasted with the noble *samurai* who fights off several attackers at once.

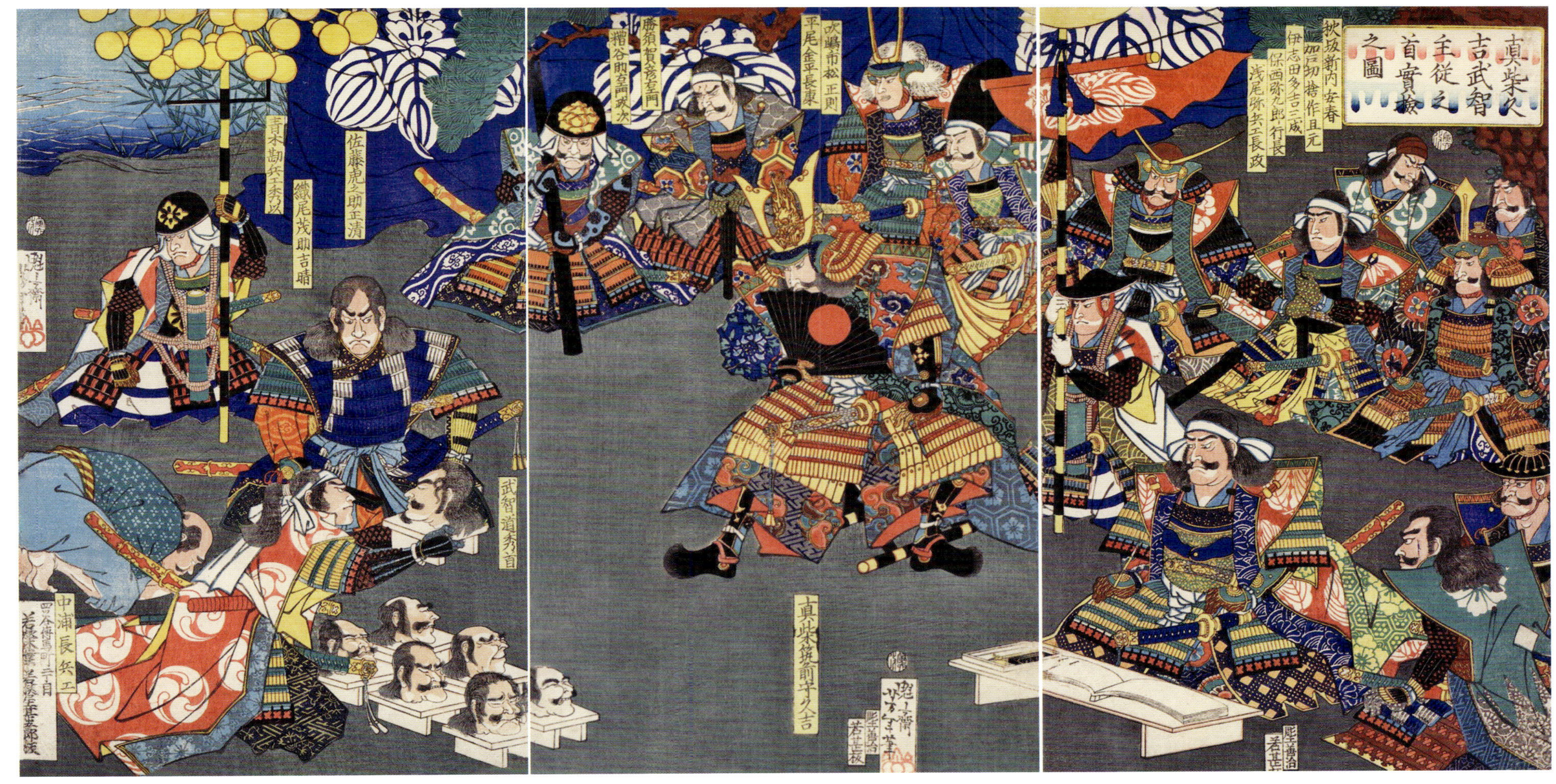

MASHIBA HISAYOSHI TAKECHI SHUJU NO KUBIJIKKEN

"Mashiba Hisayoshi Identifying The Severed Heads Of Takechi And His Close Retainers"; 1866
Mashiba Hisayoshi (Hashiba Hideyoshi) is presented with the severed heads of Takechi (Akechi Mitsuhide) and his personal guard. This would have been following the battle of Yamazaki in 1582, when the fleeing Akechi was killed. The process of *kubijikken* involved the positive identification of corpses by examining their detached heads, which were cleaned of blood after removal.

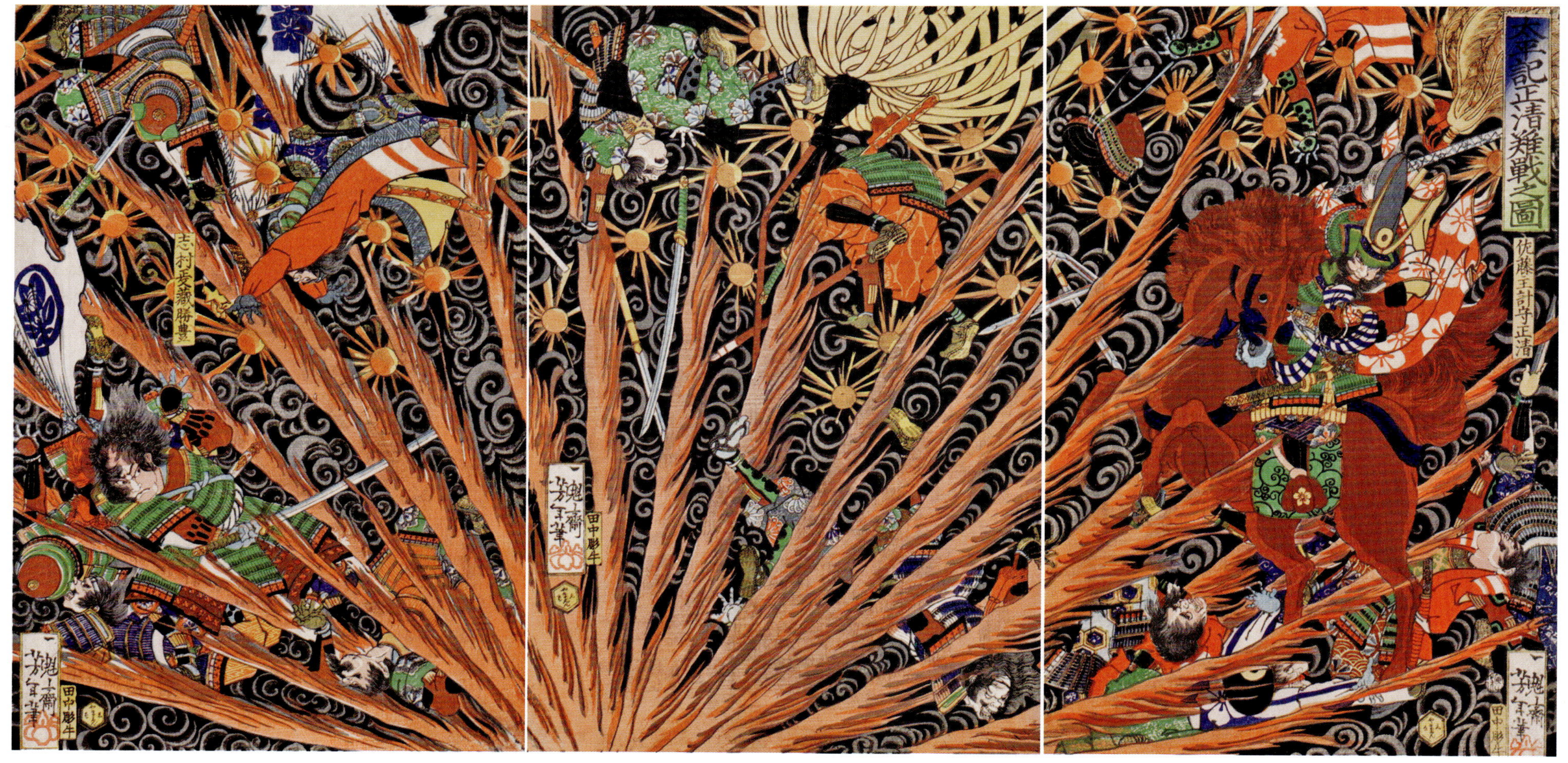

TAIHEIKI MASAKIYO NANSEN

"Scene From *Taiheiki*: Masakiyo's Dangerous Battle"; 1866
One of Yoshitoshi's most dynamic war illustrations, showing a massive explosion and carnage. Another thinly-veiled image of Kiyomasa from the *Taikoki*, which possibly also had a third, more contemporary layer of meaning relating to the *shogun* Tokugawa Iemochi's recent battle campaign against an insurgency of dissident Choshu *samurai* with a *modus operandi* of explosive artillery attacks.

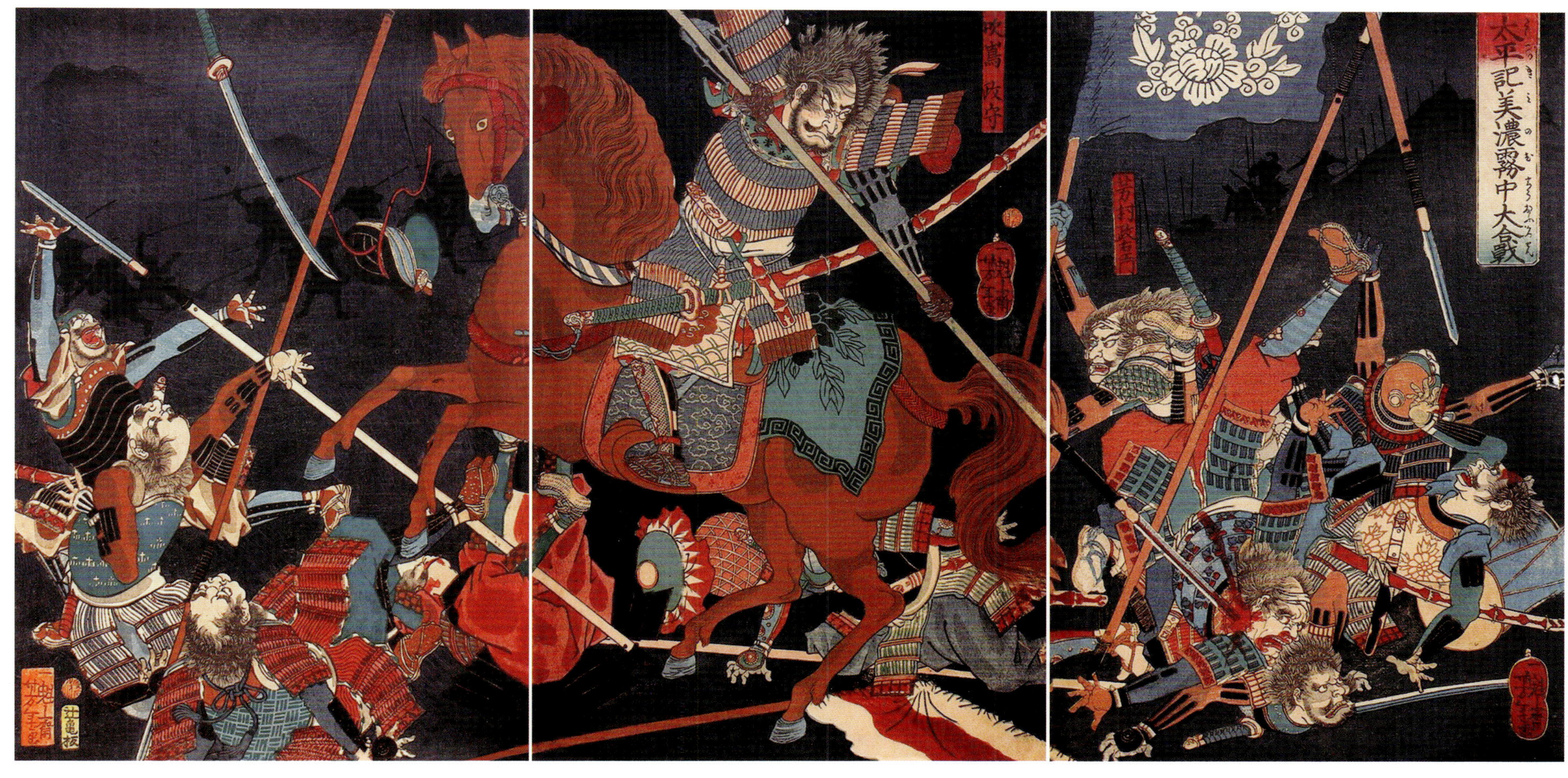

TAIHEIKI MINO MUCHU OKASSEN

"Scene From *Taiheki*: Great Battle At Mino In The Fcg"; 1866
Most likely a depiction of figting during Oda Nobunaga's campaign to defeat the Saito clan and conquer Mino Province in 1567.

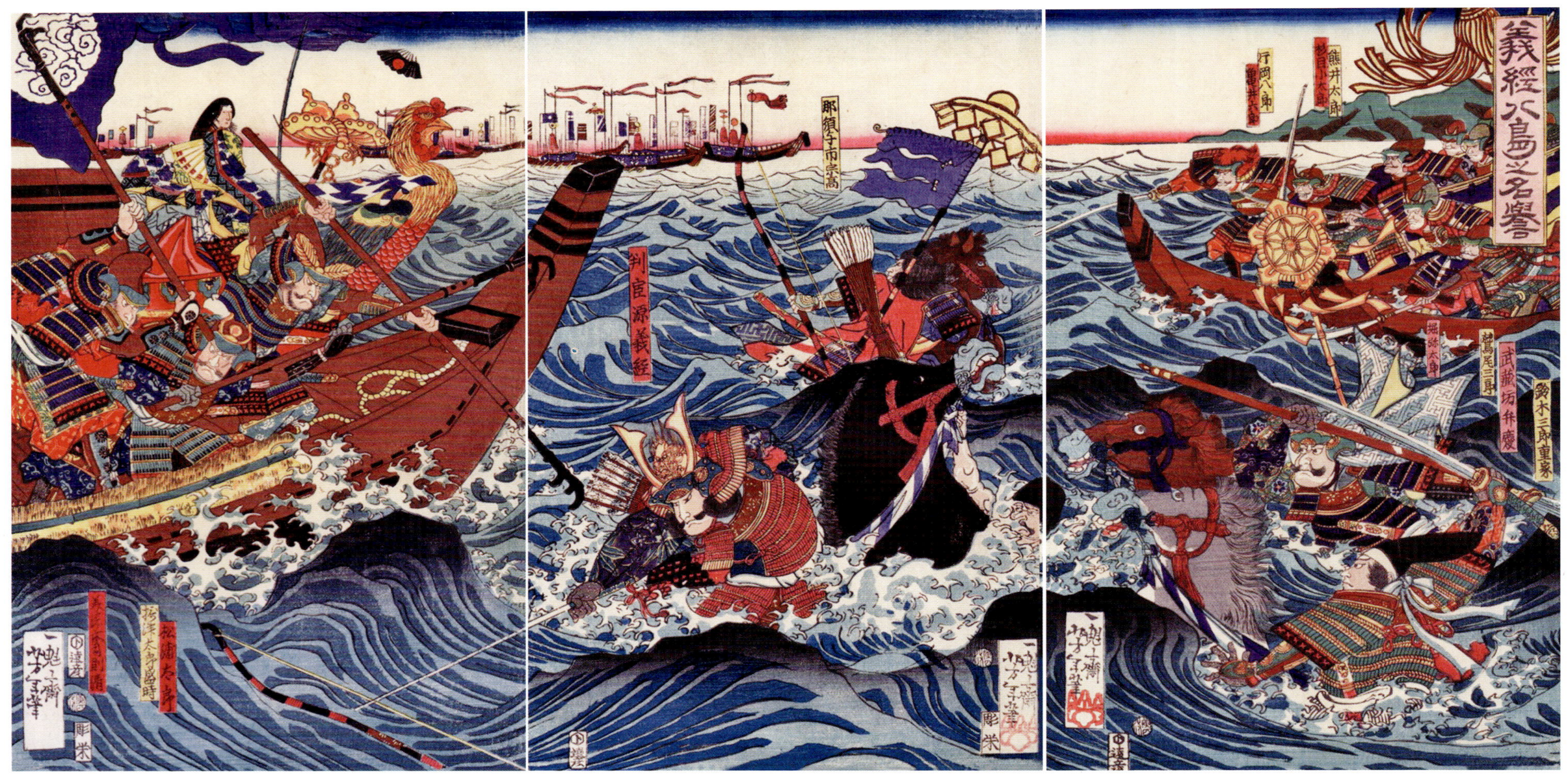

YOSHITSUNE YASHIMA NO MEIYO

"Yoshitusne's Valour At Yashima"; 1866

Yashima was a sea-battle of the Genpei Wars, from 1185; thanks to the military cunning of Minatmoto no Yoshitsune, the Taira clan were repelled and forced to make a final stand at Dan-no-Ura a month later.

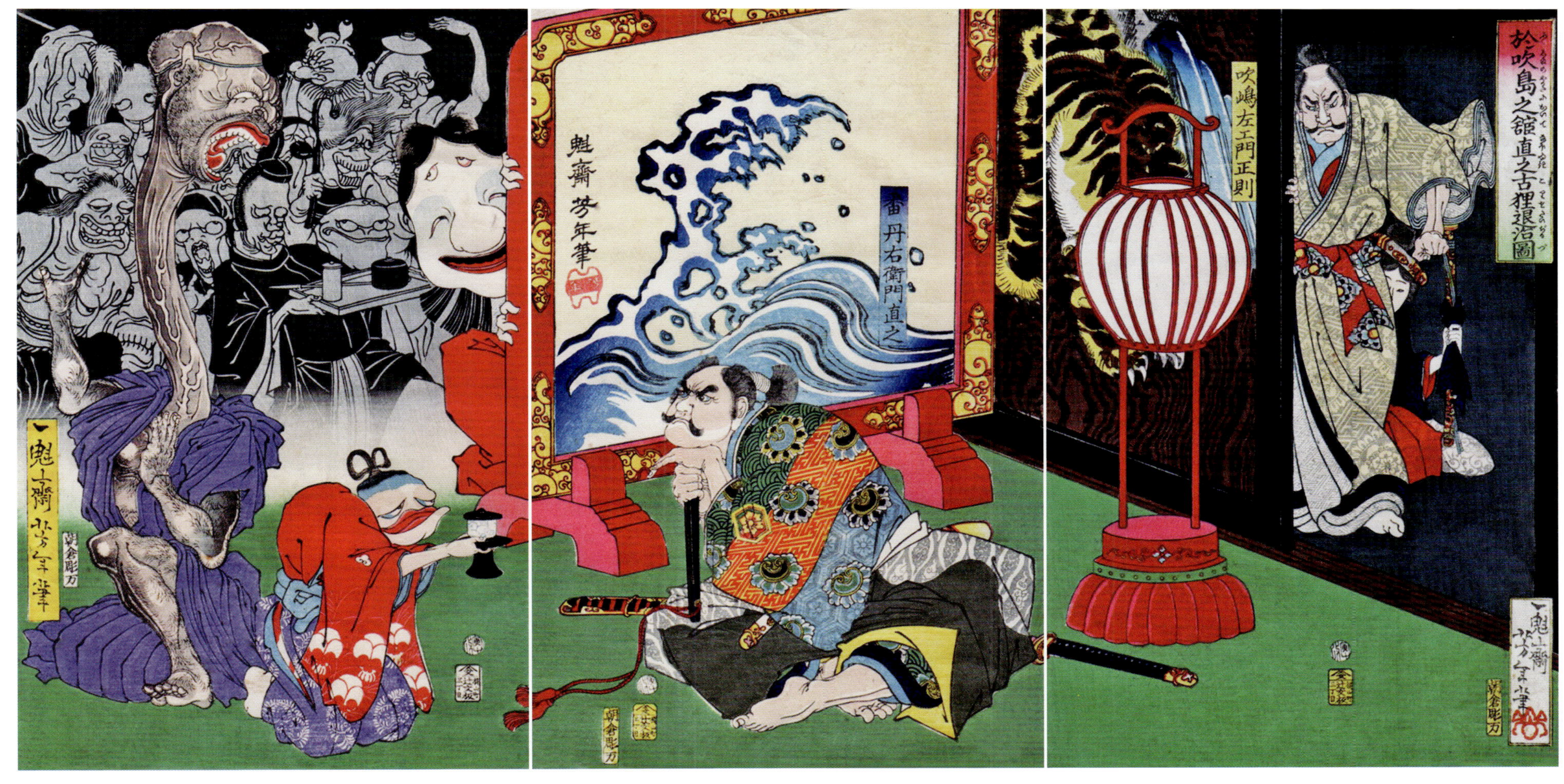

FUKUSHIMA NO YAKATA NAOYUKI FURUDANUKI TAIJI
"Naoyuki Destroys The Badger-Demon At The Old Fukushima Mansion"; 1866
Naoyuki Ban, also known as Danemon, was a 16th century *samurai* who legend tells once fought and killed a crafty old demon in a *yokai*-haunted house, in order to claim the reward money.

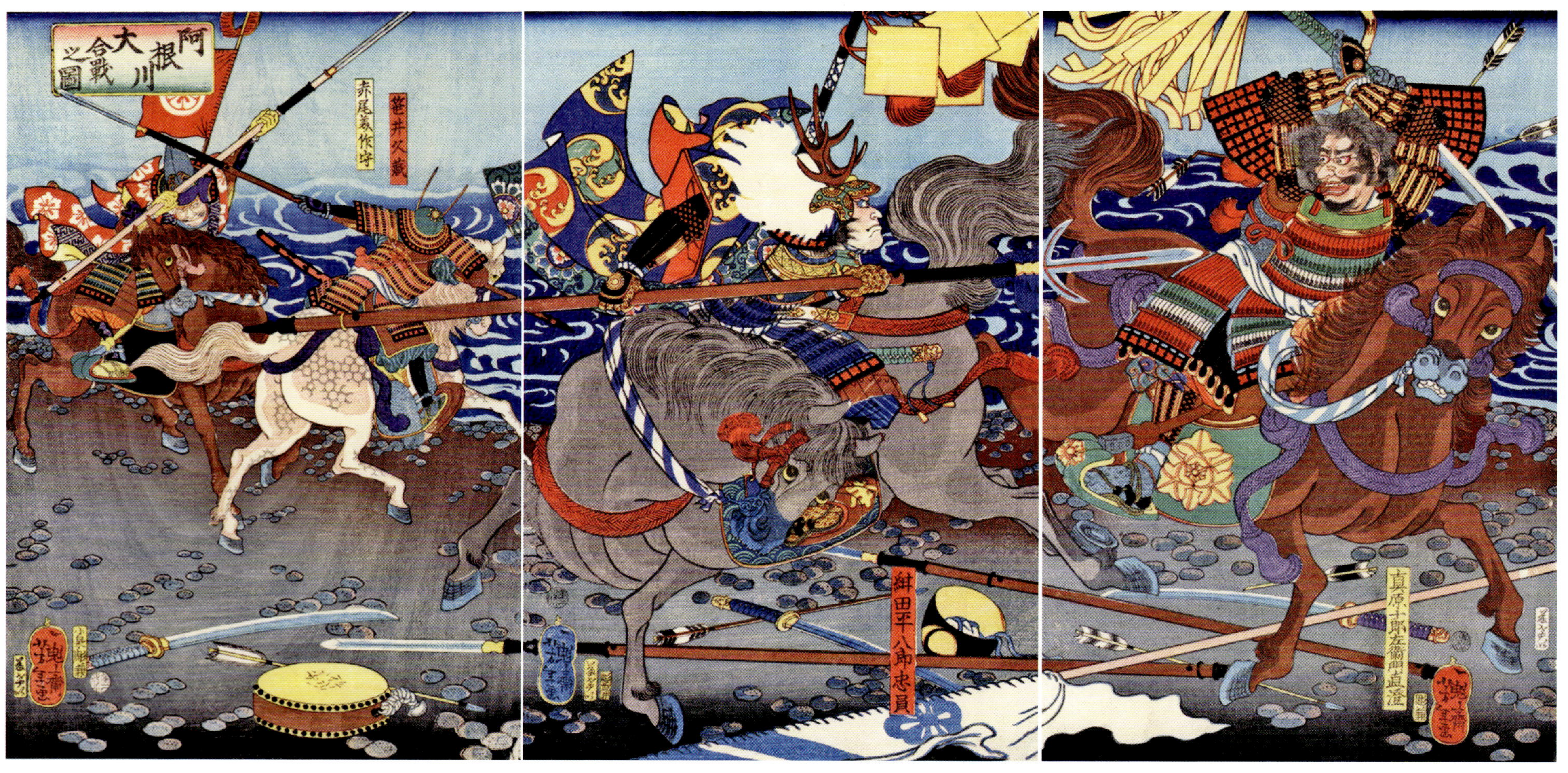

ANEGAWA OKASSEN

"The Great Battle Of Anegawa"; 1866

The battle of Anegawa took place in 1570, involving forces led by Oda Nobunaga and Tokugawa Ieyasu against an alliance of the Azai and Asakura clans. Oda and Tokugawa were victorious, and legend tells that they harvested almost 4,000 severed heads from their foe.

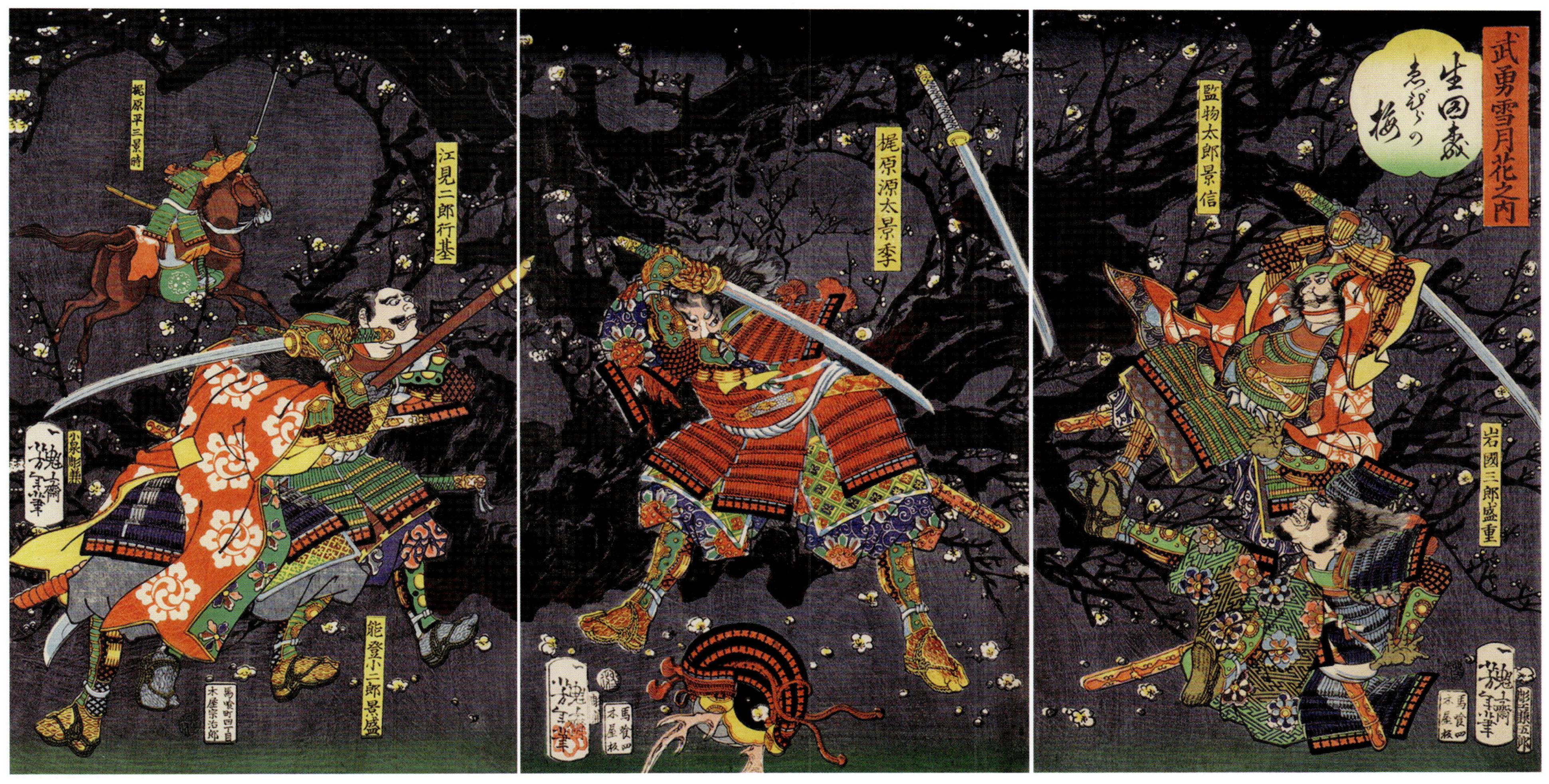

BUYU SETSUGEKKA NO UCHI IKUTA NO MORI EBIRA NO UME
"Snow Moon Flowers With Valiant Heroes: Plum Blossom In Ikuta Forest"; 1867
The first in a trilogy of *setsugekka* triptychs with warrior themes. Probably a scene representing part of the battle of Ichi-no-Tani during the Genpei Wars.

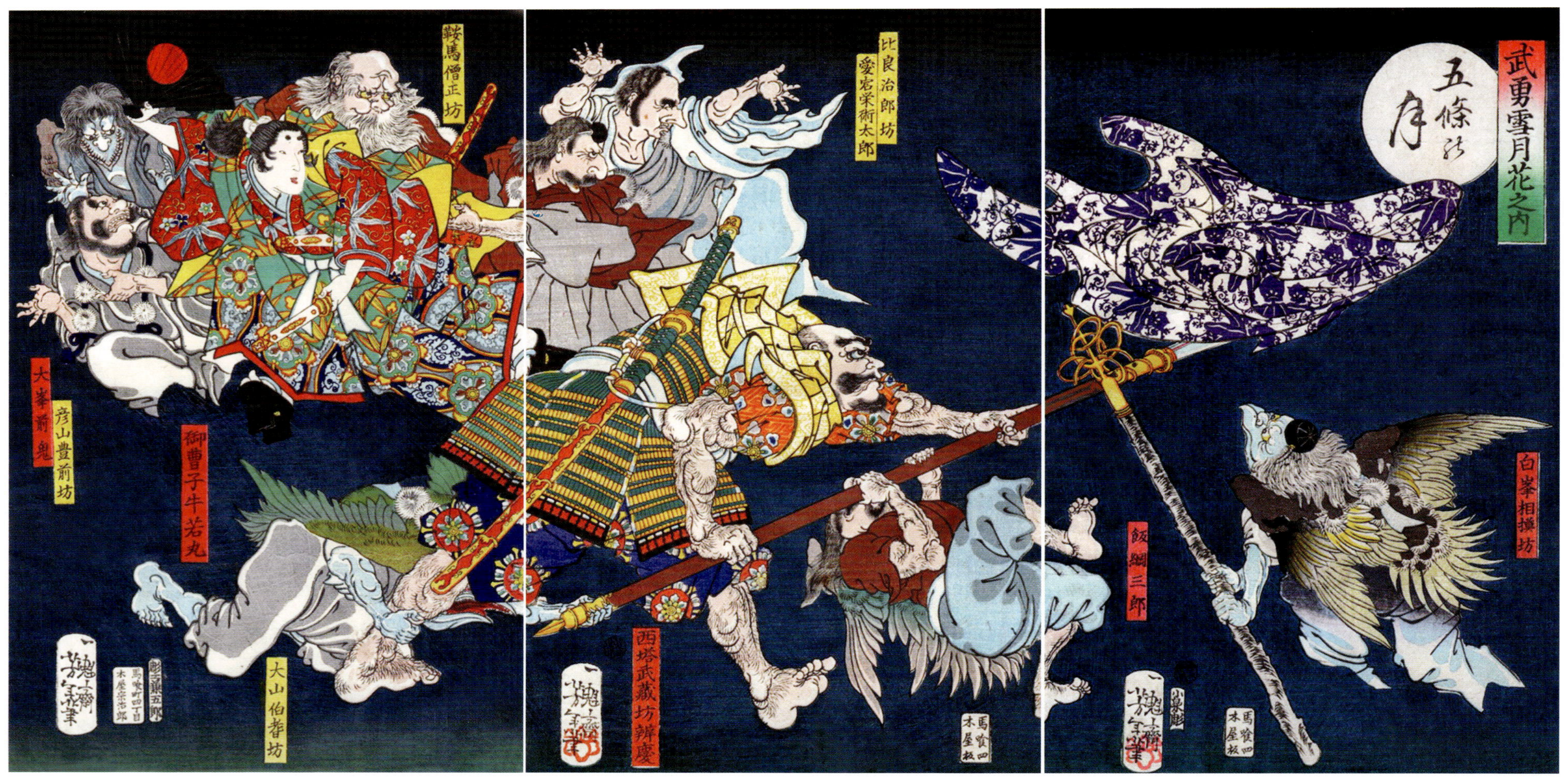

BUYU SETSUGEKKA NO UCHI GOJO NO TSUKI
"Snow Moon Flowers With Valiant Heroes: Moon Over Gojo"; 1867
The second in Yoshitoshi's *setsugekka* trilogy is taken from legend, showing the incident where the young warrior Yoshitsune (then known as Ushiwakamaru) was the first to defeat the warrior-monk Benkei and cross Gojo Bridge. The illustration includes *tengu*, mountain goblins who according to myth taught Yoshitsune his martial skills.

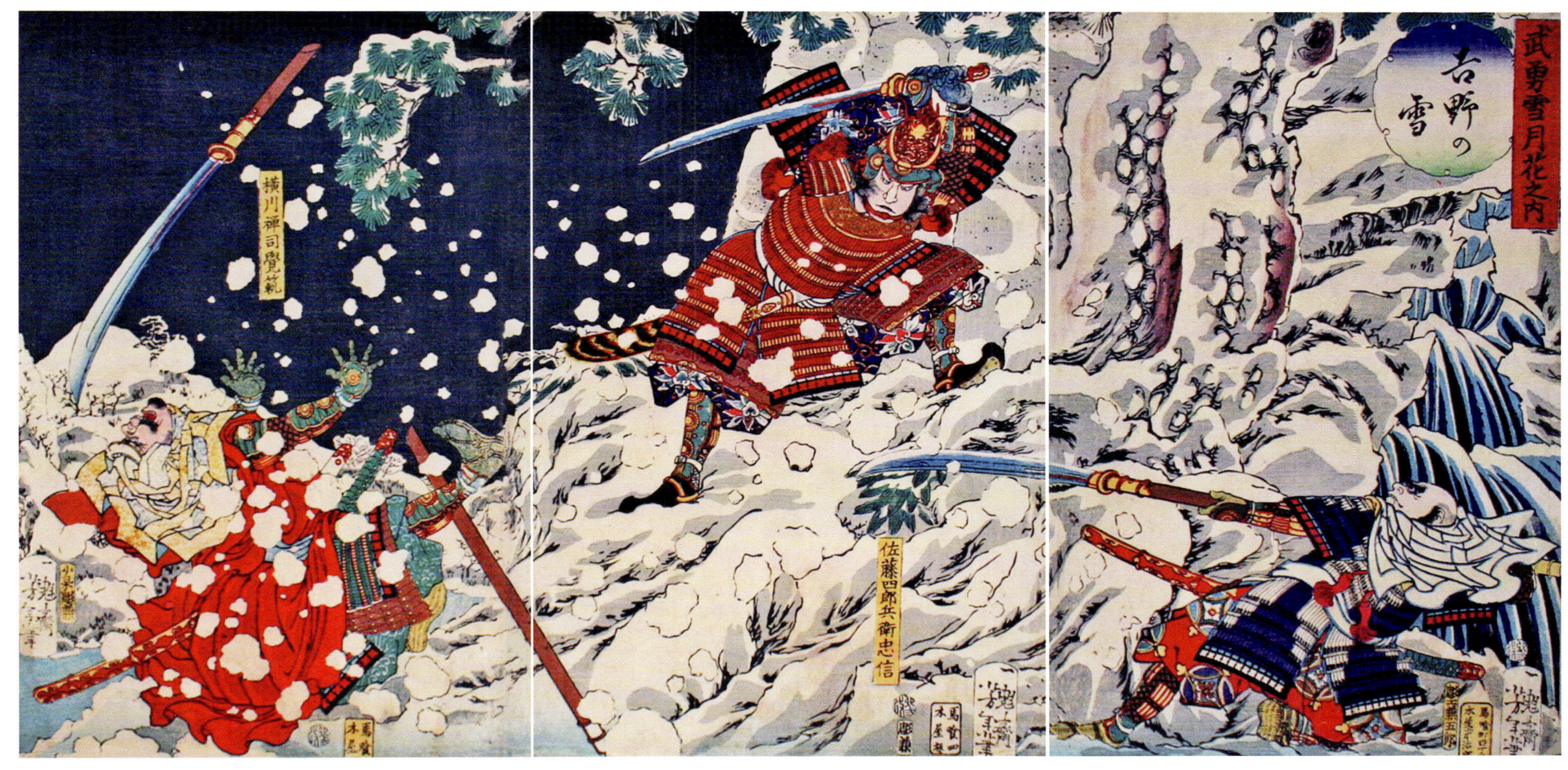

BUYU SETSUGEKKA NO UCHI YOSHINO NO YUKI

"Snow Moon Flowers With Valiant Heroes: Snow At Yoshino"; 1867
The third in Yoshitoshi's trilogy shows the *samurai* Sato Tadanobu, one of Minamoto no Yoshitsune's four "holy knights", protecting his master at Yoshino from a gang of warrior-monks loyal to Yoshitsune's brother Yoritomo. It is said that Sato killed or wounded at least twenty assailants that day.

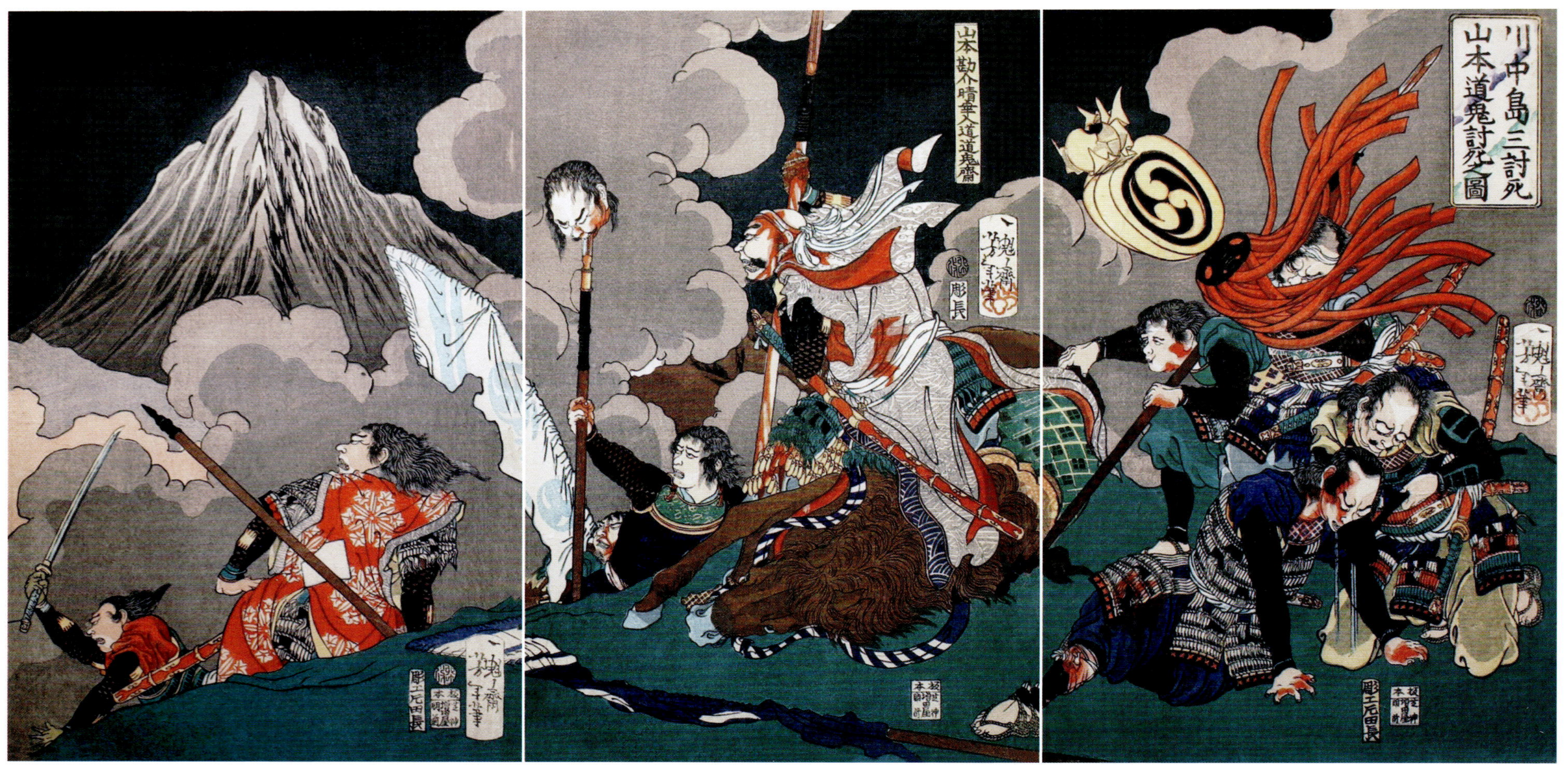

KAWANAKAJIMA SAN UCHIJINI YAMAMOTO DOSAN UCHIJINI
"Three Battle-Deaths At Kawanakajima: The Death Of Yamamoto Kansuke"; 1867
Yamamoto Kansuke was a renowned military strategist and one of Takeda Shingen's "twenty-four generals", his most trusted band of *samurai*. He was killed at the fourth battle of Kawanakajima, in 1561.

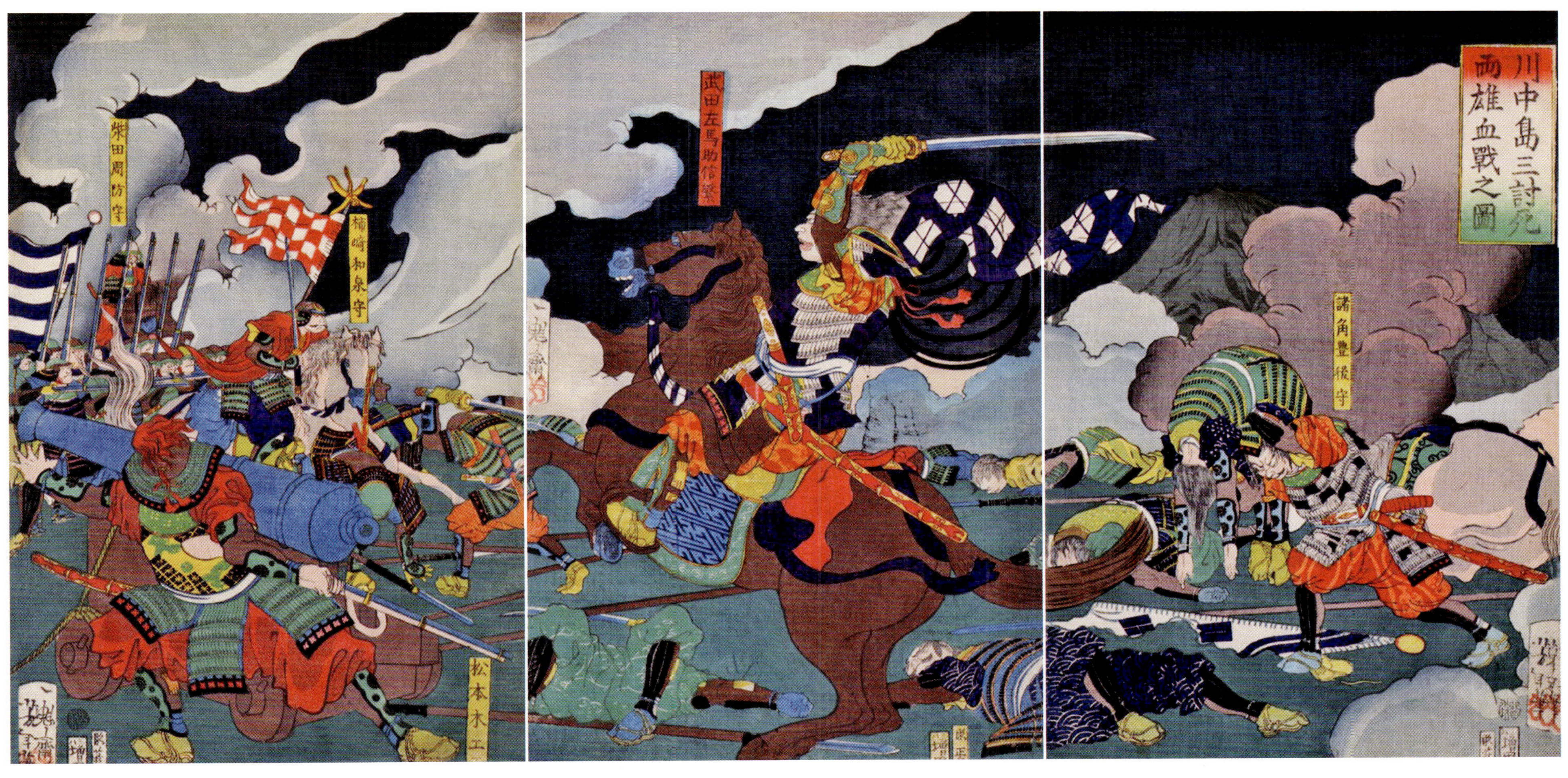

KAWANAKAJIMA SAN UCHIJINI RYOYU KESSEN

"Three Battle-Deaths At Kawanakajima: Bloody Battle Between Two Adversaries"; 1867
Another view of fighting, carnage and death at Kawanajima. It is not known if Yoshitoshi ever made a third triptych in this set.

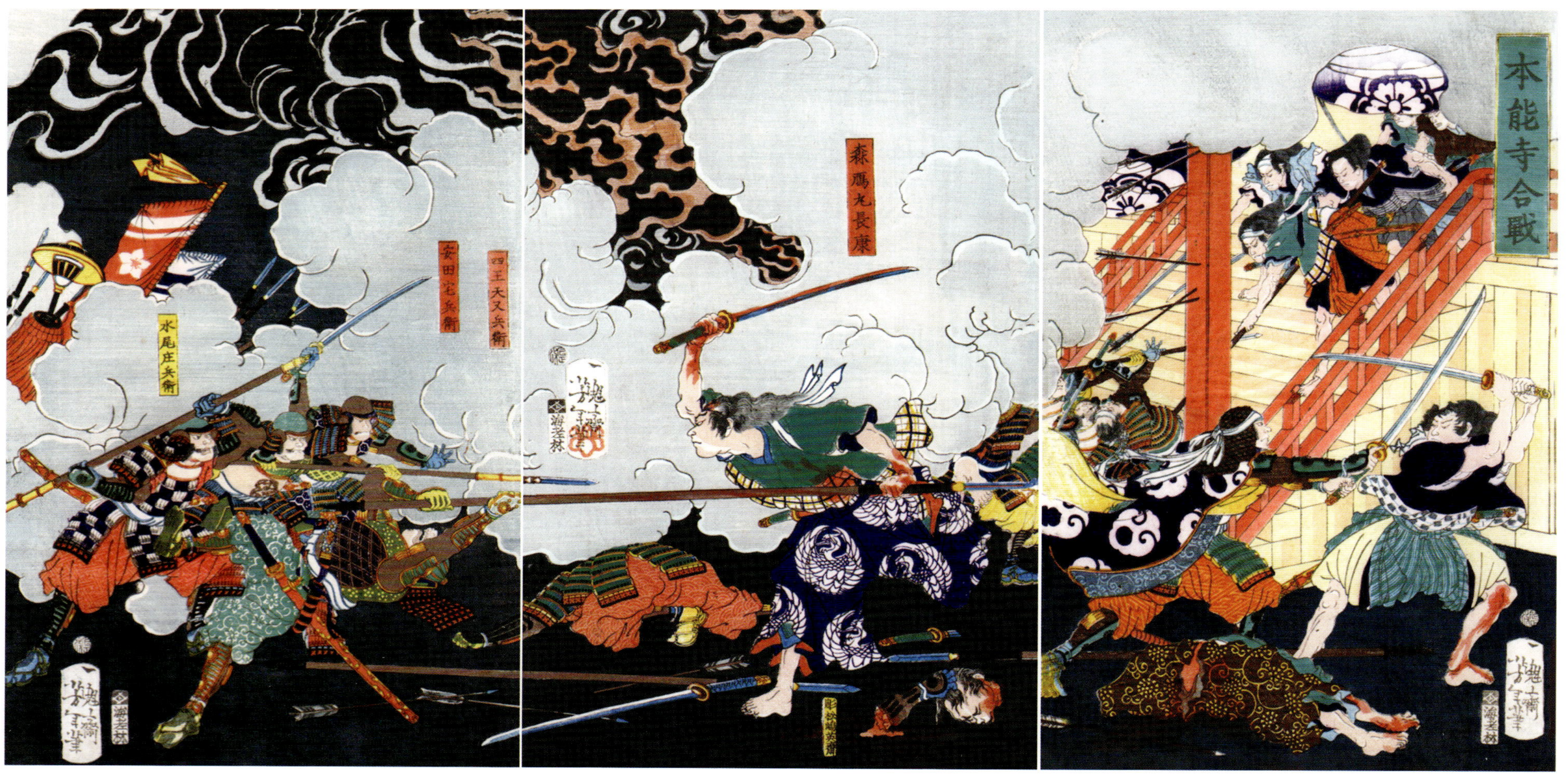

HONNO-JI KASSEN
"Battle At Honno Temple"; 1867
In 1582 the *daimyo* Oda Nobunaga was betrayed by his own general Akechi Mitsuhide, who attacked Oda at Honno temple in Kyoto, where he was relatively unprotected. Oda was forced to commit suicide, and ordered the temple to be razed so that his head could not be severed and taken as a prize by Akechi.

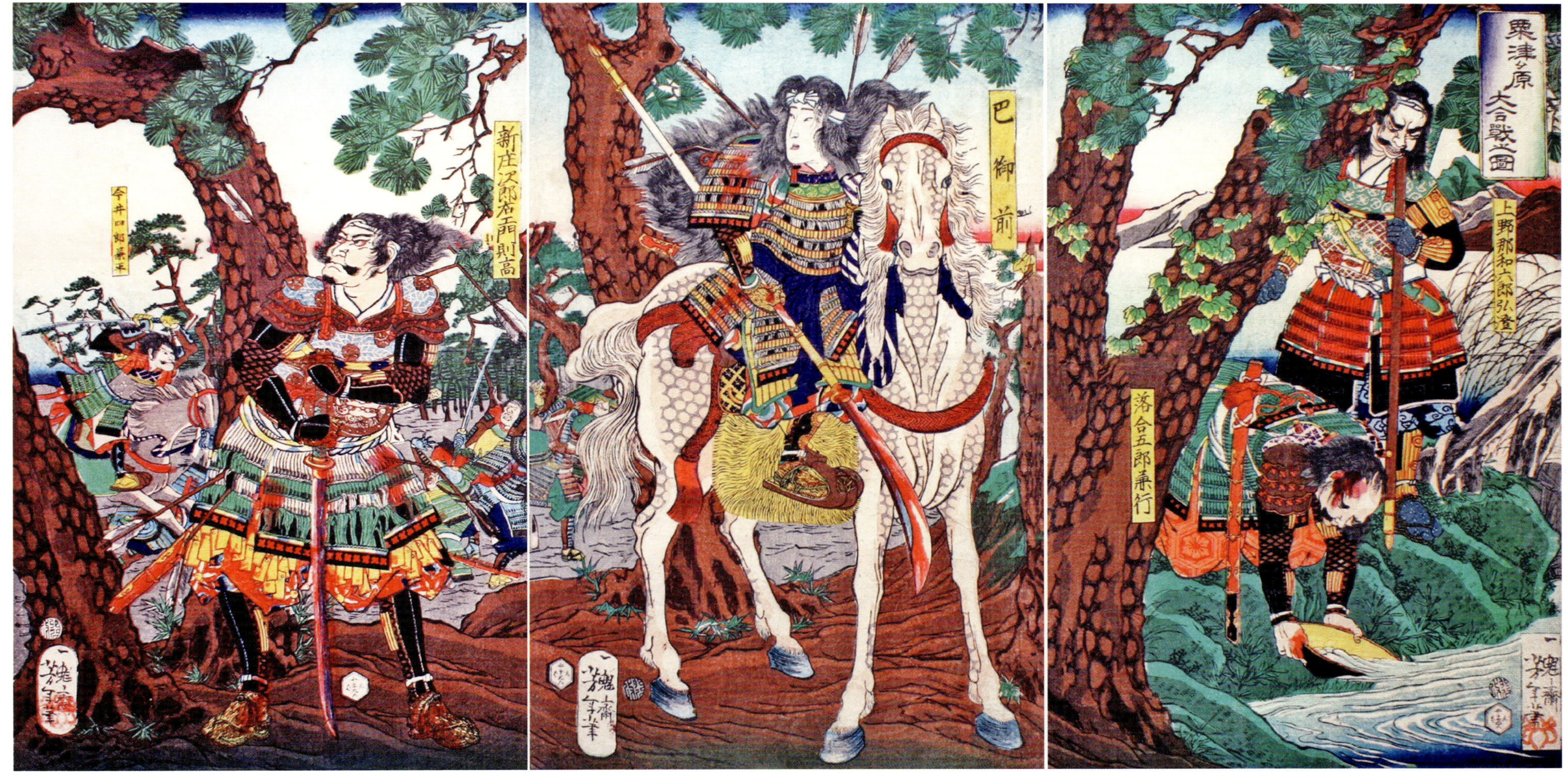

AWAZUGAHARA OKASSEN

"The Great Battle Of Awazugahara"; 1867

The battle at Awazu moor in 1184 during the Genpei Wars was the last stand of Minamoto no Yoshinaka, who was hunted down by his cousin Yoshitsune after the kidnapping of former emperor Go-Shirakawa. It is said that Yoshinaka was shot through the eye with an arrow after his horse got stuck in a rice-field. The central figure of Yoshitoshi's triptych is the legendary female *samurai* Tomoe Gozen, who was Yoshinaka's supreme warrior-concubine. It is said that during the battle of Awazu she decapitated Honda no Morishige, a notable adversary.

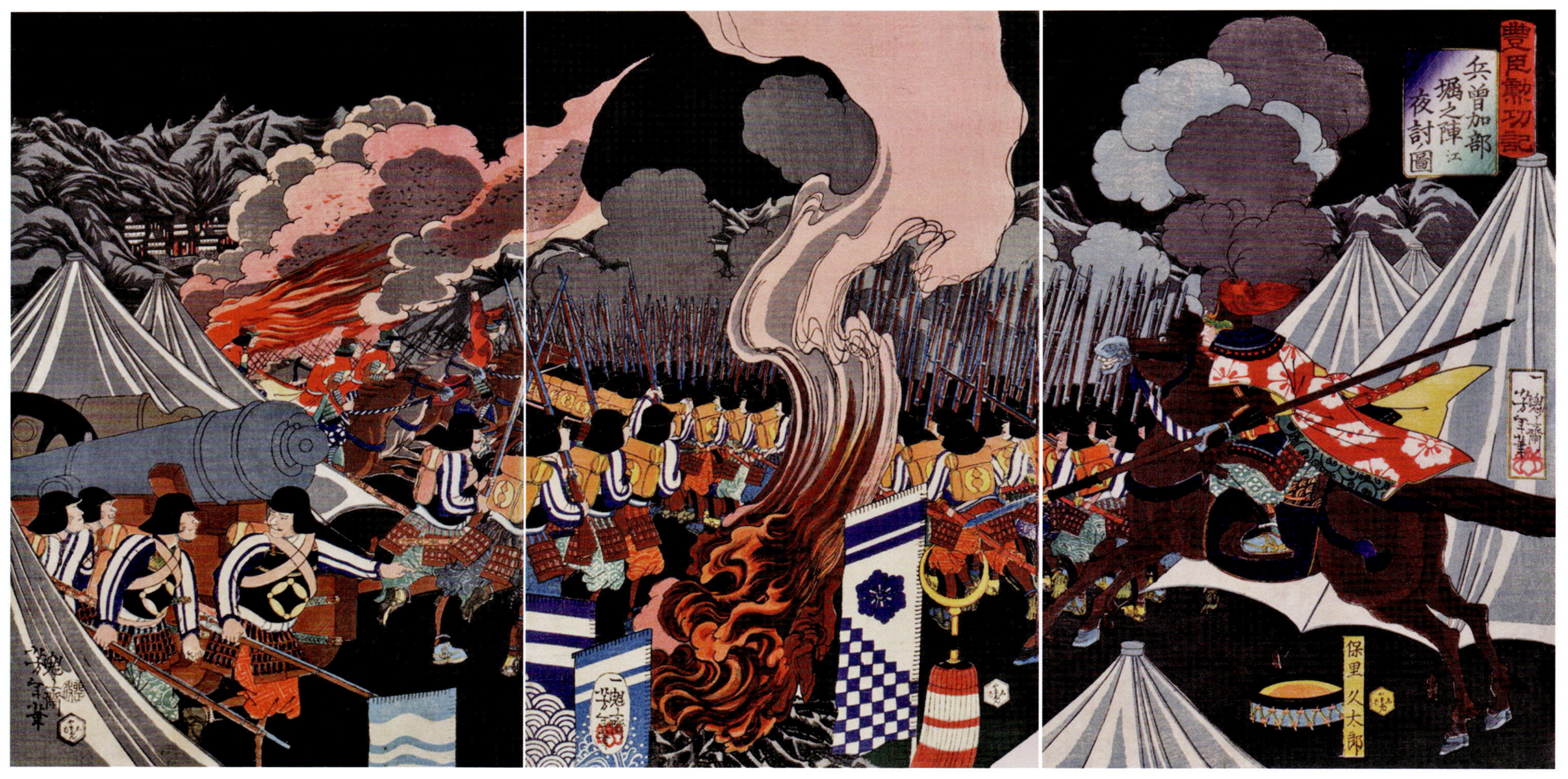

TOYOTOMI KUNKOKI HYOSOKABE HORI NO JIN YOUCHI
"Chronicles Of Toyotomi: Hyosokabe Launches A Night Attack Against Hori's Position"; 1867
In 1867 Yoshitoshi introduced a new style of art for some triptychs, notable for its relative lack of detail. This illustration is an example of this more "modern" style, which may have been simply the result of rushing to meet deadlines. Hori Hidemasa was one of Toyotomi's most ferocious *samurai*; he avoided death in battle despite waging mnay campaigns, and died in 1590 from natural causes. Hyosokabe may refer to clan leader Chosokabe Morichika, who was suppressed by Toyotomi in 1885.

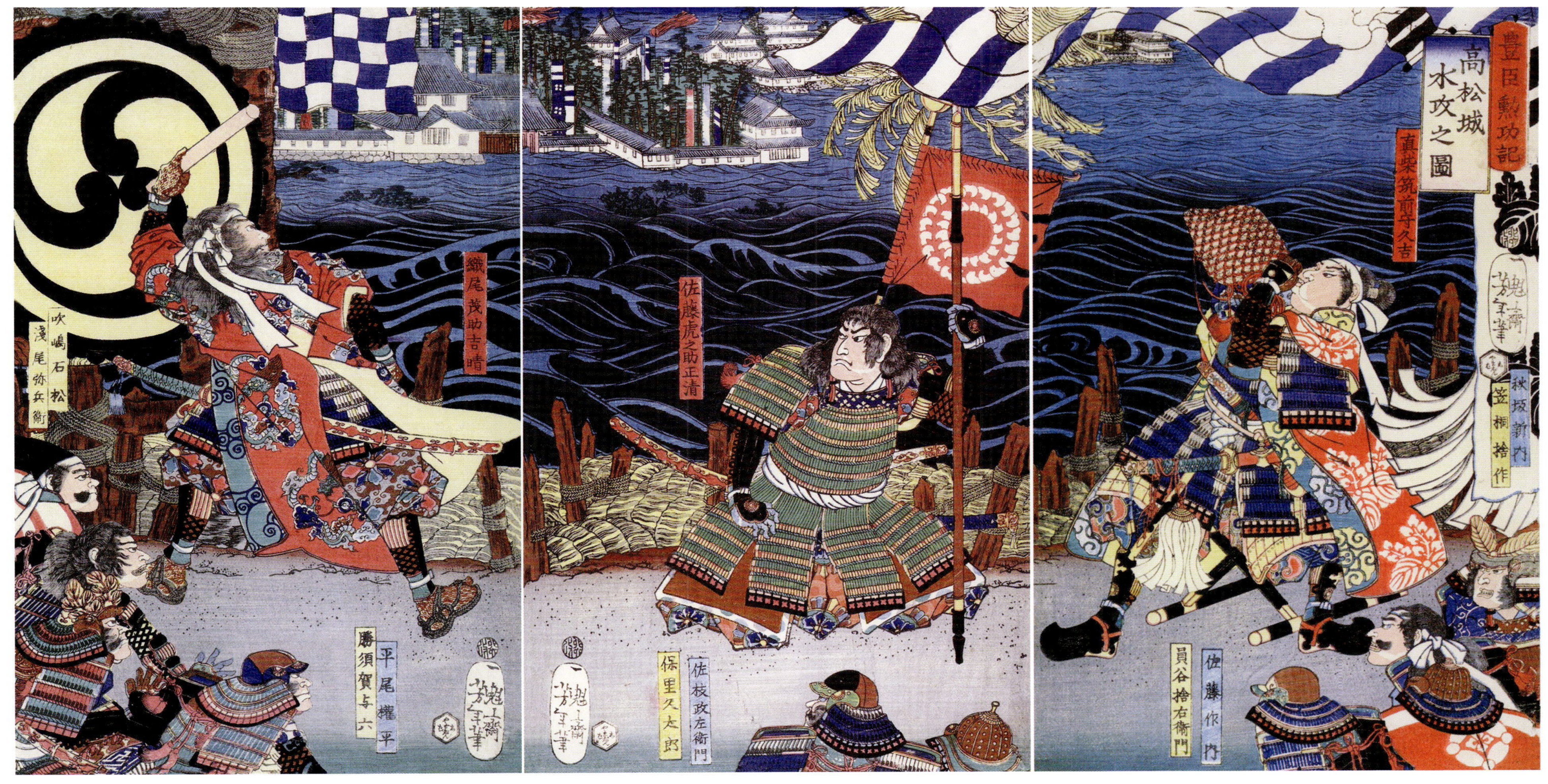

TOYOTOMI KUNKOKI TAKAMATSU-JO MIZUSEME

"Chronicles Of Toyotomi: Water Attack On Takamatsu Castle"; 1867
The siege of Takamatsu castle took place in 1582, when Toyotomi Hideyoshi attacked the Mori clan; his tactics were to flood the castle and to erect floating towers from which his archers and fuseliers could fire at will. The siege ended when the castle's commander, Shimizu Muneharu, was forced to commit ritual suicide.

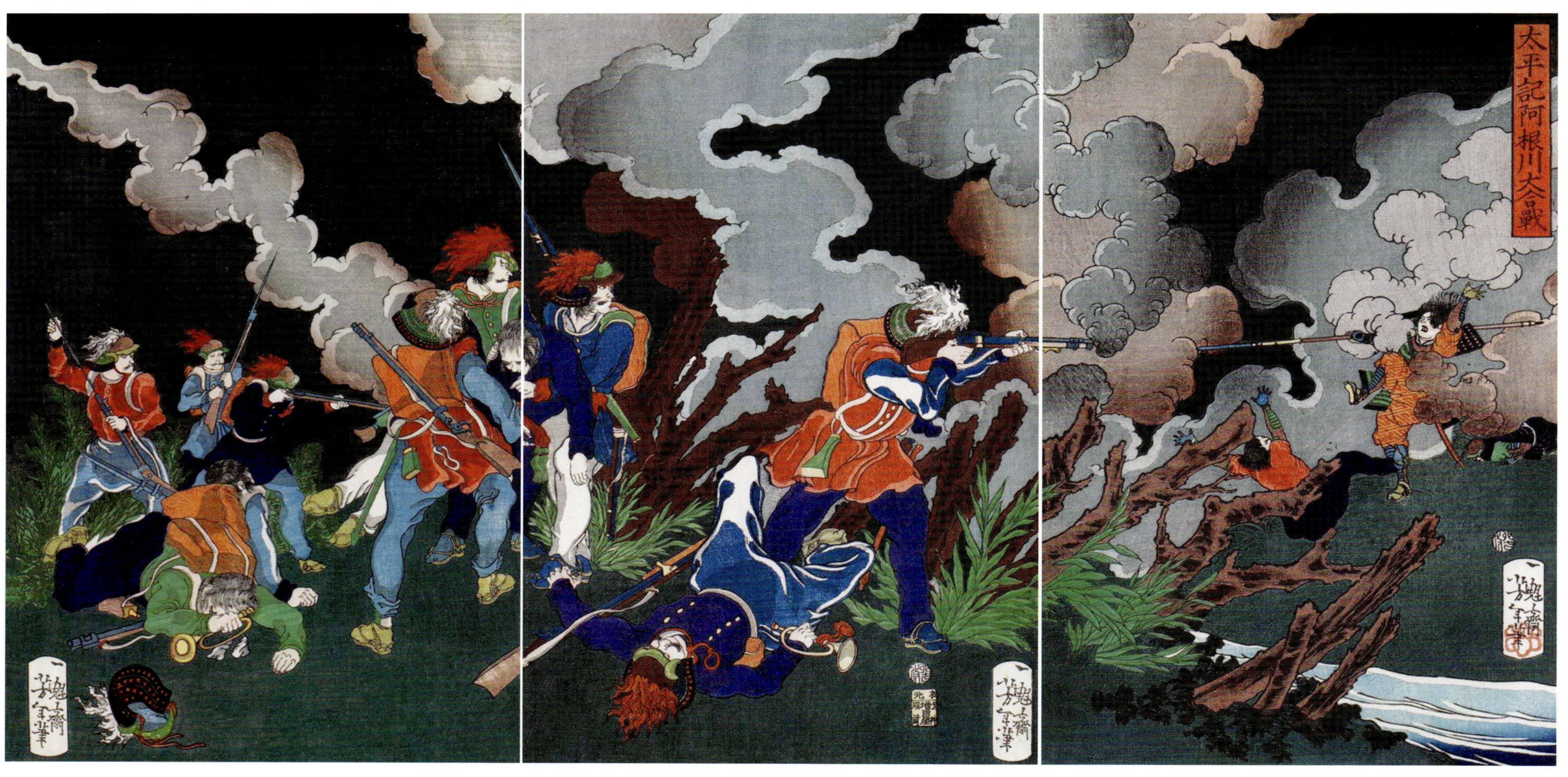

TAIHEIKI ANEGAWA OKASSEN

"Scene From *Taiheiki*: Great Battle Of Anegawa"; 1867
Clearly not from *Taiheiki* with its anachronistic depiction of gunfire, this illustration refers to the clash which took place in 1570.

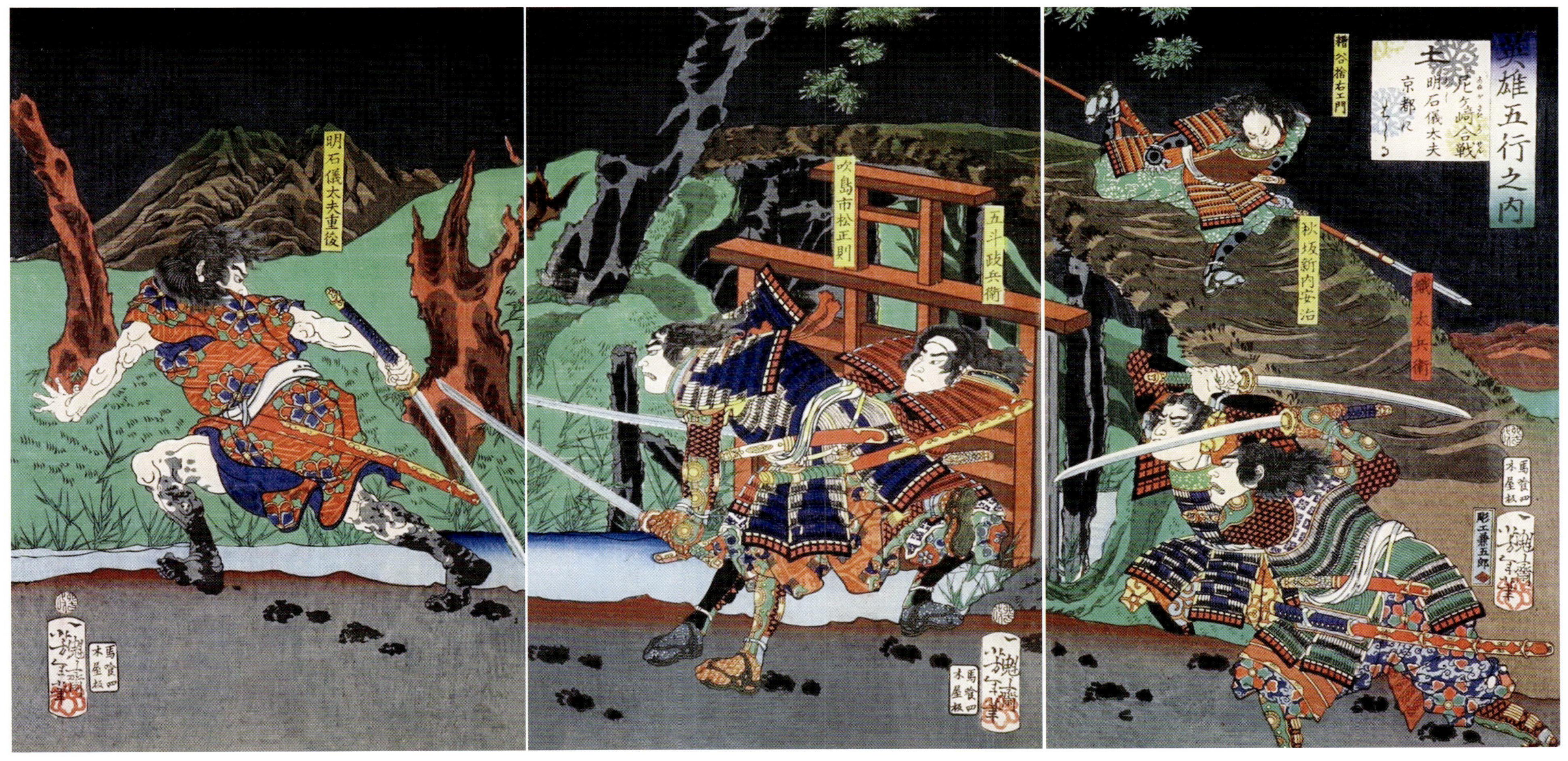

EIYU GOGYO NO UCHI TSUCHI AMAGASAKI KASSEN AKASHI GIDAYU KYOTO NI HASHIRU

"Five Element Warrior: Earth: At The Battle Of Amagasaki, Akashi Gidayu Retreats To Kyoto"; 1867

The first in Yoshitoshi's set of triptychs depicting legendary actions by heroic warriors, each themed around one of the five elements. Akashi Gidayu was one of Akechi Mitsuhide's generals, who committed ritual suicide by disembowelment in Kyoto – against his lord's wishes – after suffering defeat at Yamazaki against the vengeful troops of the recently-deceased Oda Nobunaga in 1582.

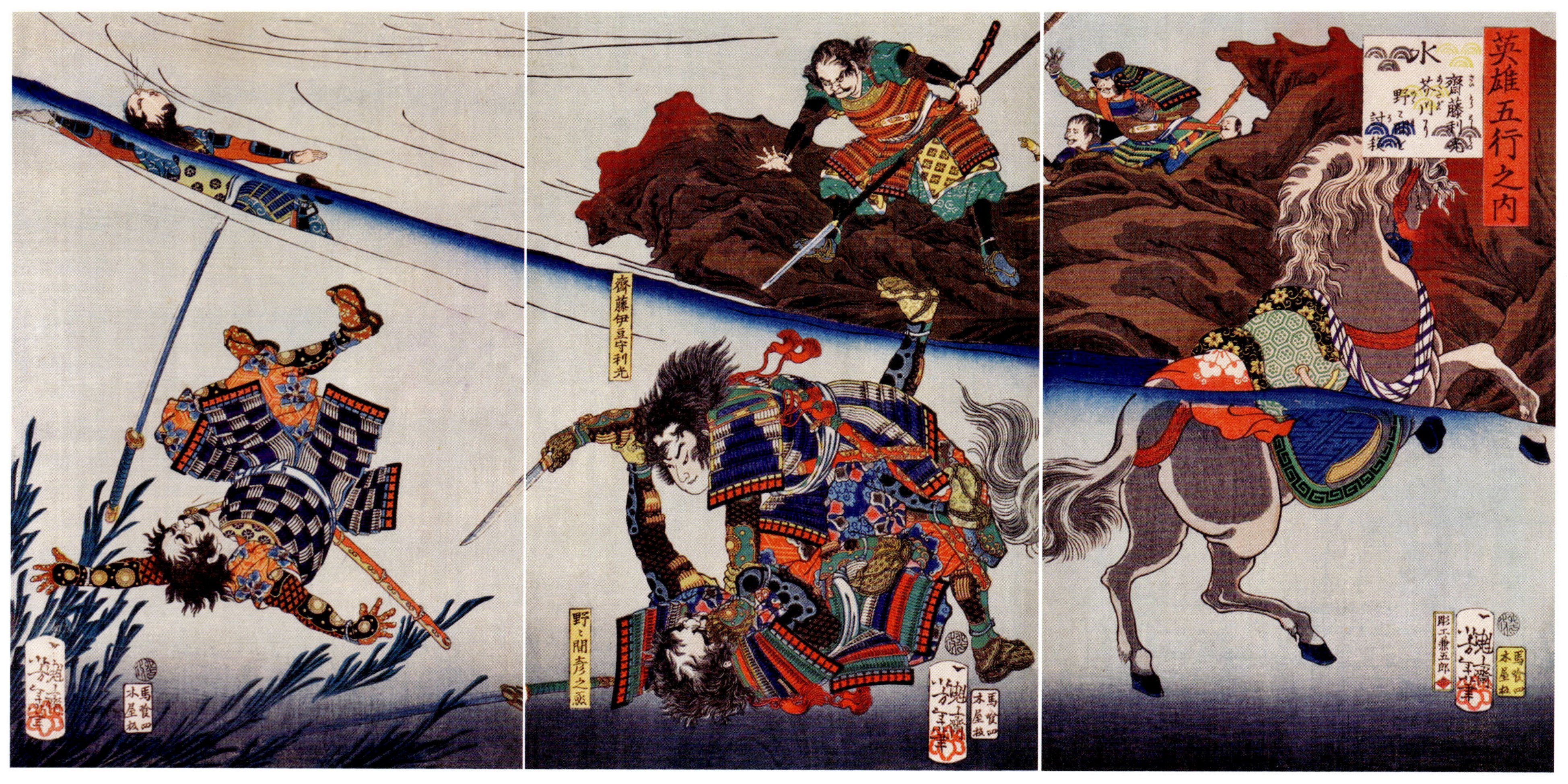

EIYU GOGYO NO UCHI MIZU SAITO TOSHIMITSU AKUTAGAWA NI NONOMA O UTSU

"Five Element Warrior: Water: Saito Toshimitsu Fighting Nonoma At Akutagawa"; 1867

The second in Yoshitoshi's elemental set depicts an underwater fight between the two *samurai* Saito Toshimitsu and Nonomiya Hikonojo in the river Akuta, where a fortress was captured by Oda Nobunaga in 1568. Saito was allied to Akechi Mitsuhide, and saw action at the storming of Honno temple and the battle of Yamazaki, where he was killed alongside his master.

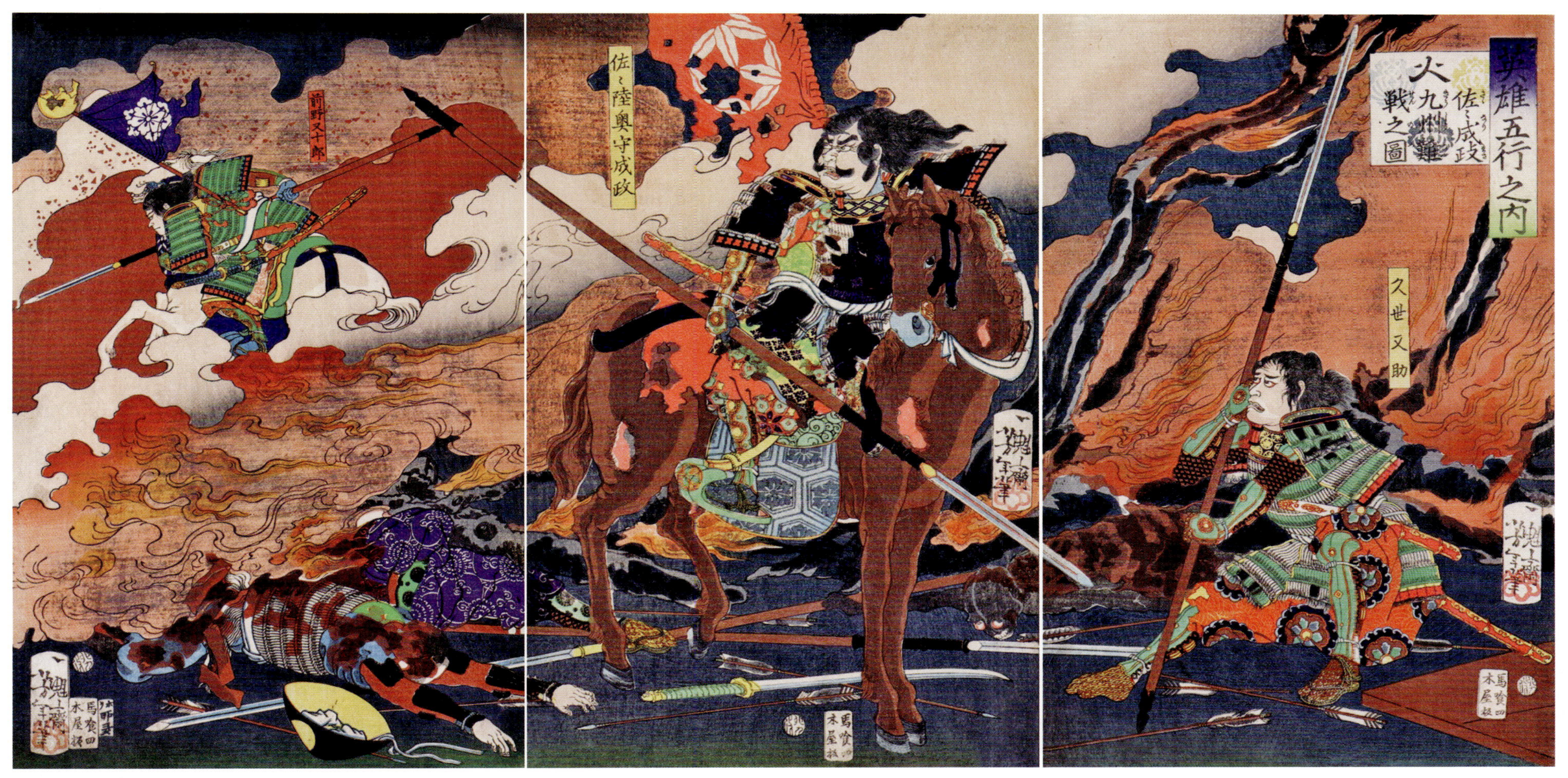

EIYU GOGYO NO UCHI HI SASSA NARIMASA KYUSHU NANSEN

"Five Element Warrior: Fire: Sassa Narimasa's Dangerous Fight At Kyushu"; 1867

Third in the elemental set, featuring the *samurai* Sassa Narimasa, who fought for Oda Nobunaga. In 1584 Narimasa surrendered to Toyotomi Hideyoshi, who spared his life and in 1587 awarded him a fief of Higo Province in Kyushu. He was ordered by Toyotomi to commit *seppuku* a year later after failing to quell a local revolt.

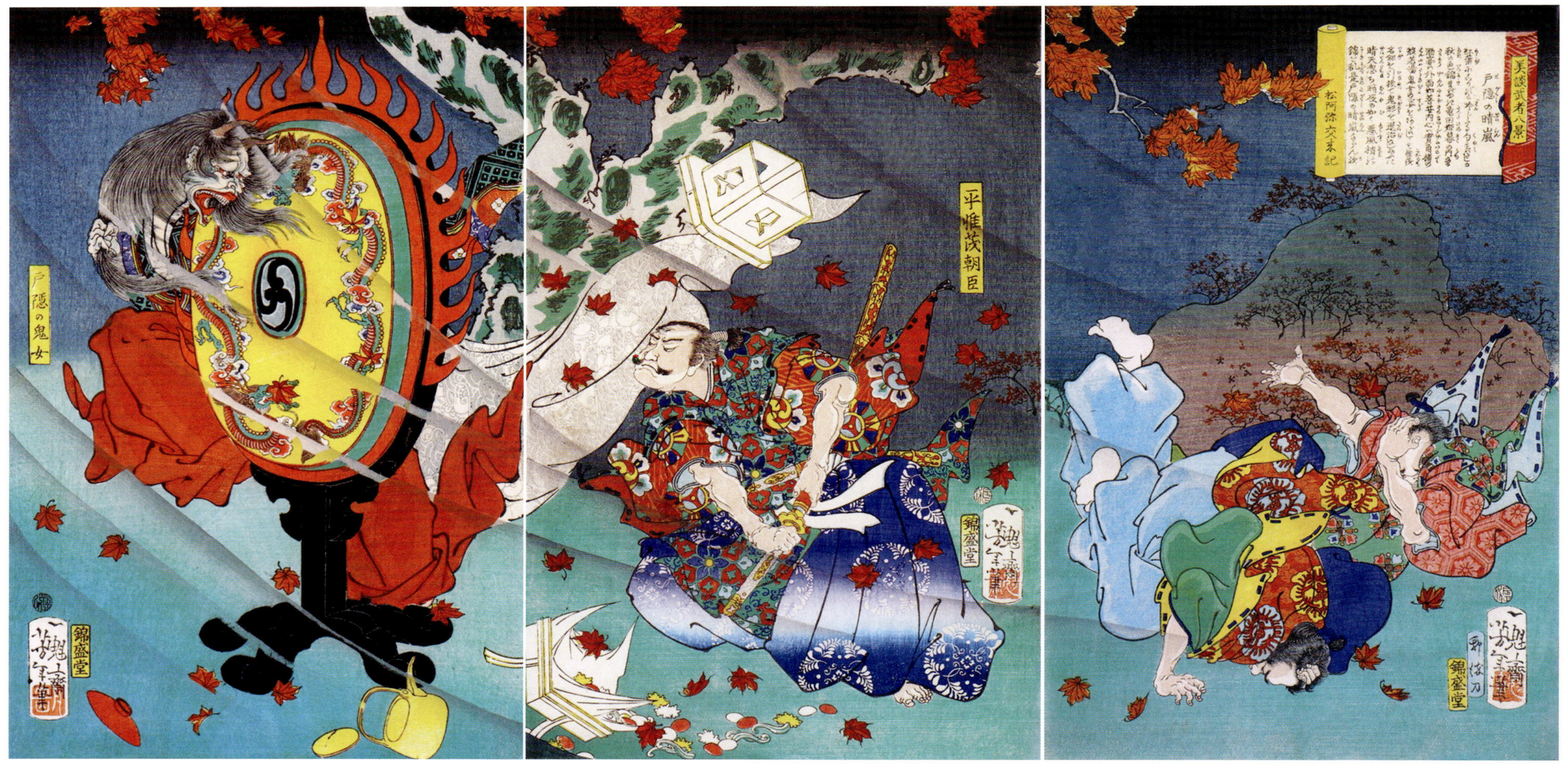

BIDAN MUSHA HAKKEI TOGAKUSHI NO SEIRAN

"Eight Views Of Impressive Warrior Tales: Storm Wind At Togakushi"; 1868
In this eight-triptych series, Yoshitoshi mostly stepped back from scenes of battle carnage to present moments from warrior history and legend marked by nature and the weather. This triptych illustrates the story of Taira-no-Koremochi, who encountered the she-demon Kijo atop Mount Togakushi. At first she took the form of a beautiful princess, Sarashina-hime, and plied the warrior with *sake* before attacking him; Koremochi fought back, killing the demon.

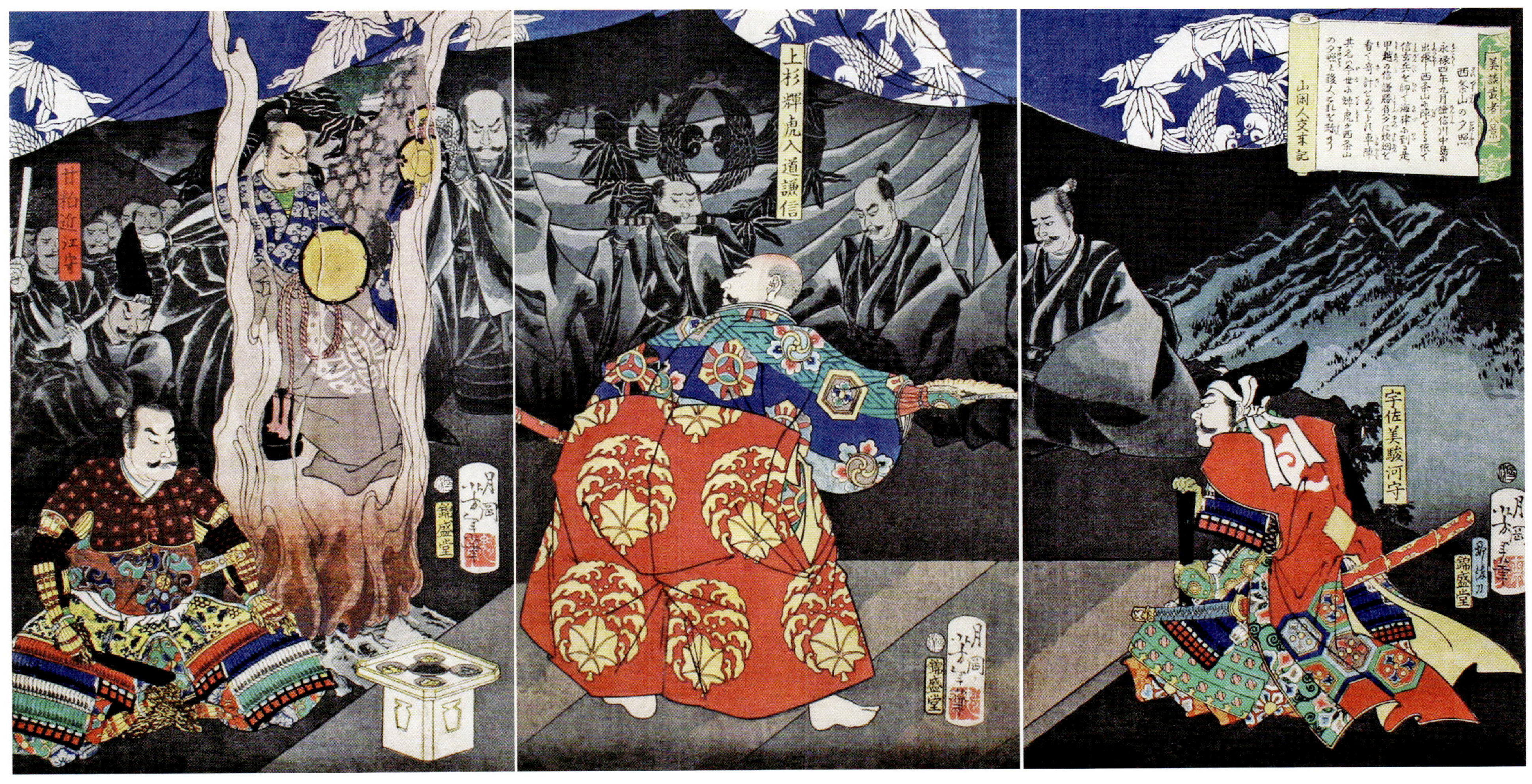

BIDAN MUSHA HAKKEI SAIJO-ZAN NO YUSHU

"Eight Views Of Impressive Warrior Tales: Evening Glow At Saijo-Zan"; 1868
This illustration from Yoshitoshi's eight-triptych series shows the renowned *daimyo* Uesugi Terutora Nyudo Kenshin viewing a stage performance at dusk.

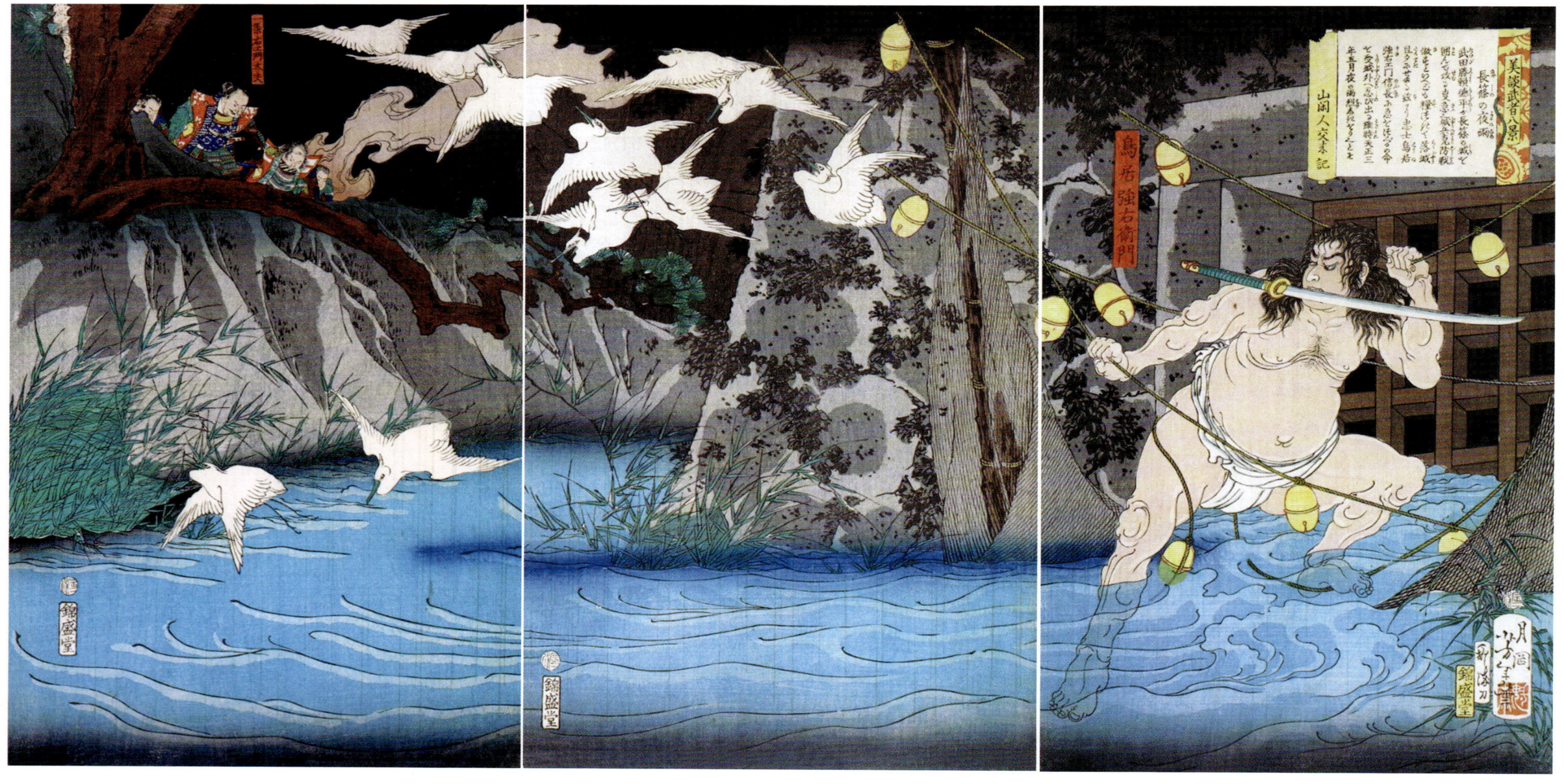

BIDAN MUSHA HAKKEI NAGASHINO NO YAU

"Eight Views Of Impressive Warrior Tales: Night Rain At Nagashino"; 1868
During the siege of Nagashino Castle by Takeda Katsuyori, the *samurai* Torii Suneemon Katsutaka was sent for help under cover of night; upon returning he tripped an alarm wire, was captured and killed. Yoshitoshi's illustration shows the moment when a flock of herons takes flight at the sound of the alarm bells.

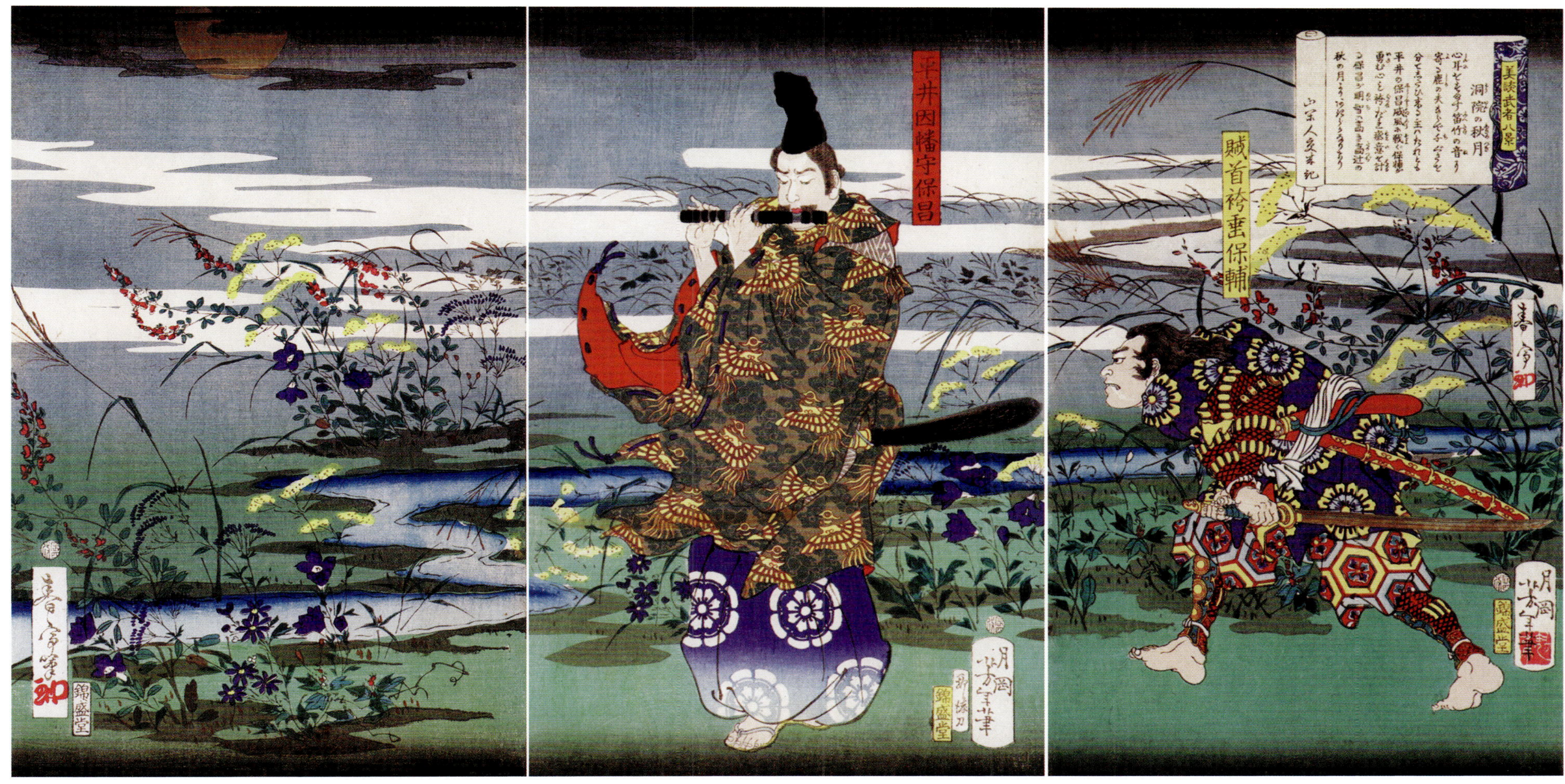

BIDAN MUSHA HAKKEI TOUIN NO AKI NO TSUKI

"Eight Views Of Impressive Warrior Tales: Autumn Moon At Touin"; 1868
The bandit Hakamadare preparing to rob Fujiwara no Yasumasa, who is playing his flute by moonlight on a deserted moor. According to the legend, Hakamadare was unable to carry through with his crime due to Yasumasa's "hypnotic" powers, which struck fear into his heart.

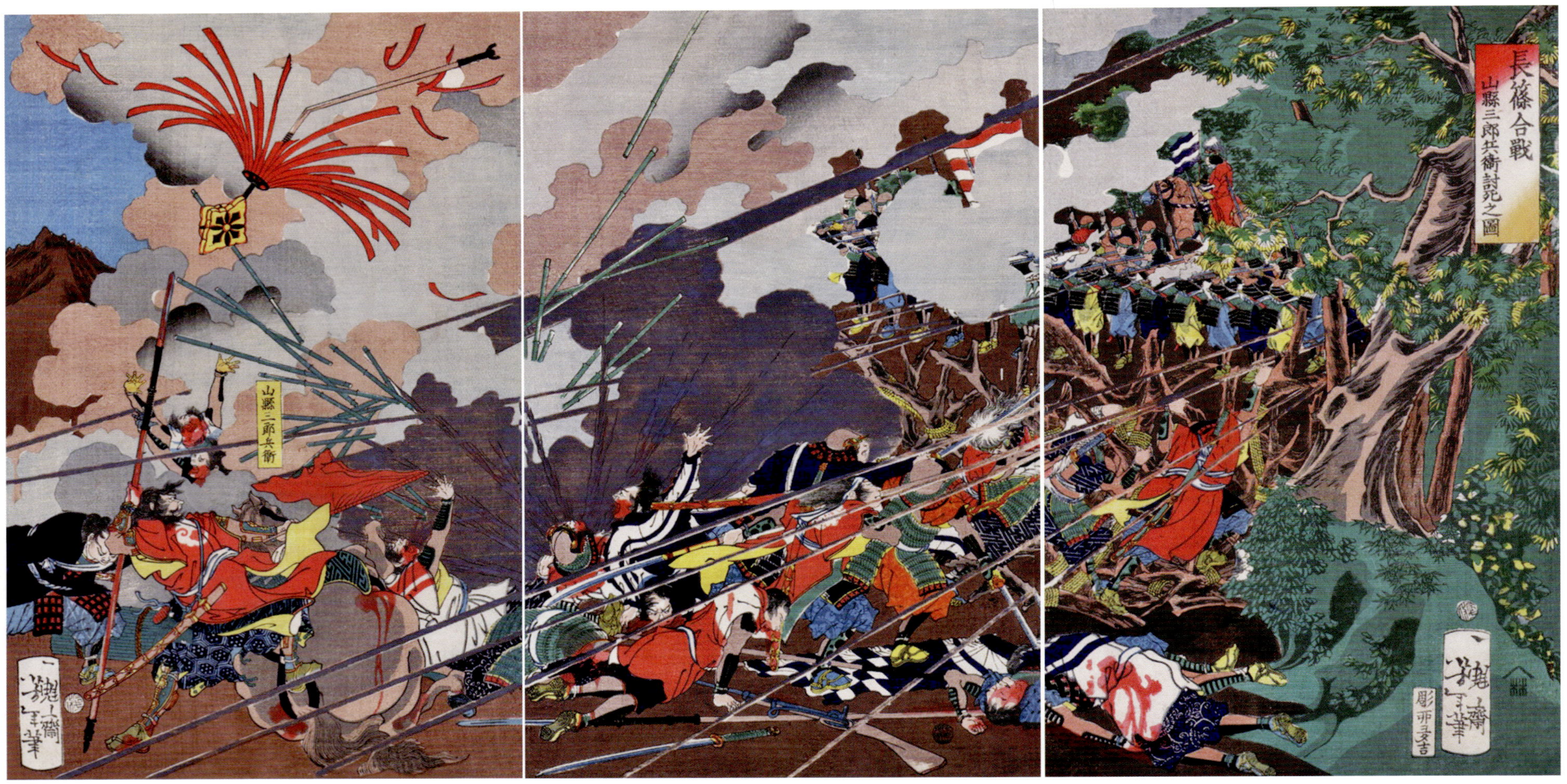

NAGASHINO KASSEN YAMAGATA SABUROBEI UCHIJINI

"The Death Of Yamagata Saburobei At The Battle Of Nagashino"; 1868

Yamagata Saburobei Masakage was another of Takeda Shingen's top twenty-four generals, who fought in many battles before meeting his doom at Nagashino in 1575, when the forces of Oda Nobunaga and Tokugawa Ieyasu were victorious over those led by Takeda Katsuyori. As shown in the illustration, Nobunaga's overwhelming rotational fire-power was the key to repelling Takeda's attempted siege of Nagashino castle.

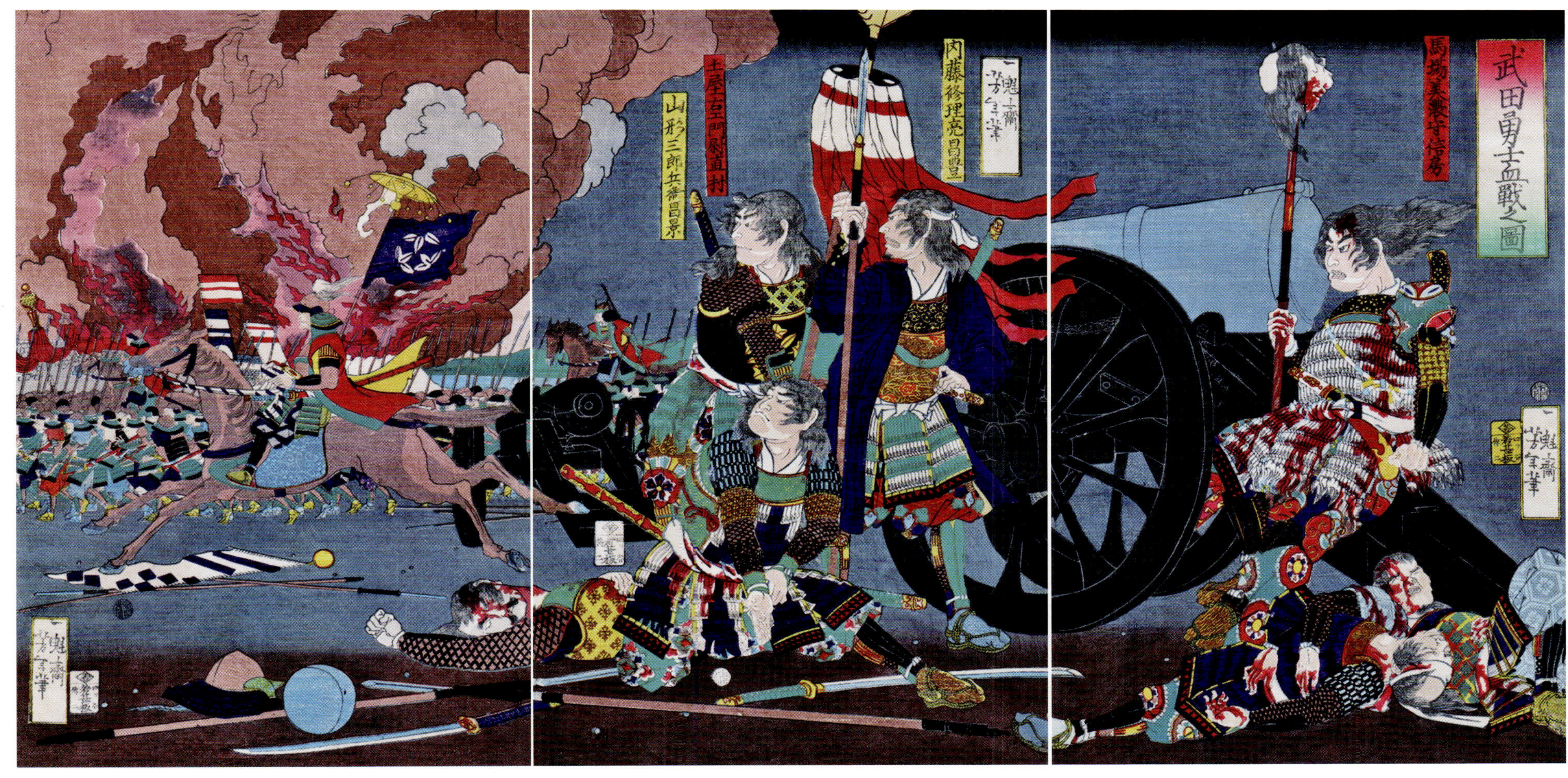

TAKEDA YUSHI KESSEN

"Bloody Battle Of The Takeda Generals"; 1868
Like Yoshitoshi's same-titled triptych of 1866, this image ostensibly refers to the bloody decimations of the Takeda clan at Kawanakajima; it may also be a covert reference to the more contemporaneous Boshin War, a civil conflict between pro-*shogun* forces and imperialists which erupted in Japan in 1868.

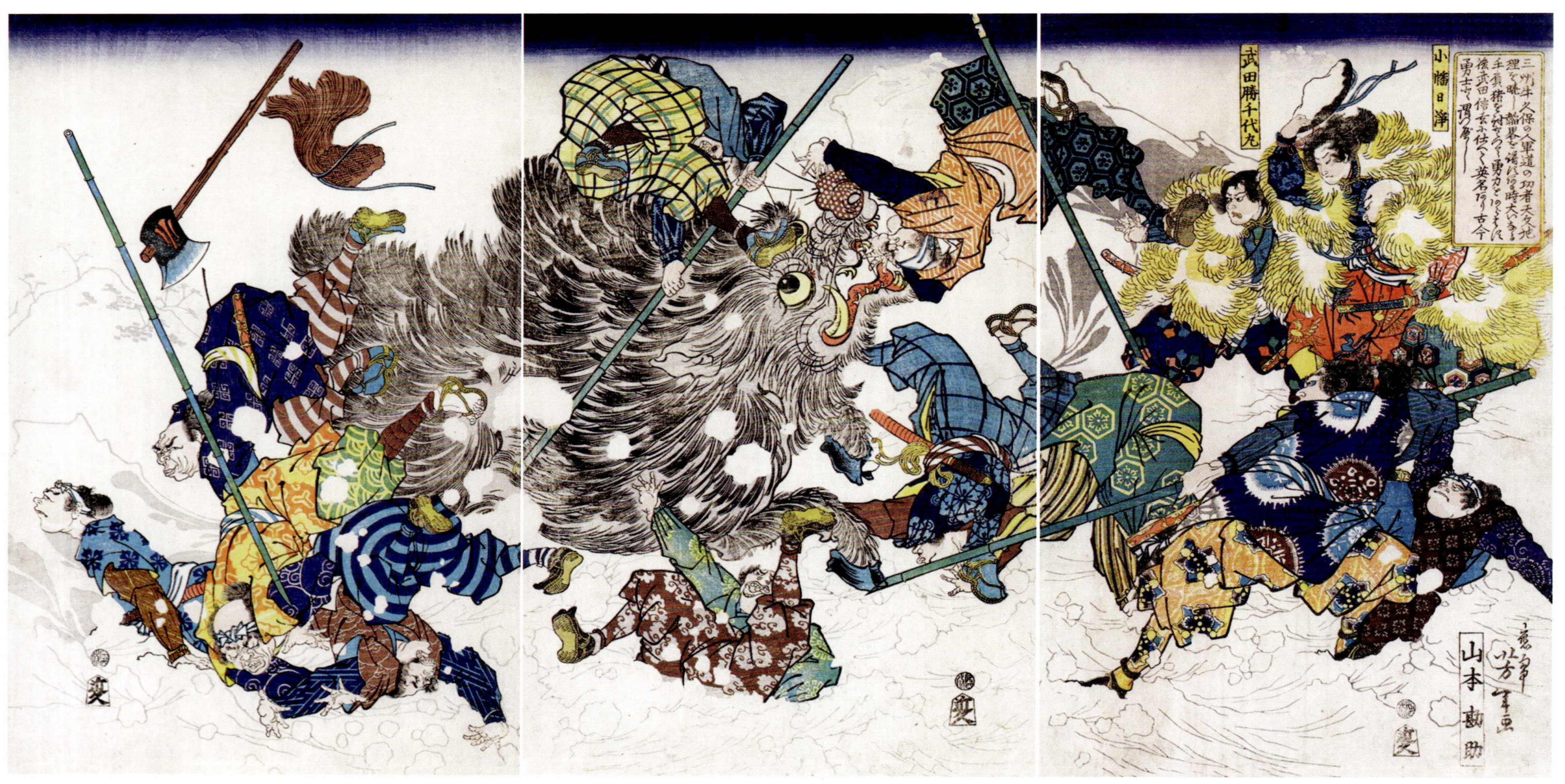

YAMAMOTO KANSUKE MOI O UTSU

"Yamamoto Kansuke Subdues A Wild Boar"; 1868

Legend tells that before he became an esteemed military general, the young Yamamoto and his comrades once hunted and overcame a gigantic wild boar.

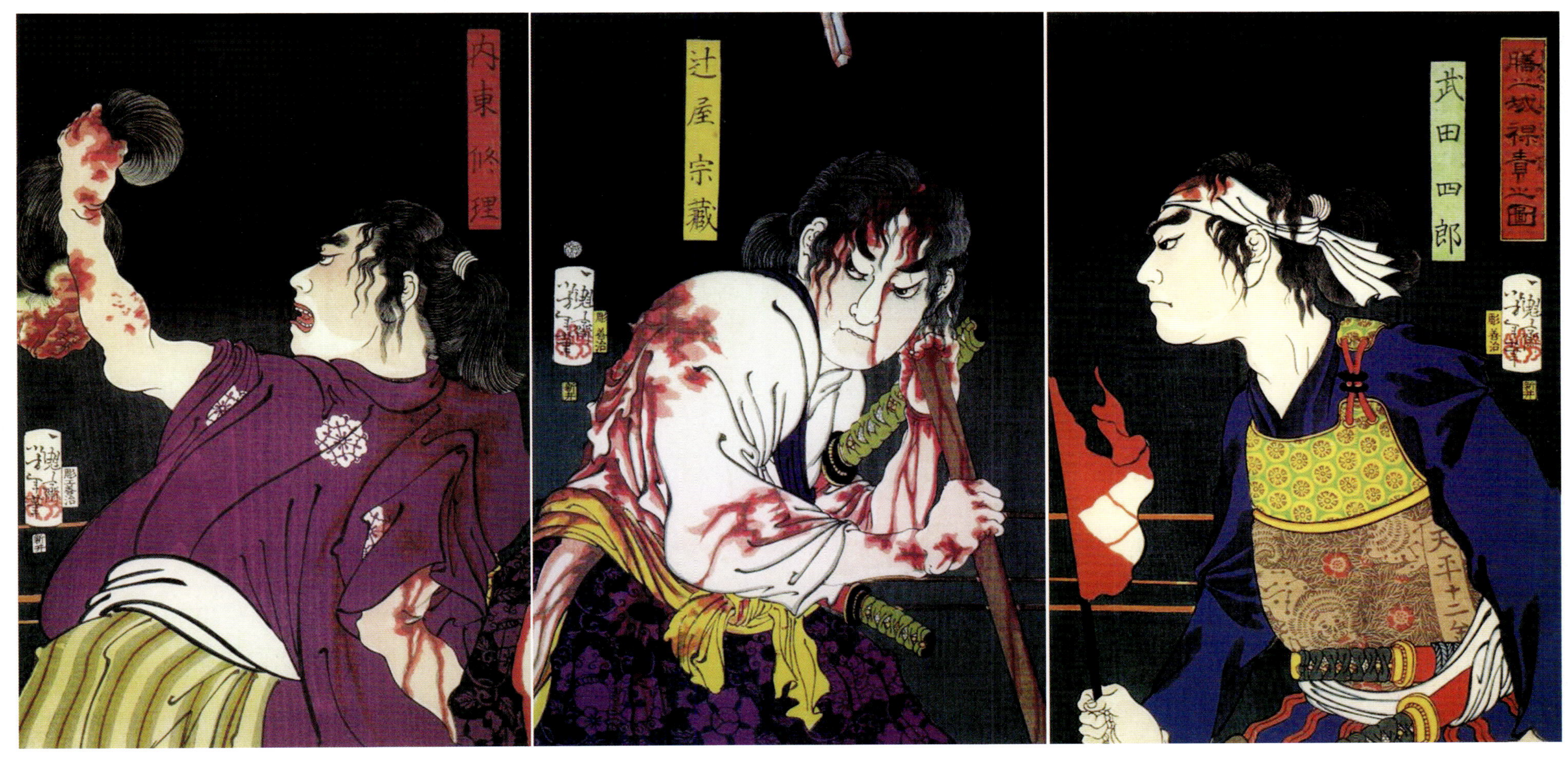

ZENNOJO HADAKA SEME

"Zennojo's Unarmed Attack"; 1868

A triptych created in the artistic style of Yoshitoshi's famous, and infamously bloody, *oban* series *Kaidai Hyaku Senso* ("One Hundred Thrusting War Portraits", 1868-69). These images, and presumably this triptych, were inspired by Yoshitoshi's first-hand witnessing of the battle of Ueno in 1868.

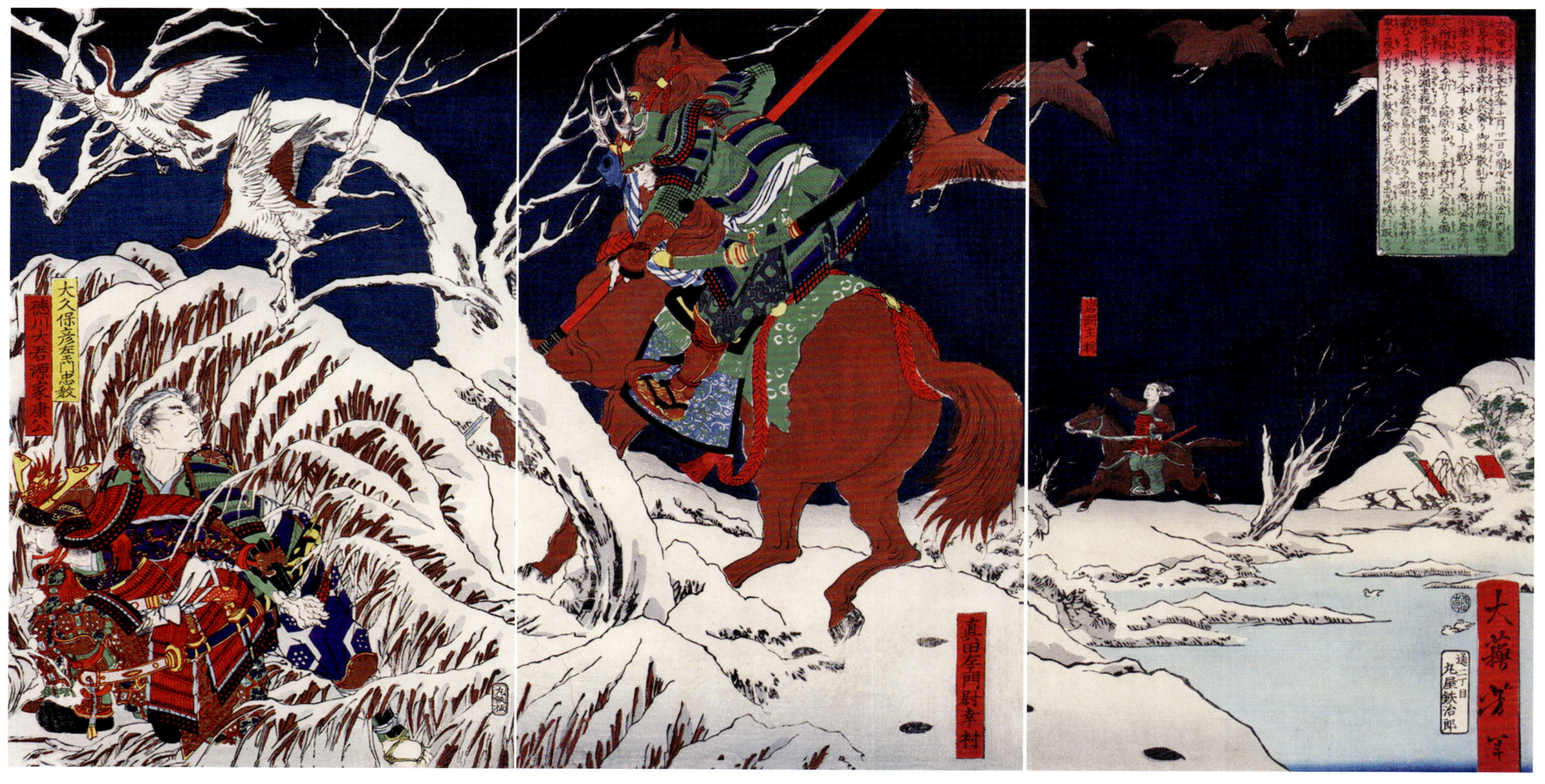

OSAKA GUNKI SANADA YUKIMURA

"Osaka War Chronicle: Sanada Yukimura"; 1873

Sanada Yukimura, sometimes called the "crimson war demon", was the celebrated and feared *samurai* who became a key defender of Osaka castle during the Tokugawa siege of 1614-15. He was killed there during the siege's terminal summer phase, but Yoshitoshi's illustration shows him hunting enemy forces in the preceding winter.

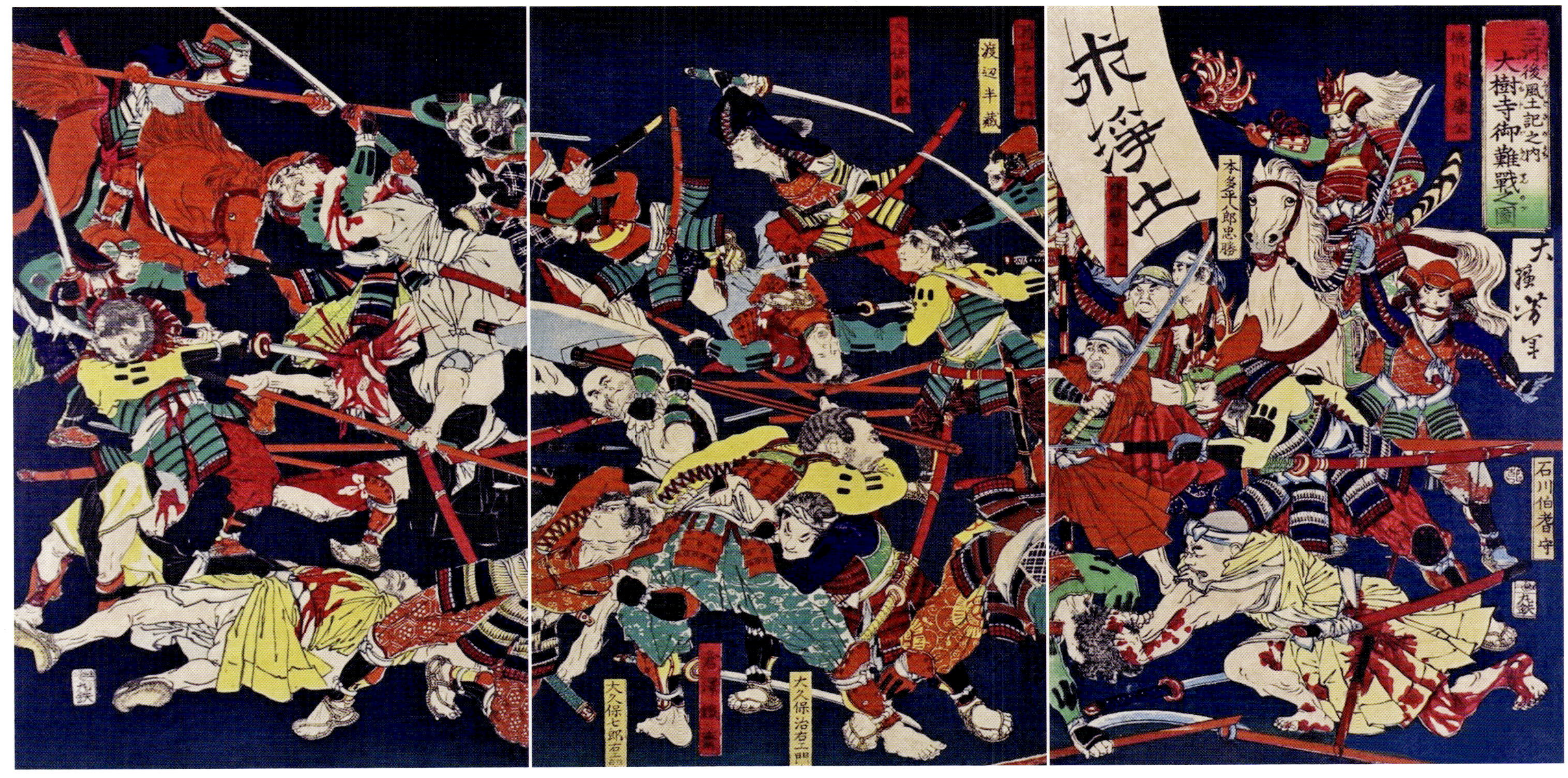

MIKAWA GOFUDOKI NO UCHI DAIJU-JI GONANSEN

"Scene From *Mikawa Go-Fudoki*: Chaotic Battle At Daiju Temple"; 1873
The *Mikawa Go-Fudoki* is a 45-volume history of the Tokugawa clan, ending with Tokugawa Ieyasu's life up to the Battle of Sekigahara in 1600. This triptych seems to illustrate the battle of Azukizaka in 1564, when the Daiju temple's warrior-monks joined forces with Ieyasu against the Ikko-Ikki, a band of anarchist renegades.

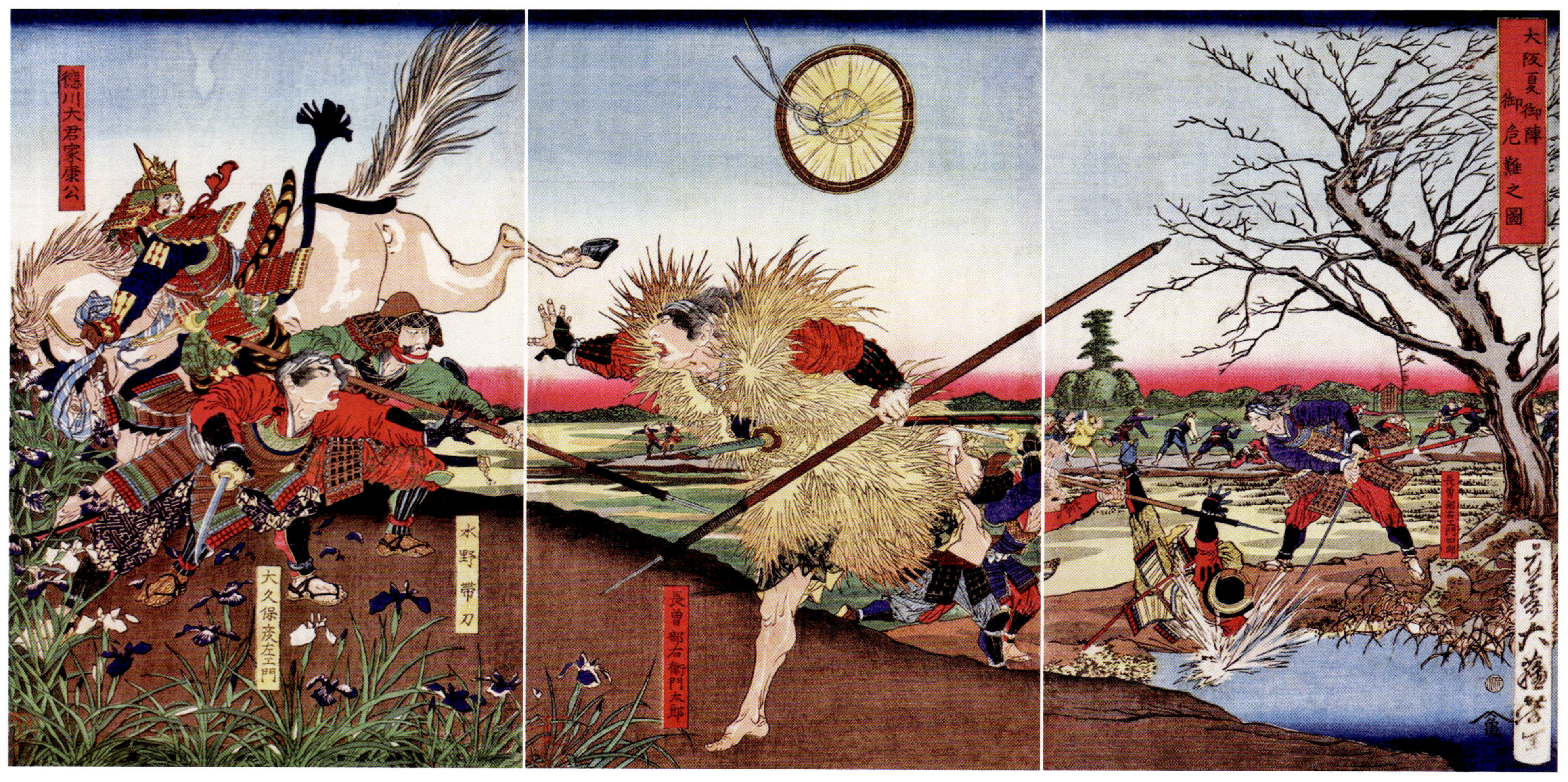

OSAKA NATSU NO GOJIN GOKINAN
"Dangerous Summer Battle At Osaka"; 1873
This triptych illustrates the conflict between Tokugawa Ieyasu and Toyotomi Hideyori in Osaka, which took place in the summer of 1615. This was the final surge in Ieyasu's siege of Osaka castle, which was finally razed with Hideyori's self-disembowelled corpse amongst the ashes.

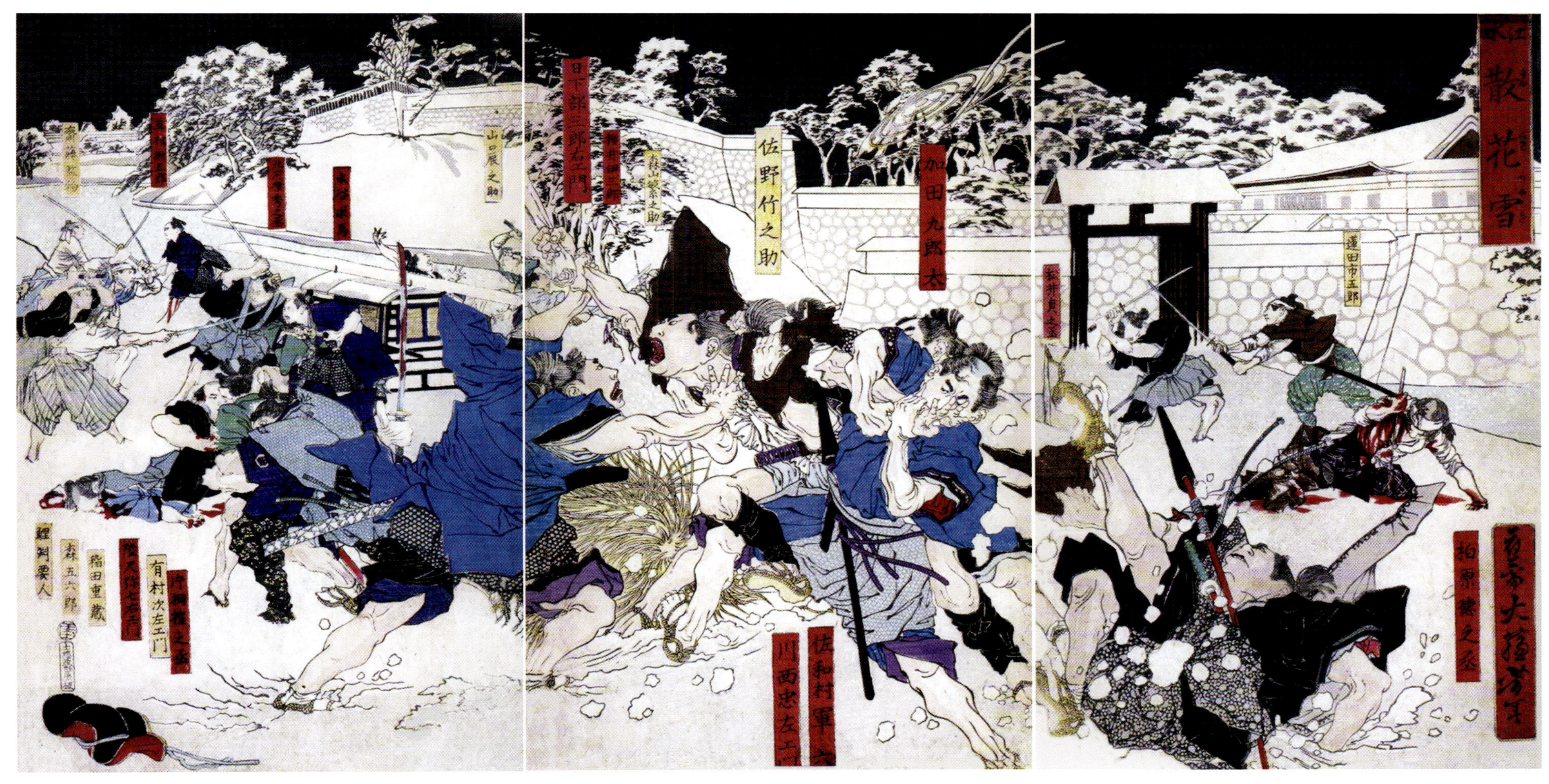

KOSUI SANKA NO YUKI

"Falling Snow Blossoms At The Lake"; 1874

This image shows the brutal assassination of the *shogun*'s chief council Ii Naosuke in 1860; Ii was attacked and butchered outside the Sakurada Gate of Edo Castle by a group of anti-shogunate *ronin*.

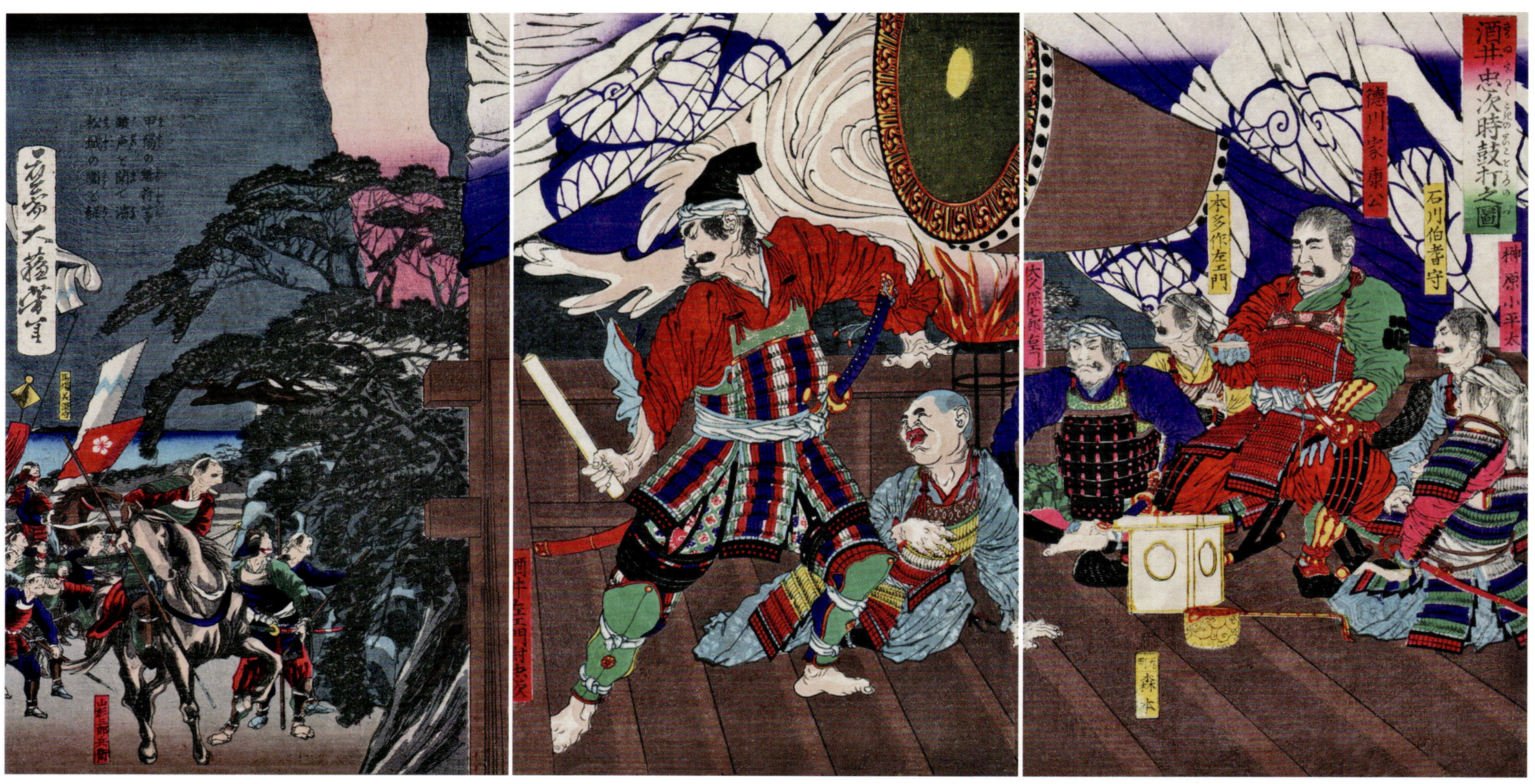

SADAI TADATSUGU-JI TSUZUMIUCHI
"Sakai Tadatsugu Strikes The Drum Clock"; 1874
Sakai Tadatsugu beating a drum during the battle of Mikatagahara in 1573, in which the forces of Tokugawa Ieyasu and his ally Oda Nobunaga opposed those of Takeda Shingen. Ieyasu retreated to Hamamatsu castle, where the relentless drum-beat and bonfires created a scene of confusion for his pursuers.

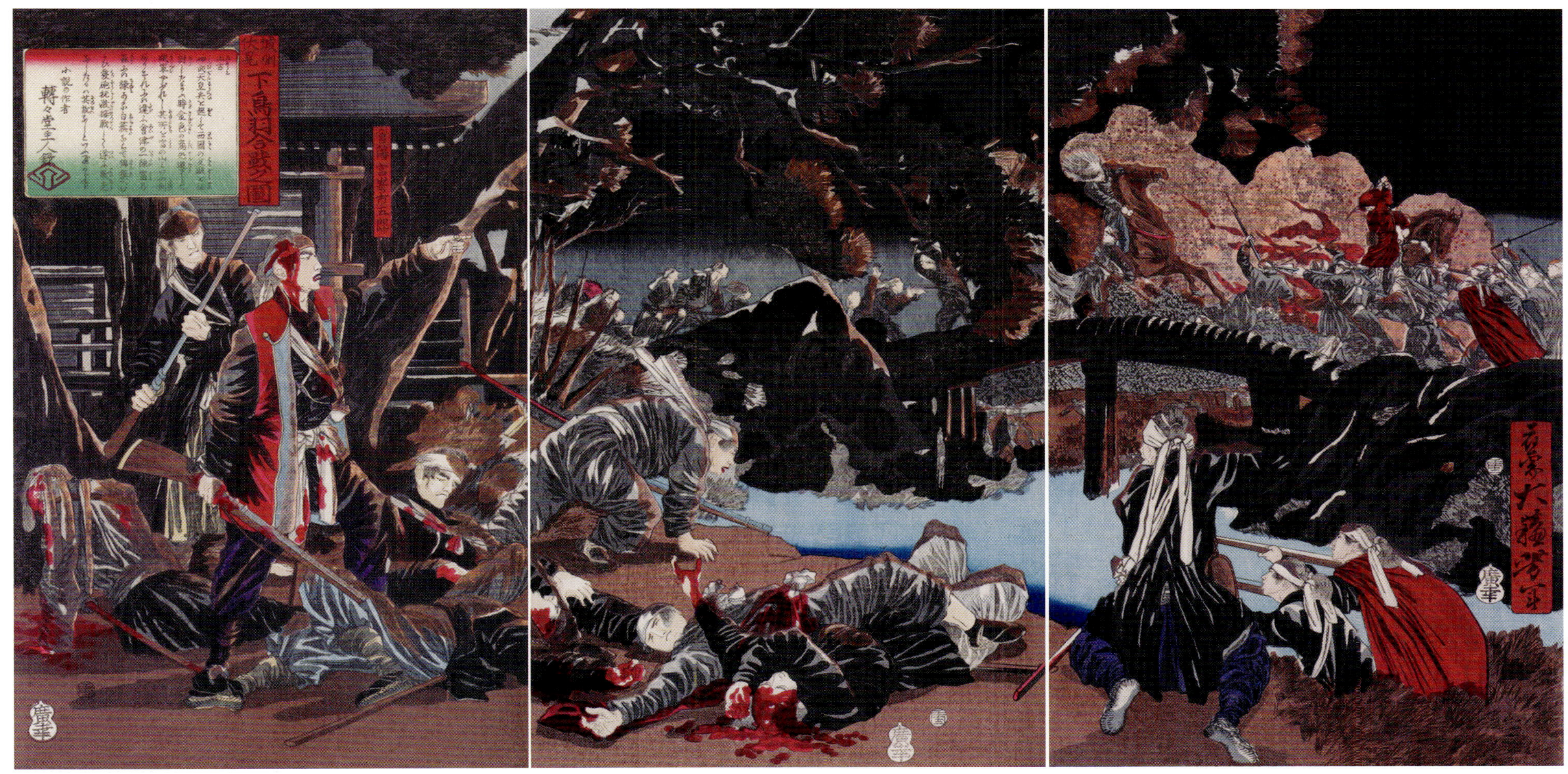

FUSHIMI SHIMOTOBA KASSEN

"The Battle Of Shimotoba-Fushimi"; 1874

This triptych illustrates a more contemporary scene, from the 1868 Boshin War between imperialist and pro-shogunate forces; the battle at Toba-Fushimi took place in January of that year.

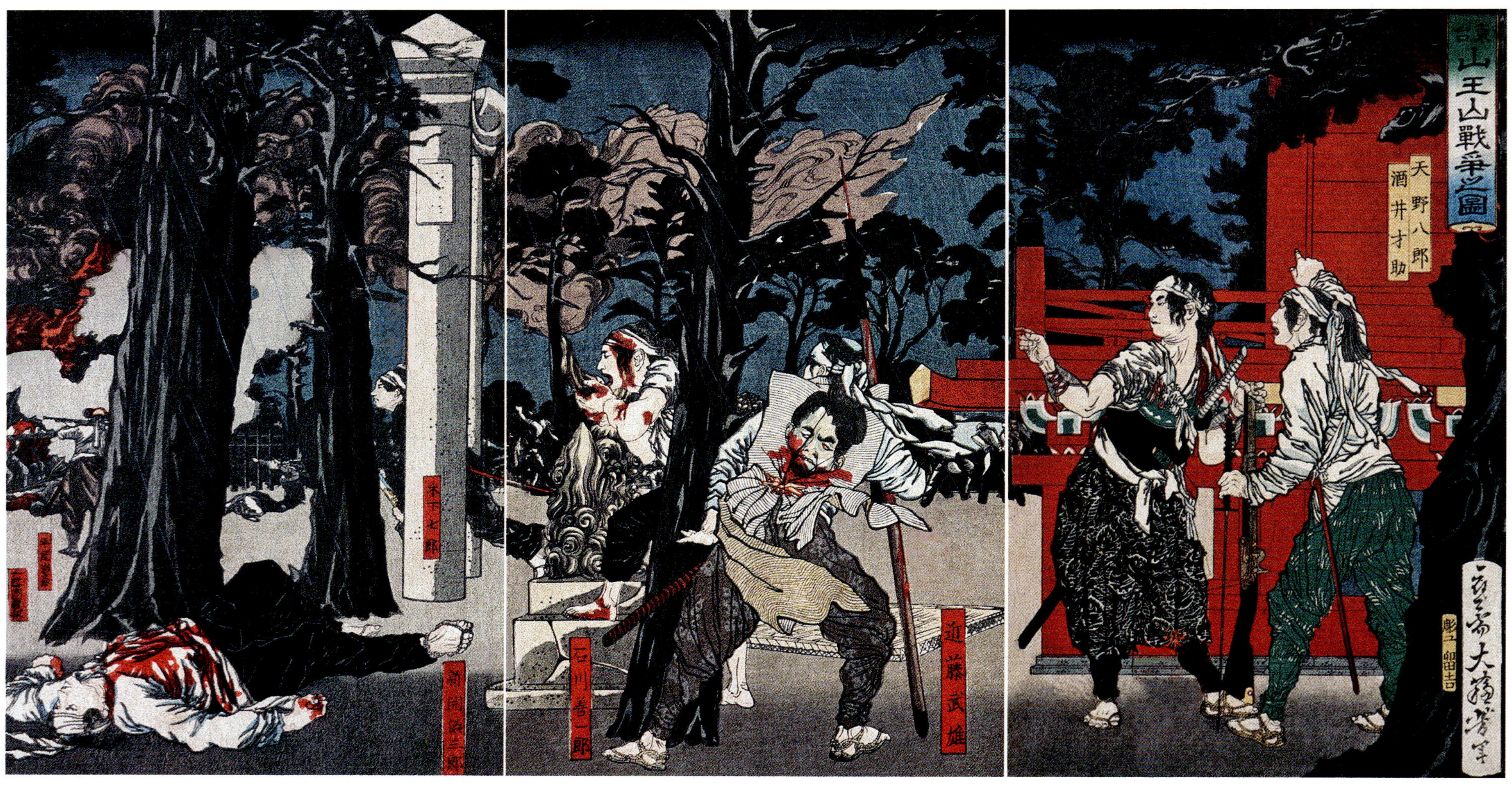

TODAI SANNOZAN SENSO
"Warfare At Sannozan-Todai"; 1874
Another triptych which relates to the battle of Ueno in 1868, when bloody fighting spread to the Toeizan shrine on Mount Sanno.

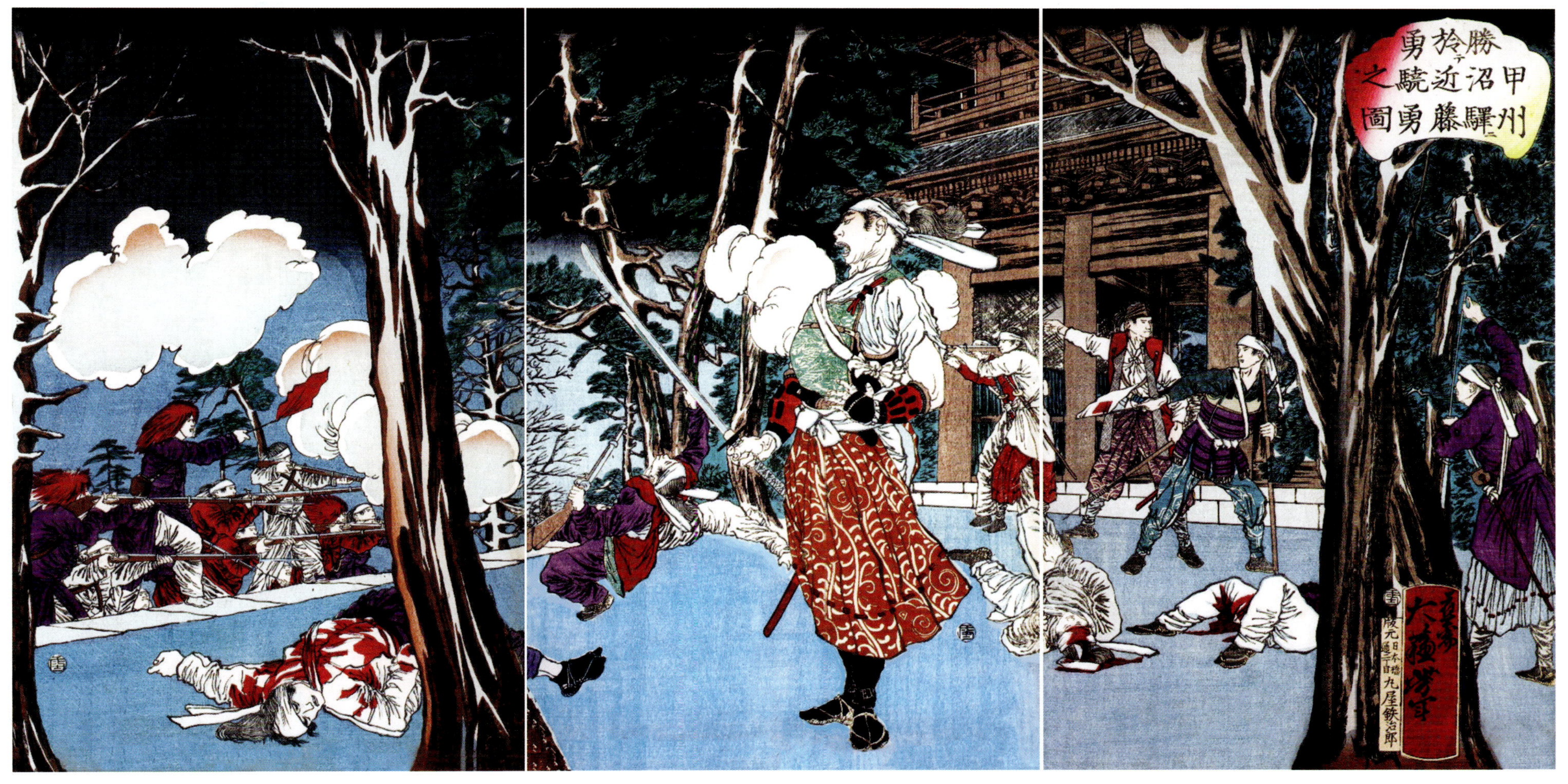

KOSHU KATSUNUMA EKI NIOTE KONDO ISAMU GYOYU

"The Bravery Of Kondo Isamu At Koshu-Katsunuma"; 1874

The battle of Koshu-Katsunuma was a clash which followed soon after the battle of Toba-Fushimi, in which pro-imperialist forces were intercepted by the Koyo Chinbutai, an elite pro-shogunate unit led by famed warrior Kondo Isami. Despite Kondo's fearless valour, as illustrated here by Yoshitoshi, the imperialists were eventually victorious. Kondo fled but soon afterwards was captured and beheaded. This defeat proved decisive in ending the Boshin War.

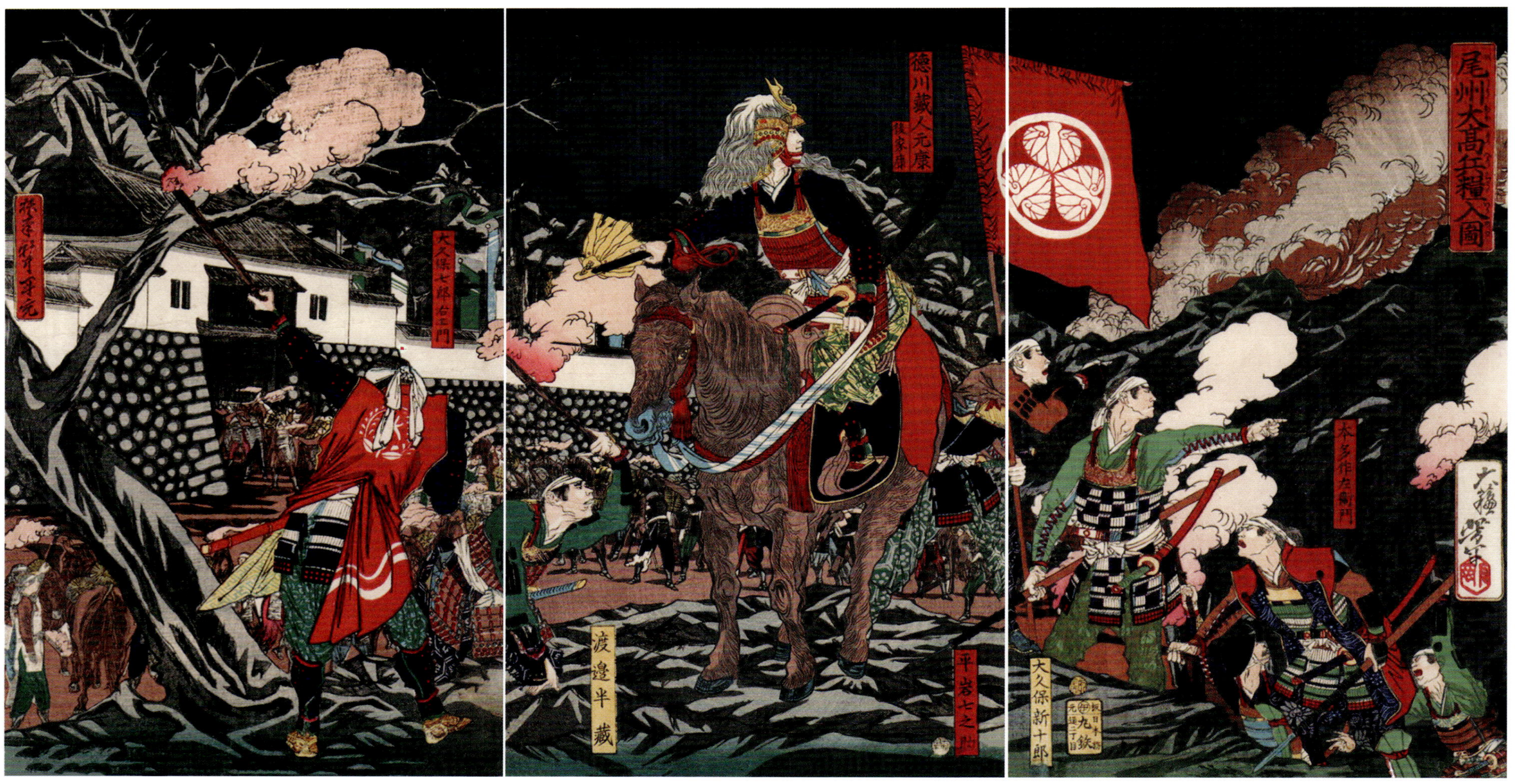

BISHU ODAKA HYOROIRI

"Troop Provisions Reaching Odaka-Bishu"; 1875
An illustration of Tokugawa troops at the siege of Odaka castle in 1559; Tokugawa Ieyasu was able to deliver vital provisions to the troops by launching diversionary attacks on two nearby forts.

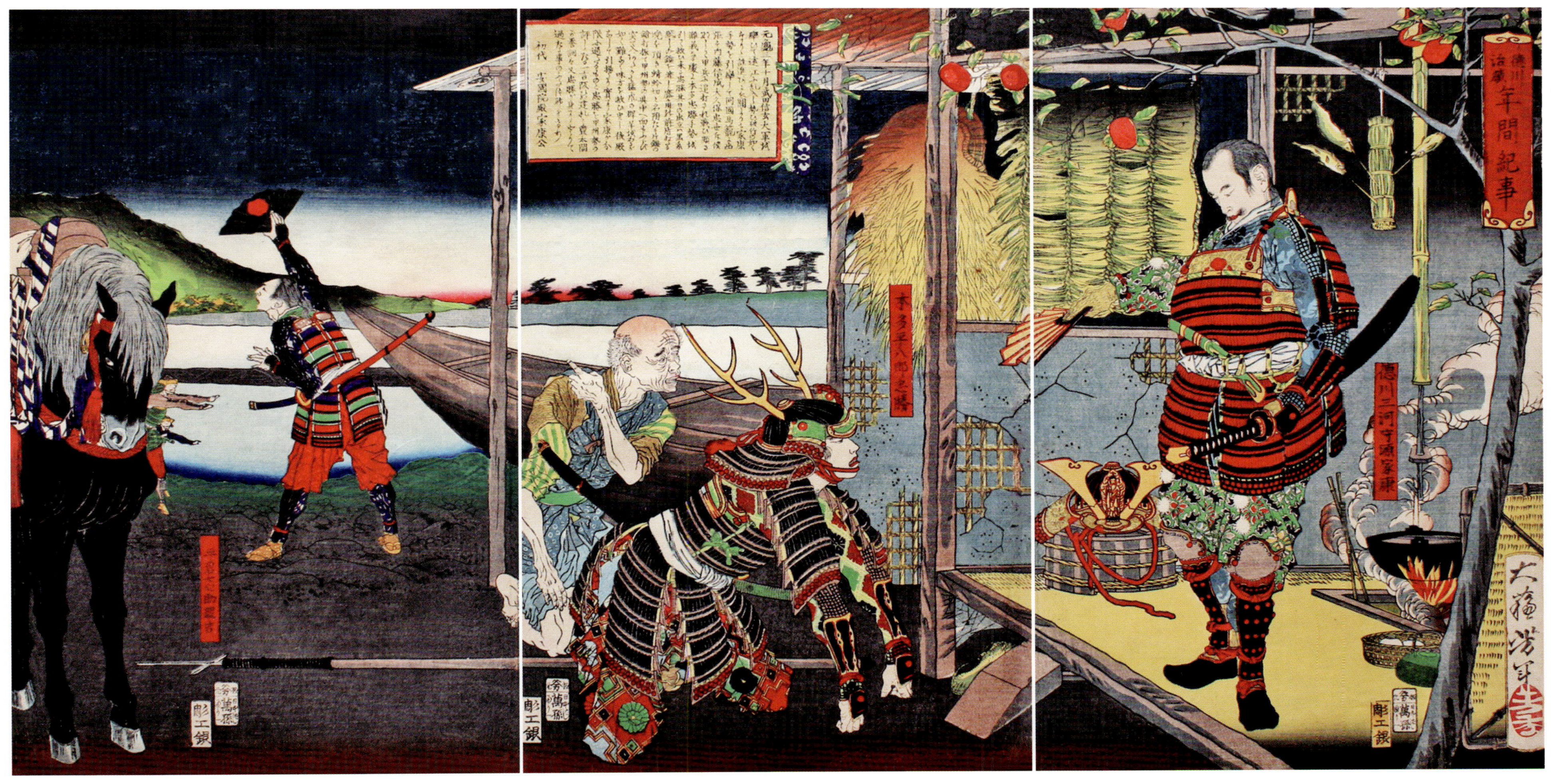

TOKUGAWA CHISEKI NENKAN KIJI SHODAI YASUKUNI-IN IEYASU-KO

"Annals Of The Tokugawa Administration: The Founder, Lord Ieyasu Yasukuni-In"; 1875

The first in a series of triptychs in honour of the Tokugawa shogunate, this illustration shows Tokugawa Ieyasu receiving a messenger during the battle of Sekigahara in 1600, which paved the way for him to become *shogun* in 1603.

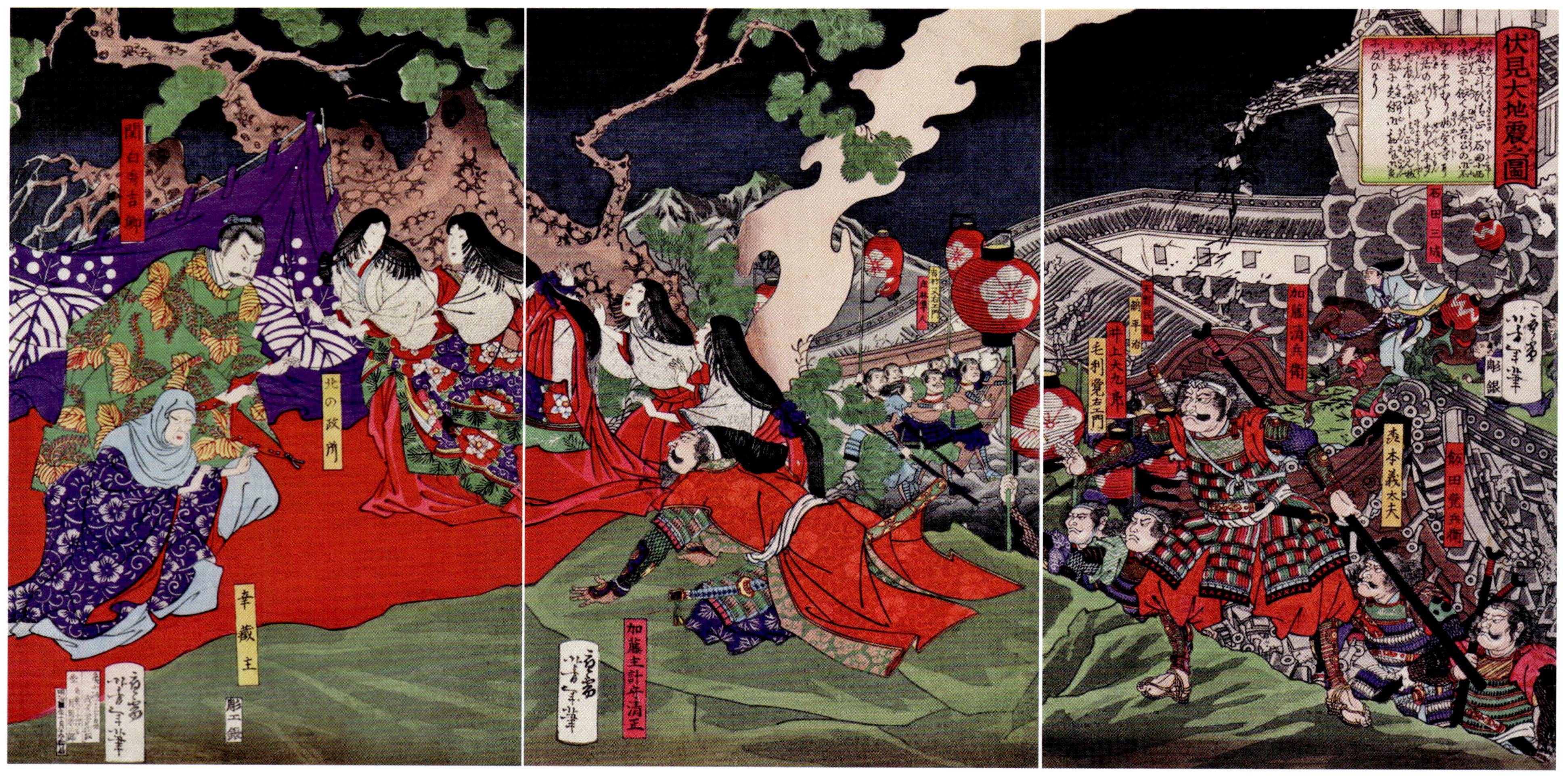

FUSHIMI DAIJISHIN MOMOYAMA GOTEN

"Great Earthquake At Momoyama Palace In Fushimi"; 1876
Momoyama Palace, also known as Fushimi castle, was built by Toyotomi Hideyoshi between 1592 and 1598. During that period, in 1596, a large inland earthquake struck the region killing around 1,500 people. Yoshitoshi's illustration shows Kiyomasa Kato protecting Toyotomi.

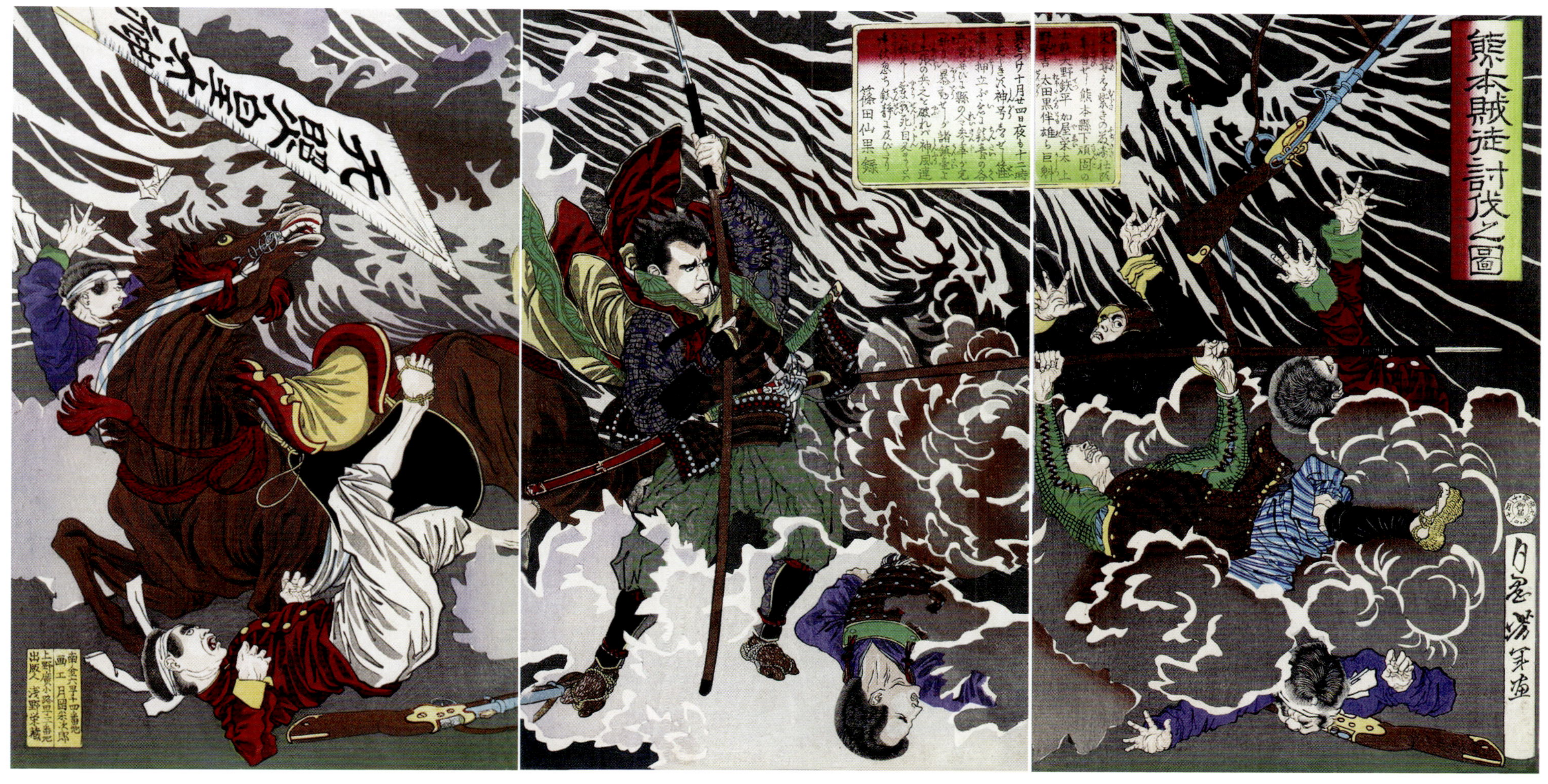

KUMAMOTO ZOKUTO TOBATSU

"Violent Suppression Of The Kumamoto Rebels"; 1876
From this point on Yoshitoshi largely documented absolutely contemporary events, in particular the violent *samurai* uprisings against the Meiji government. One such event was the Shinpuren rebellion which began Kumamoto on 24 October 1876. The rebels were finally defeated by modern firepower, and their leader Otaguro led a mass *seppuku* of his followers.

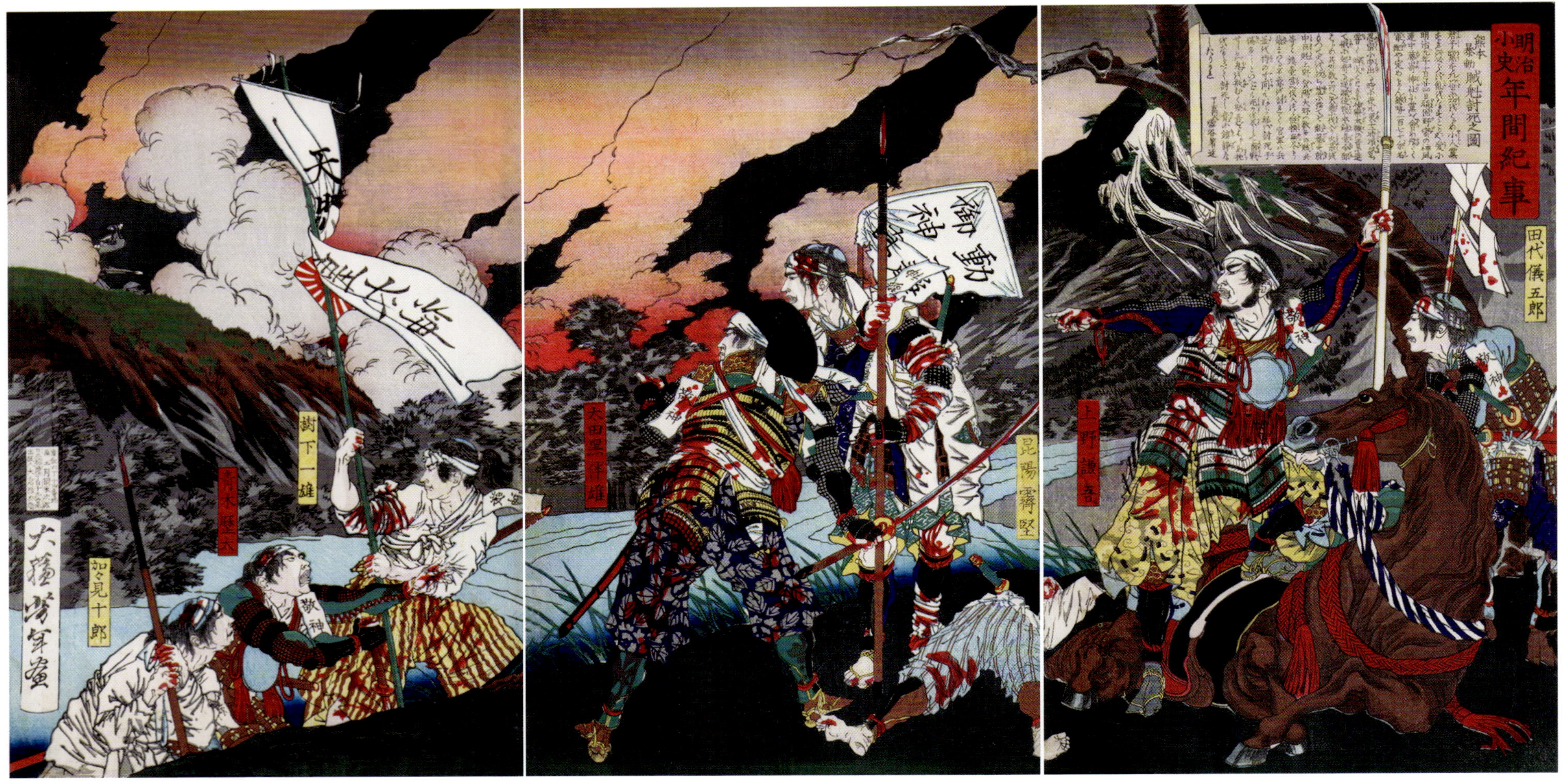

MEIJI SHOSHI NENKAN KIJI KUMAMOTO BODO ZOKU SAKIGAKE UCHIJINI

"A Short History Of The Meiji Period: Battle-Death Of The Rebel Leaders In The Kumamoto Uprising"; 1876

The first in a series of five triptychs documenting events of the Meiji period, which began in 1868. This illustration is another depiction of the Kumamoto rebels, who came to a bloody end but inspired other uprisings which would follow.

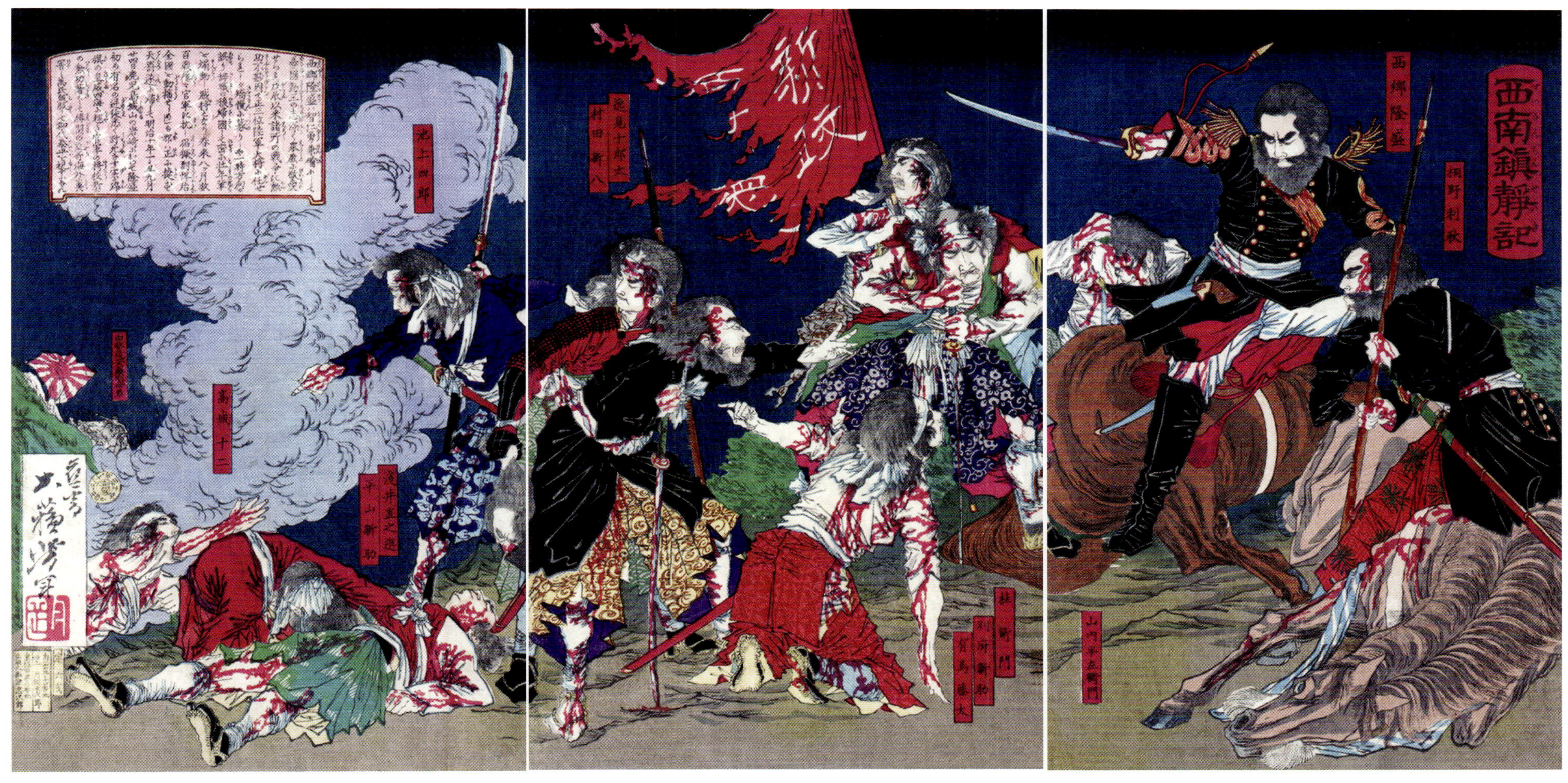

SEINAN CHINSEIKI

"Record Of Seinan Pacification"; 1877

The Seinan War, also known as the Satsuma Rebellion, was a *samurai* uprising which lasted from January to September 1877 when it was brutally crushed and its leader, Saigo Takamori (shown in the right panel of Yoshitoshi's triptych) reportedly committed *seppuku*. Most of Yoshitoshi's 1877 triptychs are illustrations of this rebellion.

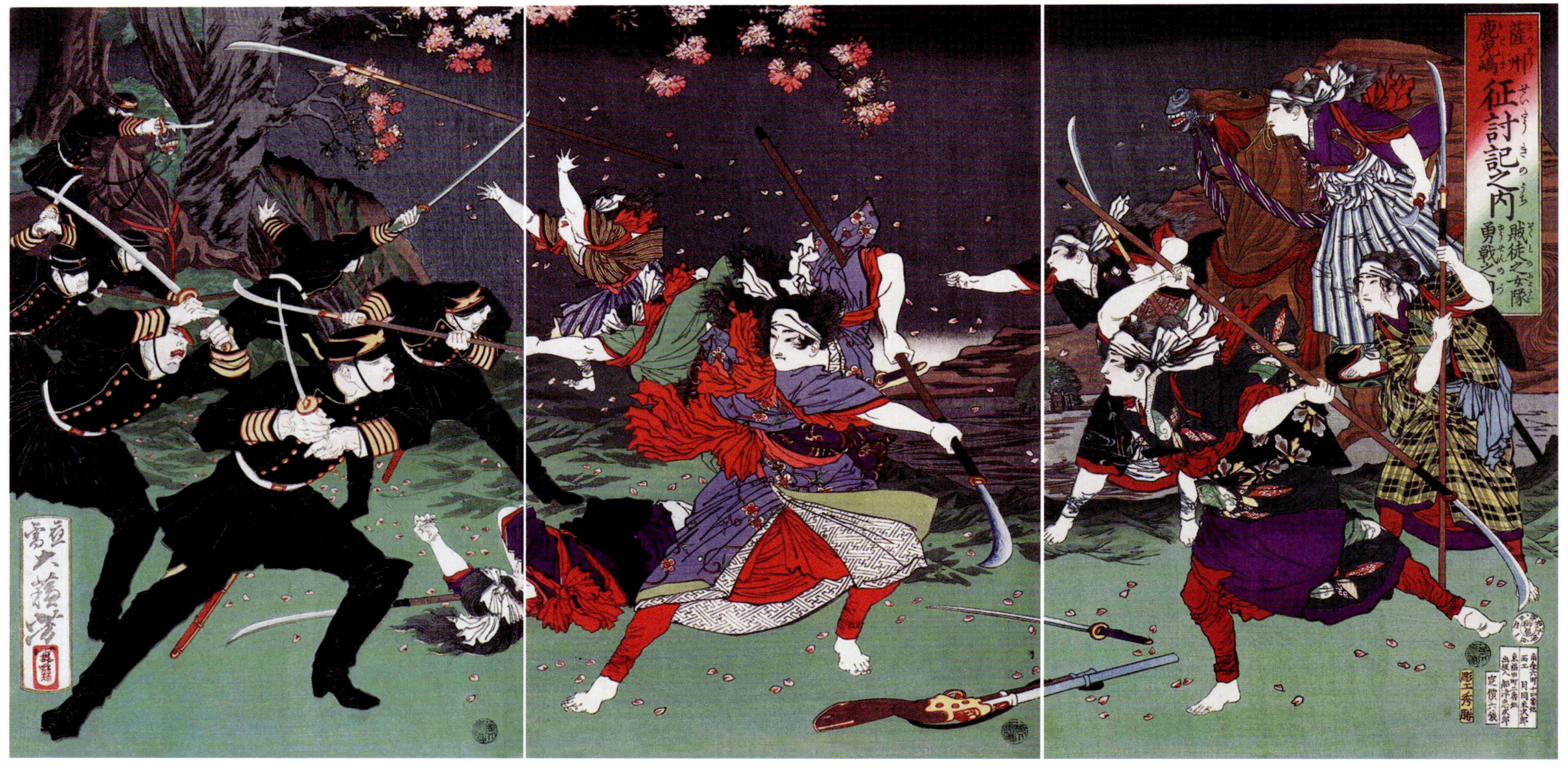

SASSHU KAGOSHIMA SEITOKI NO UCHI ZOKUTO NO JOTAI YUSEN

"Chronicle Of the Subjugation Of Kagoshima-Satsuma: Ferocious Assault Of The Female Rebel Brigade"; 1877
One of numerous illustrations which showed female fighters pitched against government troops during the Satsuma Rebellion. These *onna-bugeisha*, or female *samurai*, were increasingly marginalized in the early years of Meiji rule.

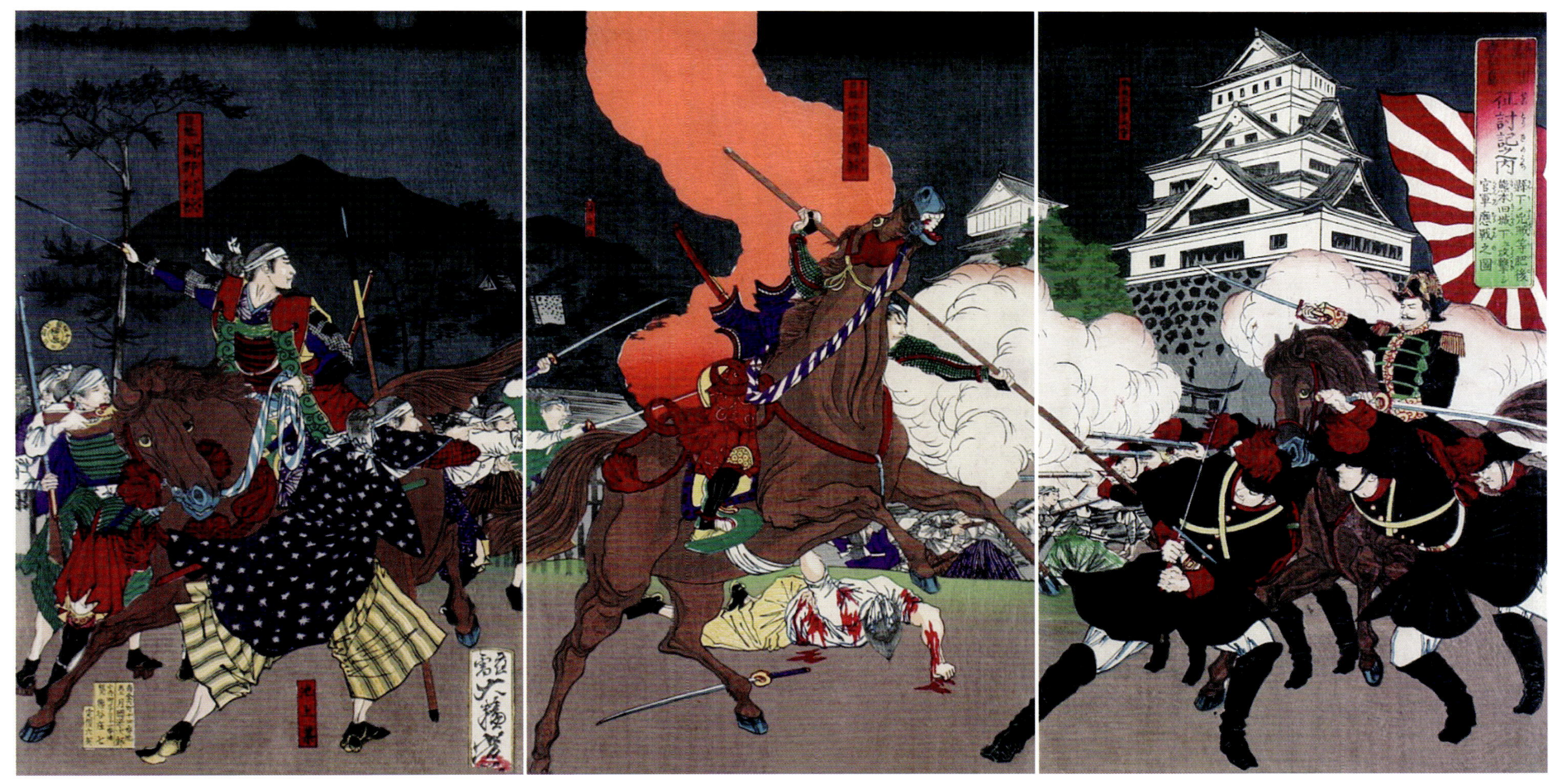

SASSHU KAGOSHIMA SEITOKI NO UCHI
"Chronicle Of the Subjugation Of Kagoshima-Satsuma"; 1877
Rebel leaders battling against government forces outside Kumamoto castle (built by Kiyomasa Kato between 1601 and 1607). Although this bulwark of defensive architecture could not be successfully stormed, Takamori's troops caused mass damage to many of its structures.

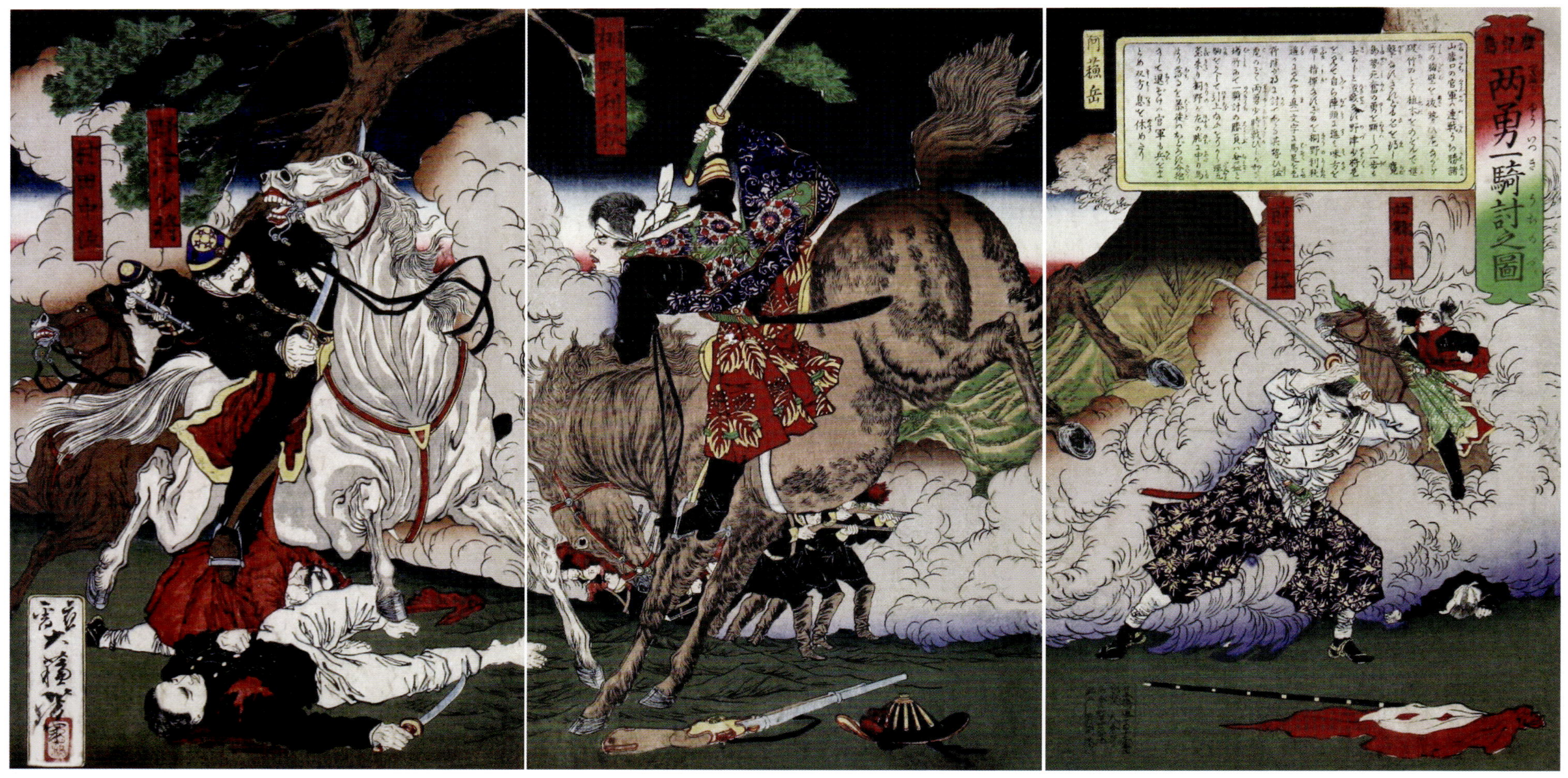

KAGOSHIMA RYOYU IKKIUCHI

"Two Brave Heroes Of Kagoshima In One-To-One Combat"; 1877
A horseback clash between Colonel Nozu Michitsura of the Imperial army and Kirino Toshiaki, a former army general who defected and joined the rebel forces of Saigo Takamori during the Satsuma Rebellion.

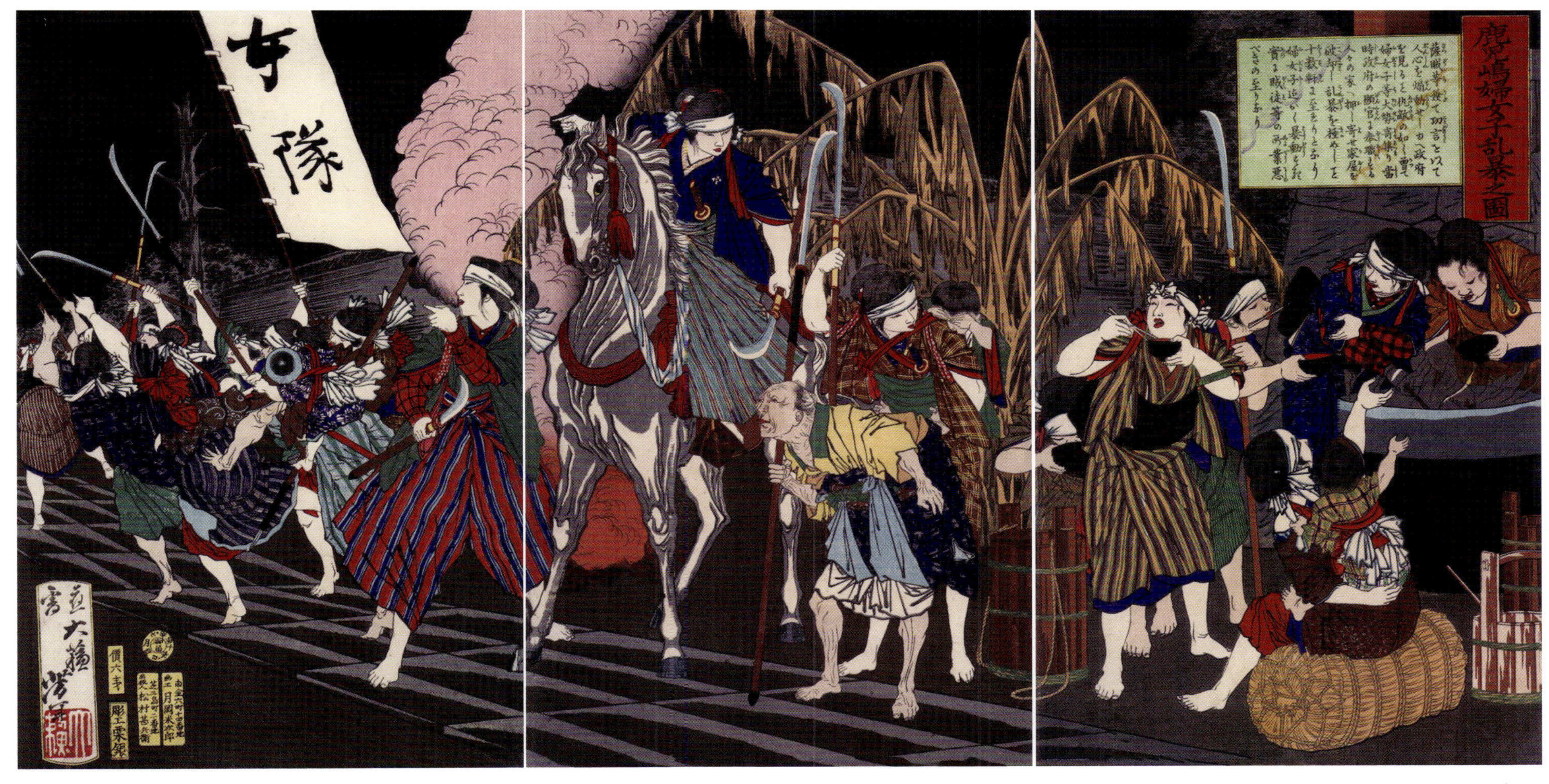

KAGOSHIMA FUJOSHI RANBO
"Feral Rampage Of Women And Children At Kagoshima"; 1877
Another image showing the participation of female fighters in the Satsuma Rebellion.

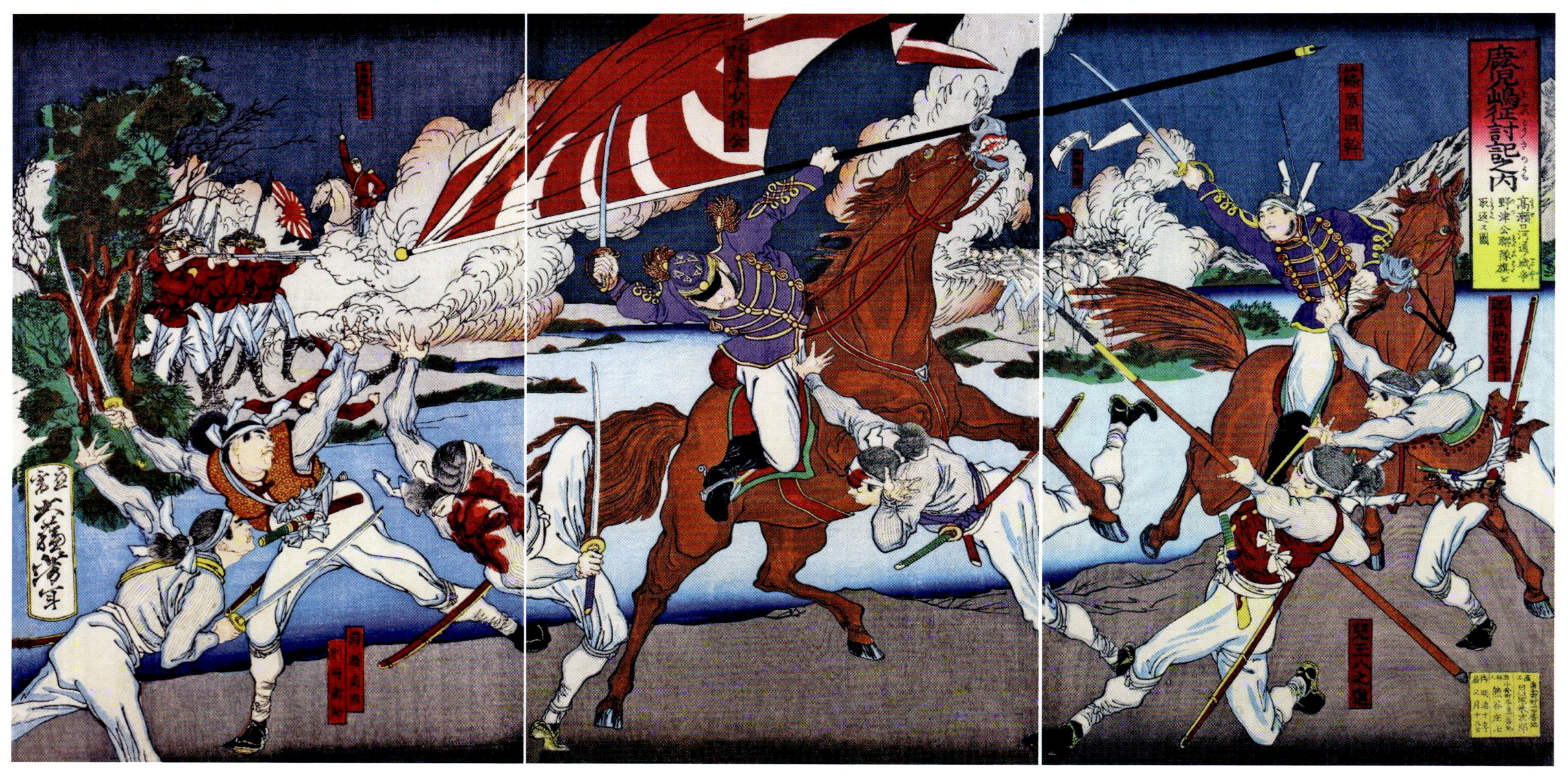

KAGOSHIMA SEITOKI NO UCHI

"Chronicle Of The Conquest Of Kagoshima"; 1877

This illustration of events from the Satsuma Rebellion shows General Nozu wielding the national flag as a weapon whilst in combat with insurgents at the Takase river.

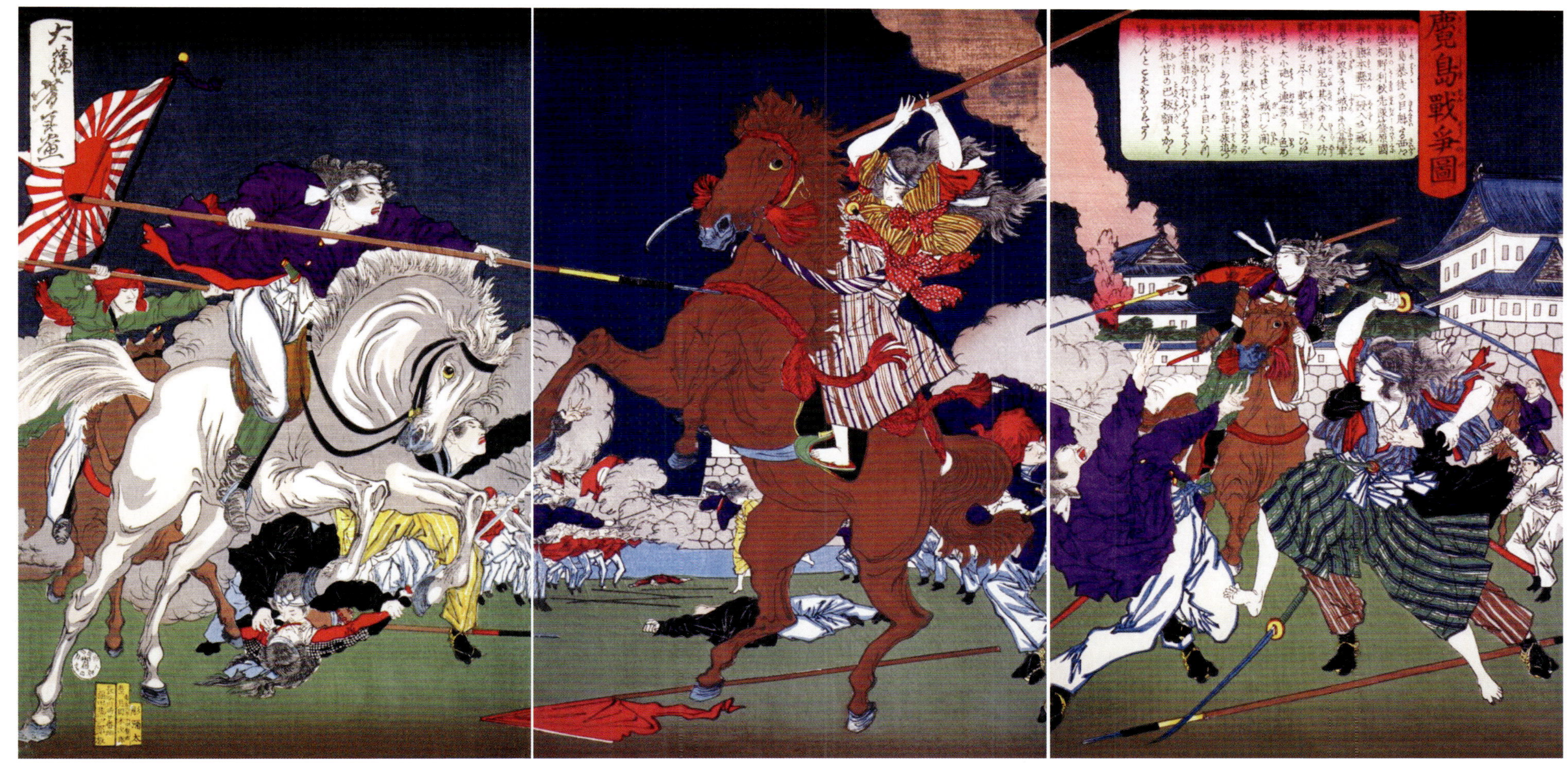

KAGOSHIMA SENSO

"War At Kagoshima"; 1877

One of numerous illustrations by Yoshitoshi showing a battle at Kumamoto castle, this time with female rebels attacking govermnent forces.

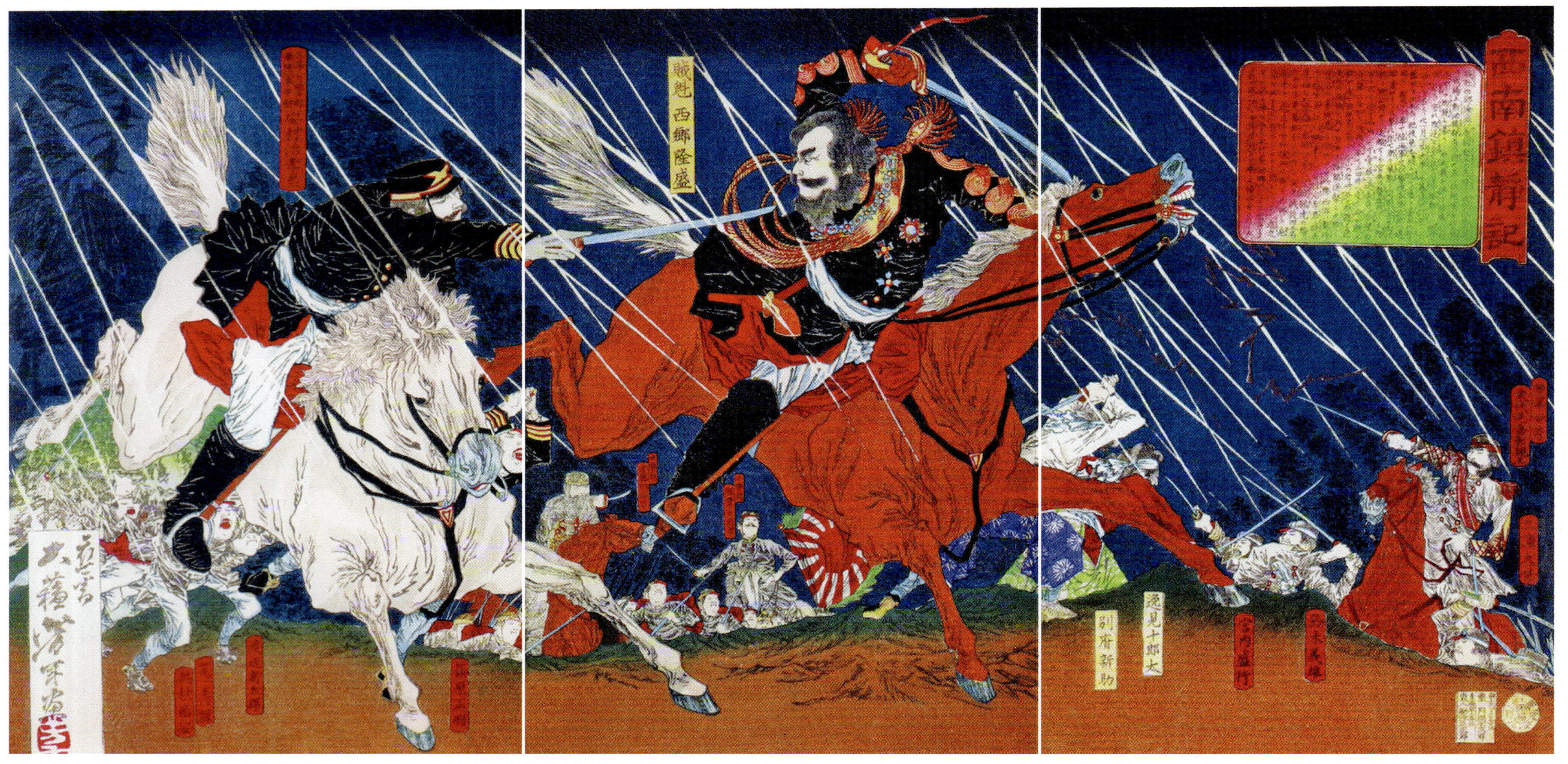

SEINAN CHINHOKI

"Seinan Pacification News Report"; 1877
Horseback duel in the rain between rebel leader Saigo Takamori and a government trooper.

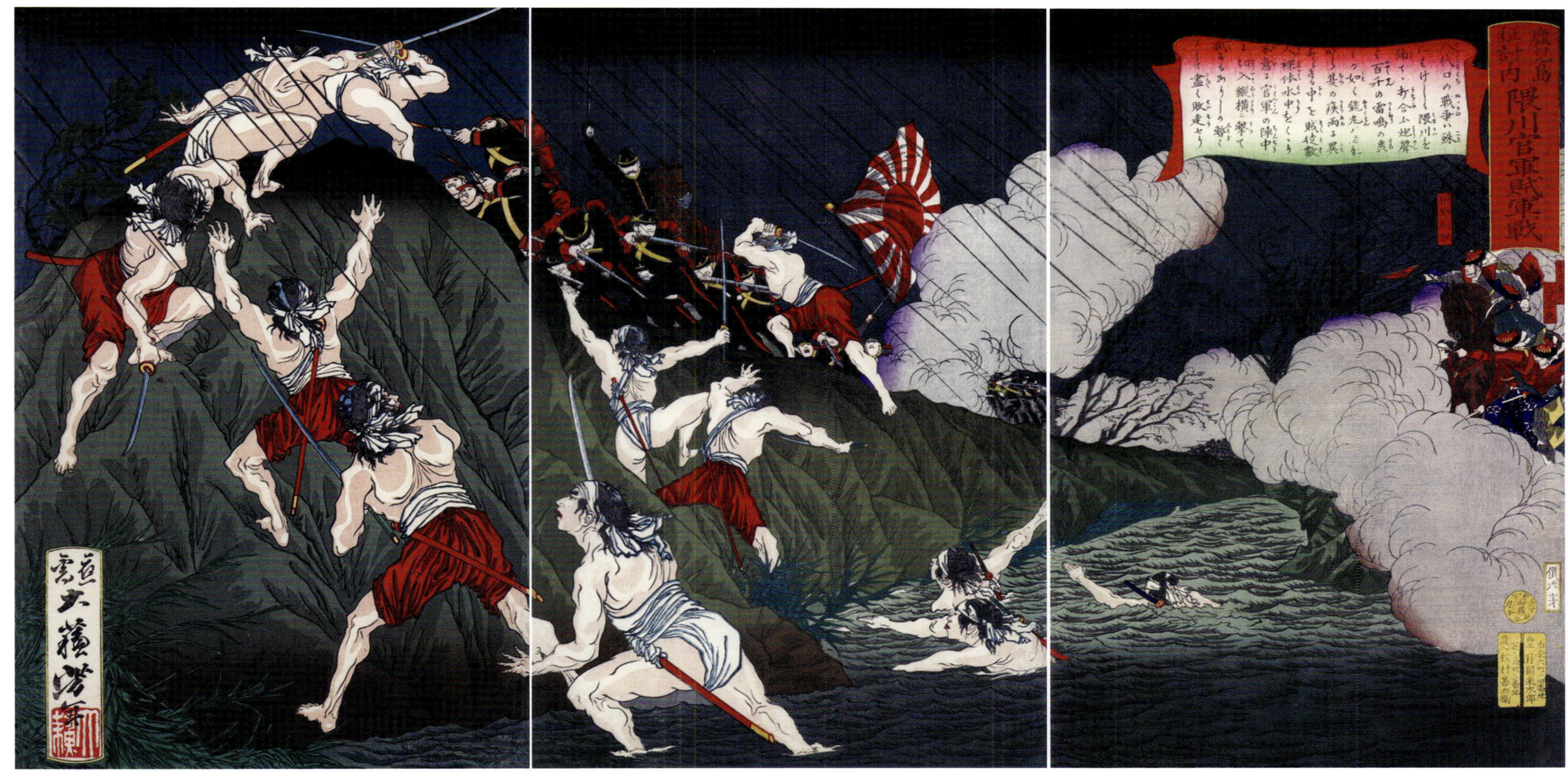

KAGOSHIMA SEITO NAI KUMAKAWA KANGUN ZOKUGUN SEN

"Chronicle Of The Subjugation Of Kagoshima: Clash Of Government Forces And Rebels At Kumagawa"; 1877
A nocturnal, rain-driven battle between two starkly contrasted factions, the uniformed government troops and the half-naked Satsuma rebels, at the Kuma river near Kumamoto.

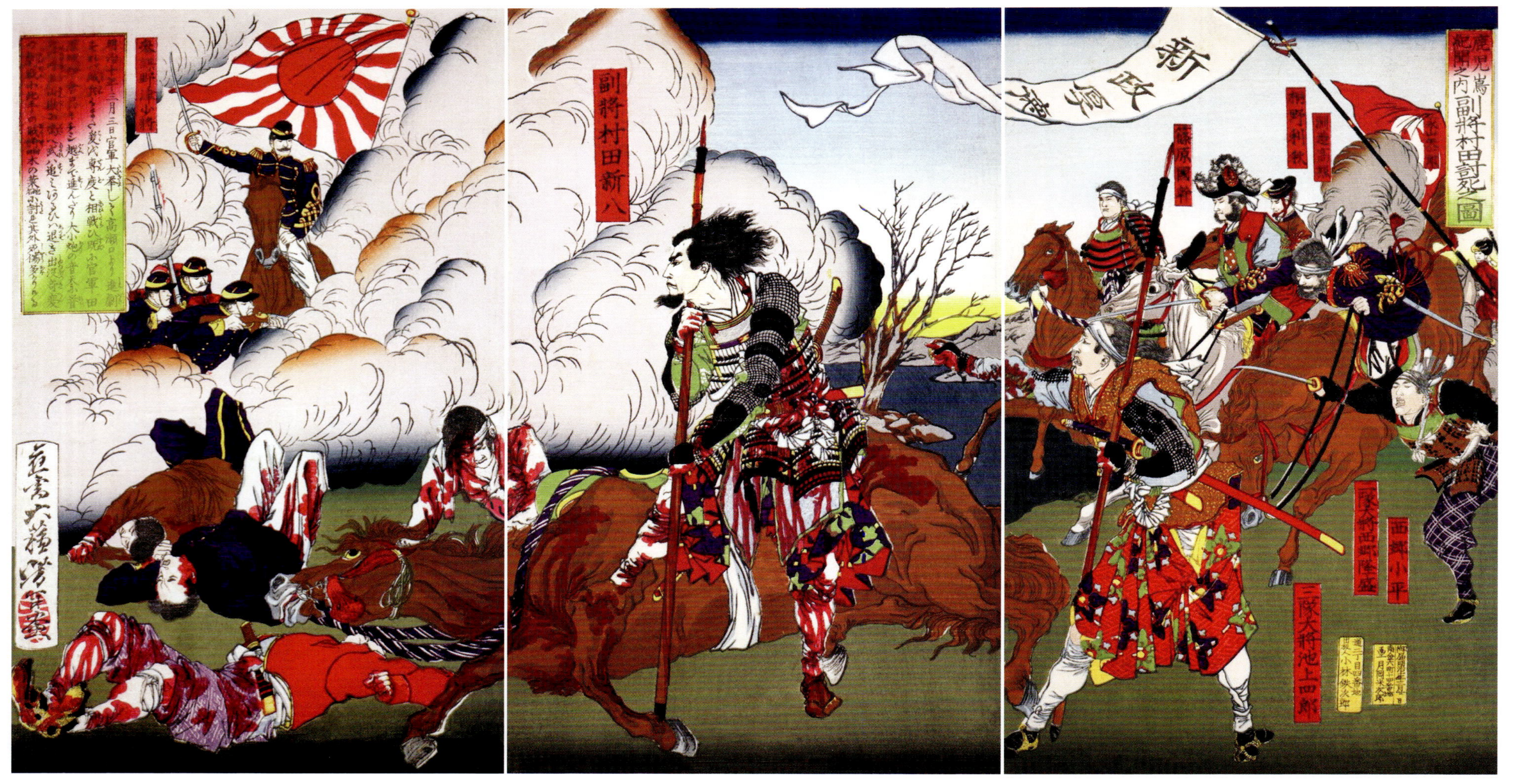

KAGOSHIMA KIBUN NO UCHI FUKUSHO MURATA UCHIJINI
"Annals Of Kagoshima: Battle-Death Of Second-In-Command Murata"; 1877
A scene from the battle of Shirayama, which marked the end of the Satsuma Rebellion; after witnessing the suicide-death of his leader Saigo Takamori, second commander Murata Sansuke also took his own life.

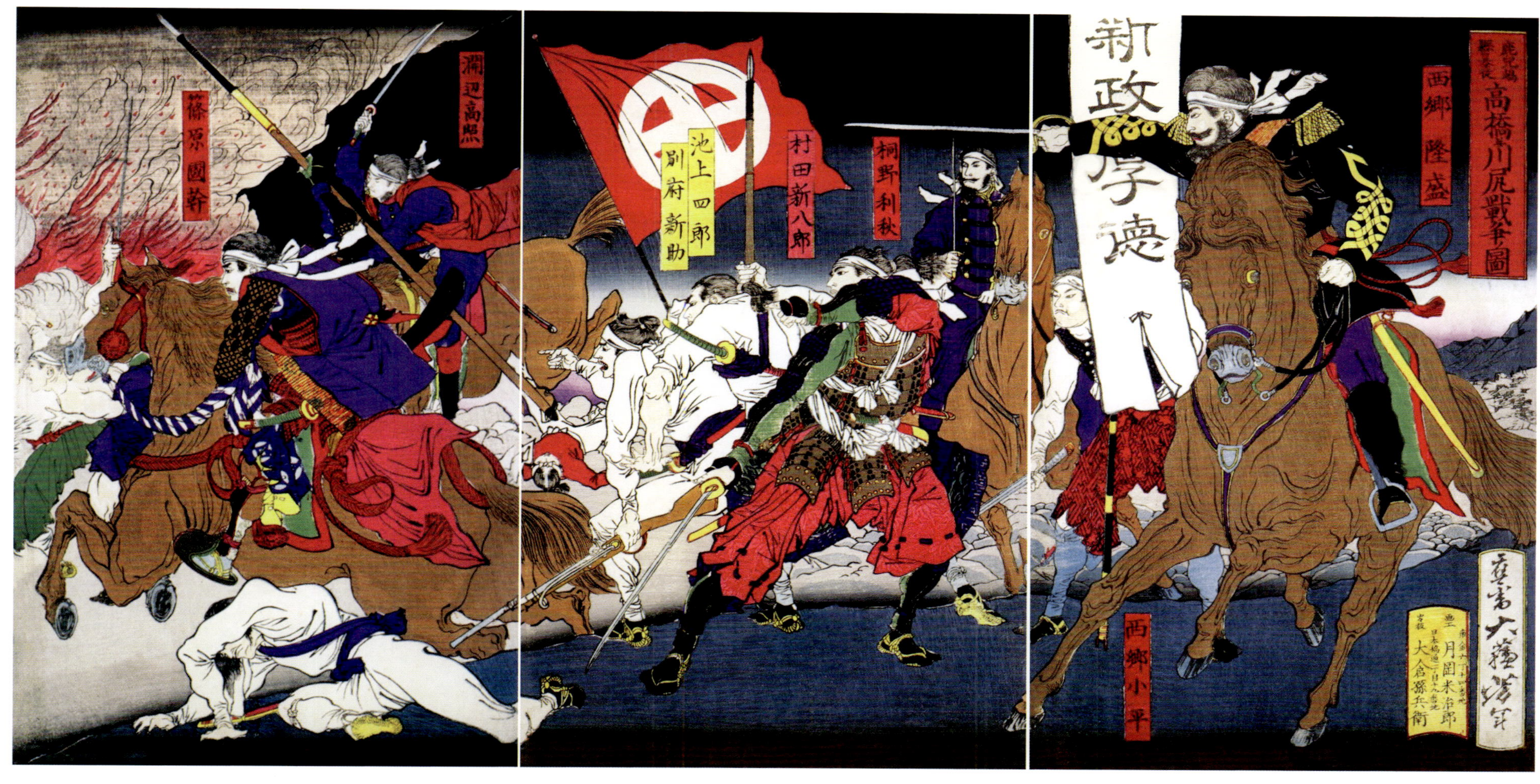

KAGOSHIMA-KEN BOTO TAKABA NARABI KAWAJIRI SENSO
"War At Takaba-Kawajiri In Kagoshima"; 1877
One of Yoshitoshi's most dynamic Kagoshima illustrations. Rebel leader Saigo Takamori is shown in the right-hand panel directing his troops into battle, while other notable figures represented include *samurai* Kirino Toshiaki and Beppu Shinsuke.

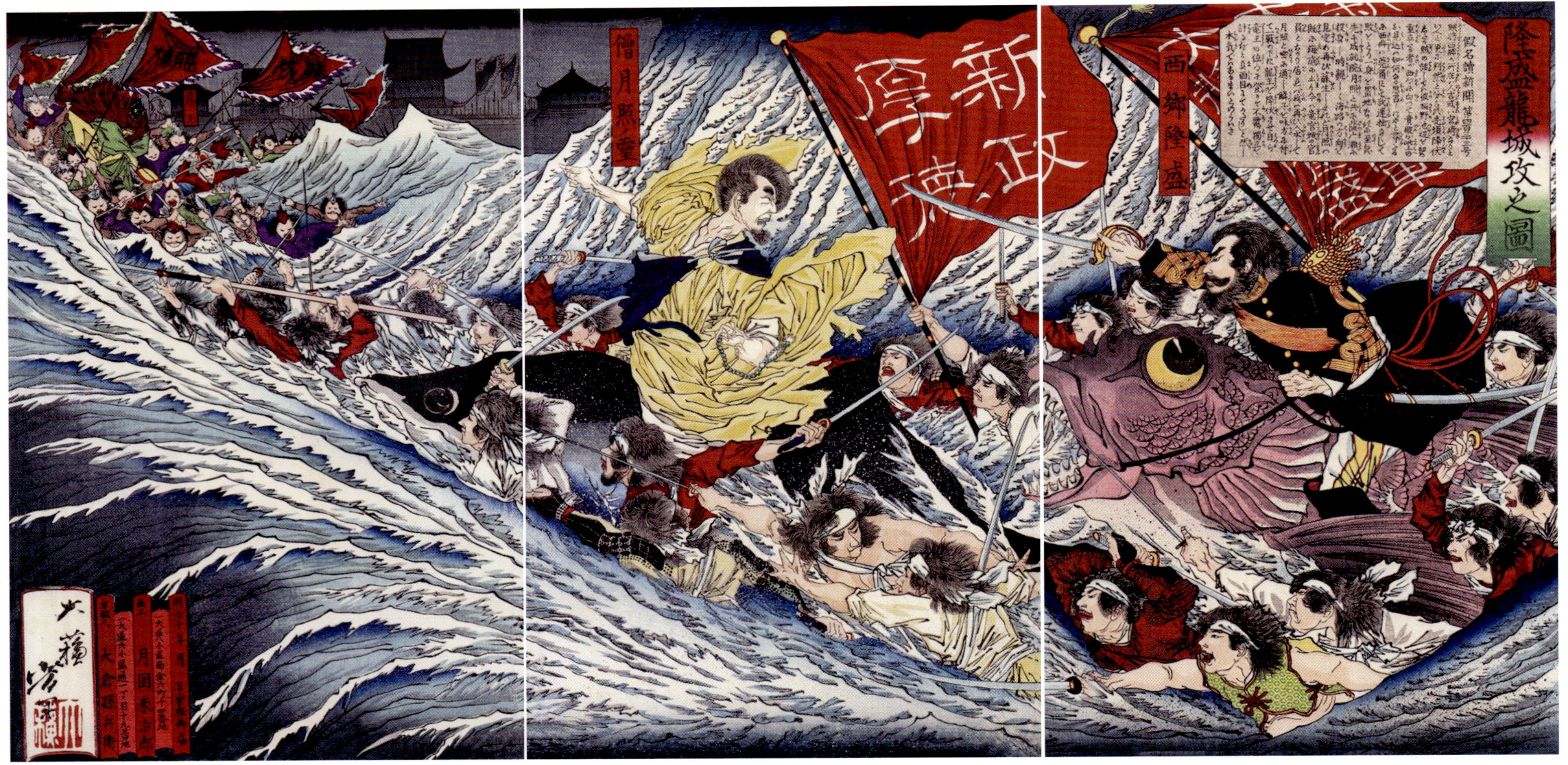

TAKAMORI RYU-JO ZEME
"Takamori Storms The Dragon Palace"; 1877
Yoshitoshi created a rare (for 1877) fantasy illustration with this mythic depiction of rebel leader Saigo Takamori, who is shown leading an oceanic charge towards the palace of Ryujin, the Dragon-King. Presumably intended as an allegory of Takamori's struggle against the Imperialists.

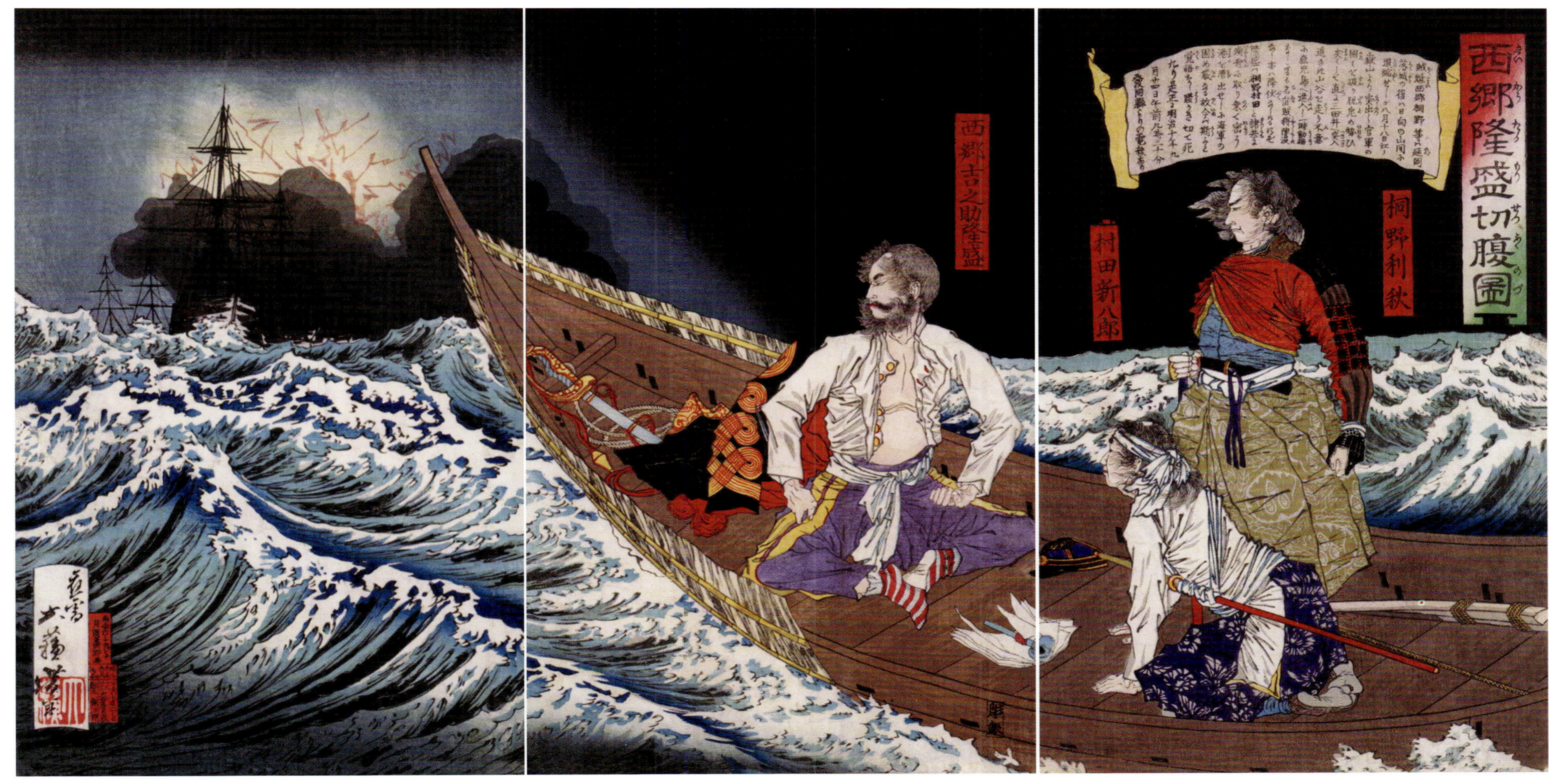

SAIGO TAKAMORI SEPPUKU

"Suicide Of Saigo Takamori"; 1877

Yoshitoshi's romanticized depiction of Takamori's death sees him serenely drifting out to sea, accompanied by the *samurai* Murata Sansuke and Kirino Yoshiaki, where his corpse might be sunken without trace after an honourable death. In reality, it is believed that the rebel leader was crippled by a bullet wound to the femoral artery at the battle of Shiroyama, and beheaded by his loyal follower Beppu Shinsuke. Some say that Takamori's head was never found.

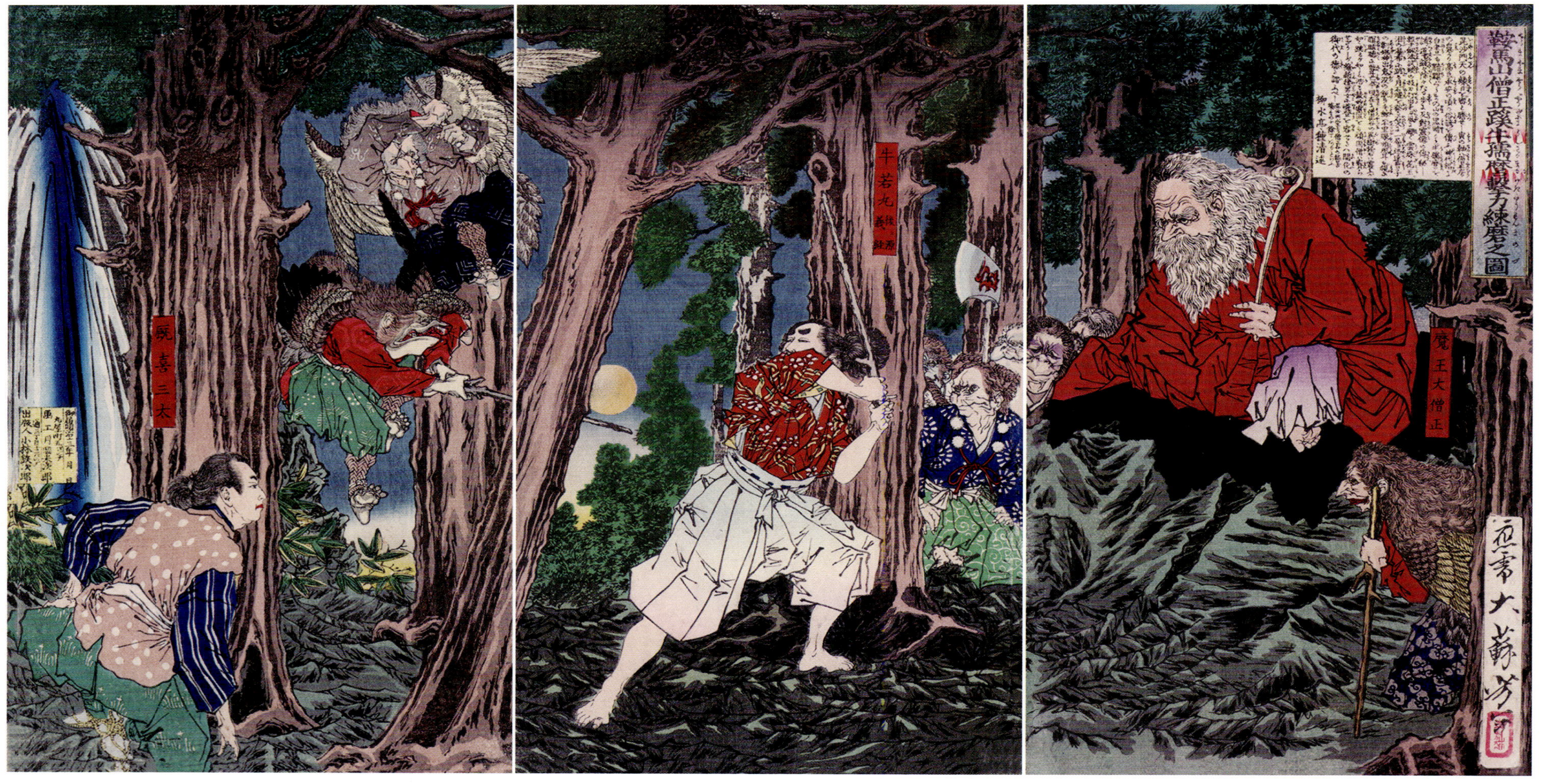

KURAYAMA SOJOKEI NI USHIWAKAMARU GEKITO REMMA

"Ushiwakamaru Learns Swordsmanship From Sojobo At Kurayama"; 1880
The young warrior Yoshitsune is trained in martial arts and combat by the king of the *tengu*. A new version of a scene first illustrated as a triptych by Yoshitoshi in 1865, and which derives from Kuniyoshi's definitive print of 1851. A sign that after years of war documentation Yoshitoshi was ready to explore historical subjects and myth once again in a new, refined style which was now much closer to Western aesthetics.

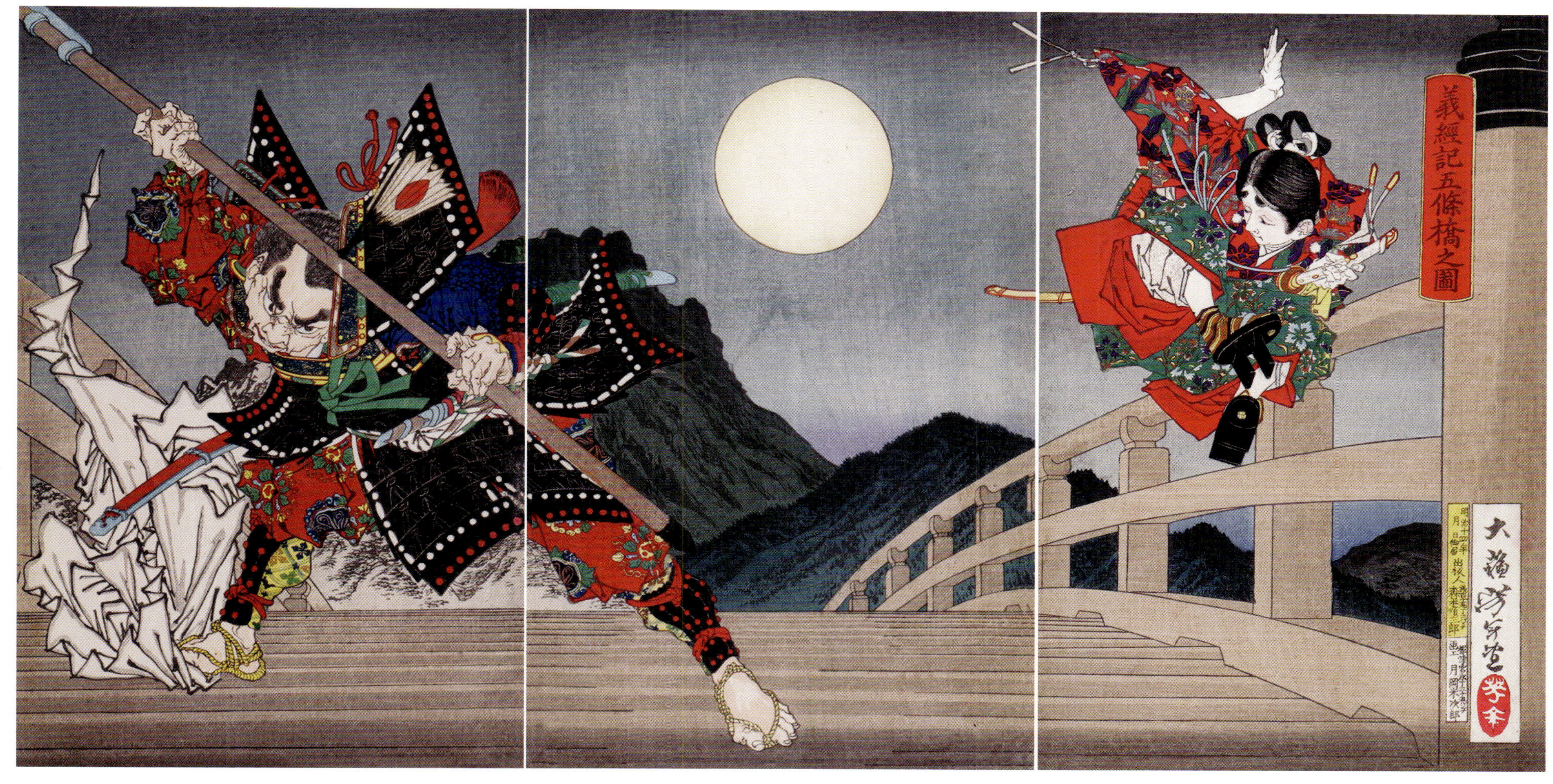

GIKEIKI GOJO-BASHI

"Annals Of Yoshitsune: Gojo-Bashi"; 1881

Another myth from the life of Yoshitsune revisited by Yoshitoshi, this time the besting of the warrior-monk Benkei on Gojo bridge by the boy Ushiwaka. This illustration showcased a striking new triptych design strategy by the artist, placing the main figures in the far left and far right panels as opposed to either left and centre or right and centre.

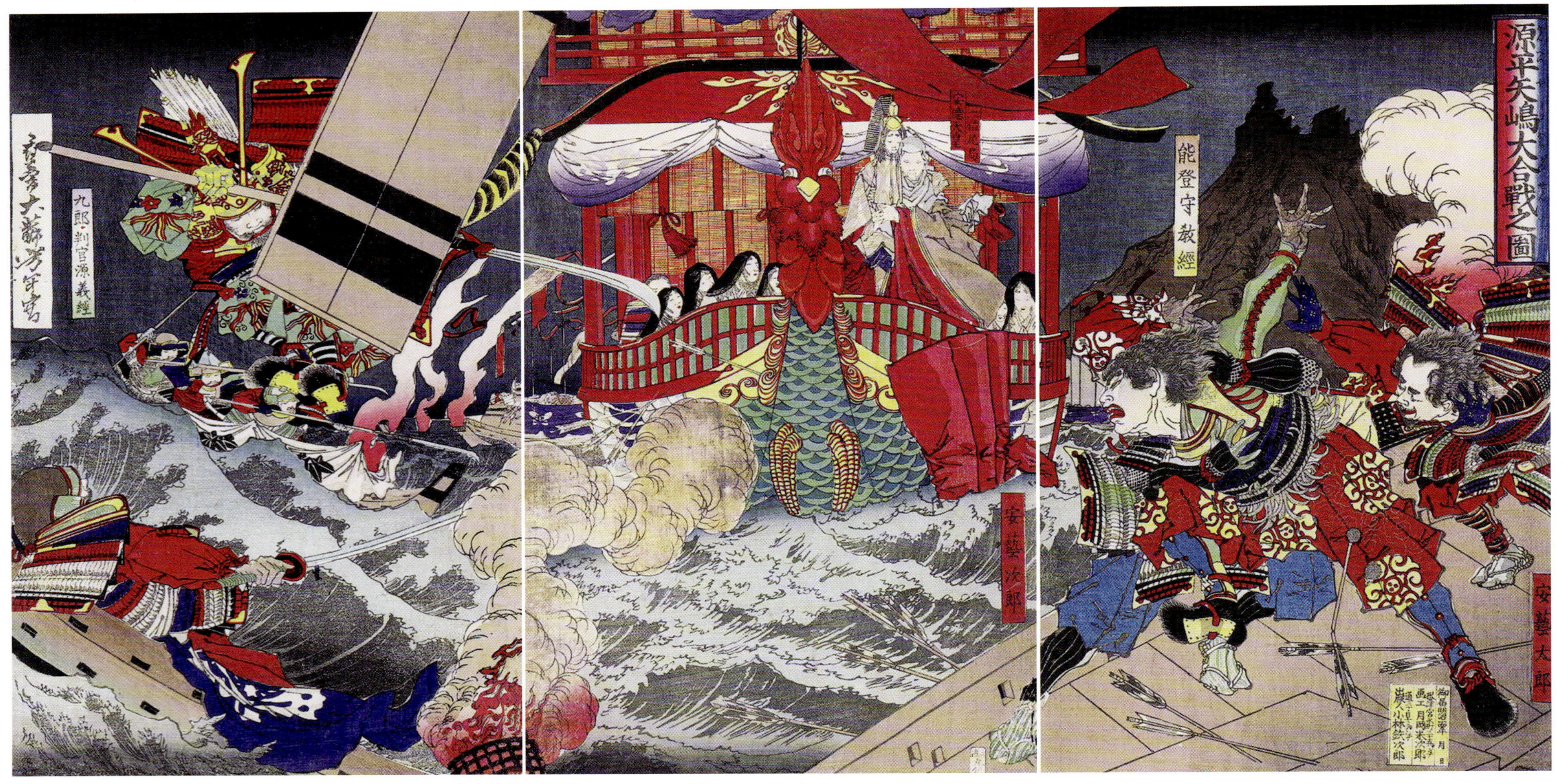

GENPEI YASHIMA DAIKASSEN

"The Great Genpei War Battle Of Yashima"; 1881

The legendary "eight-boat" leap by Yoshitsune at Yashima, with Taira royalty watching from their flagship.

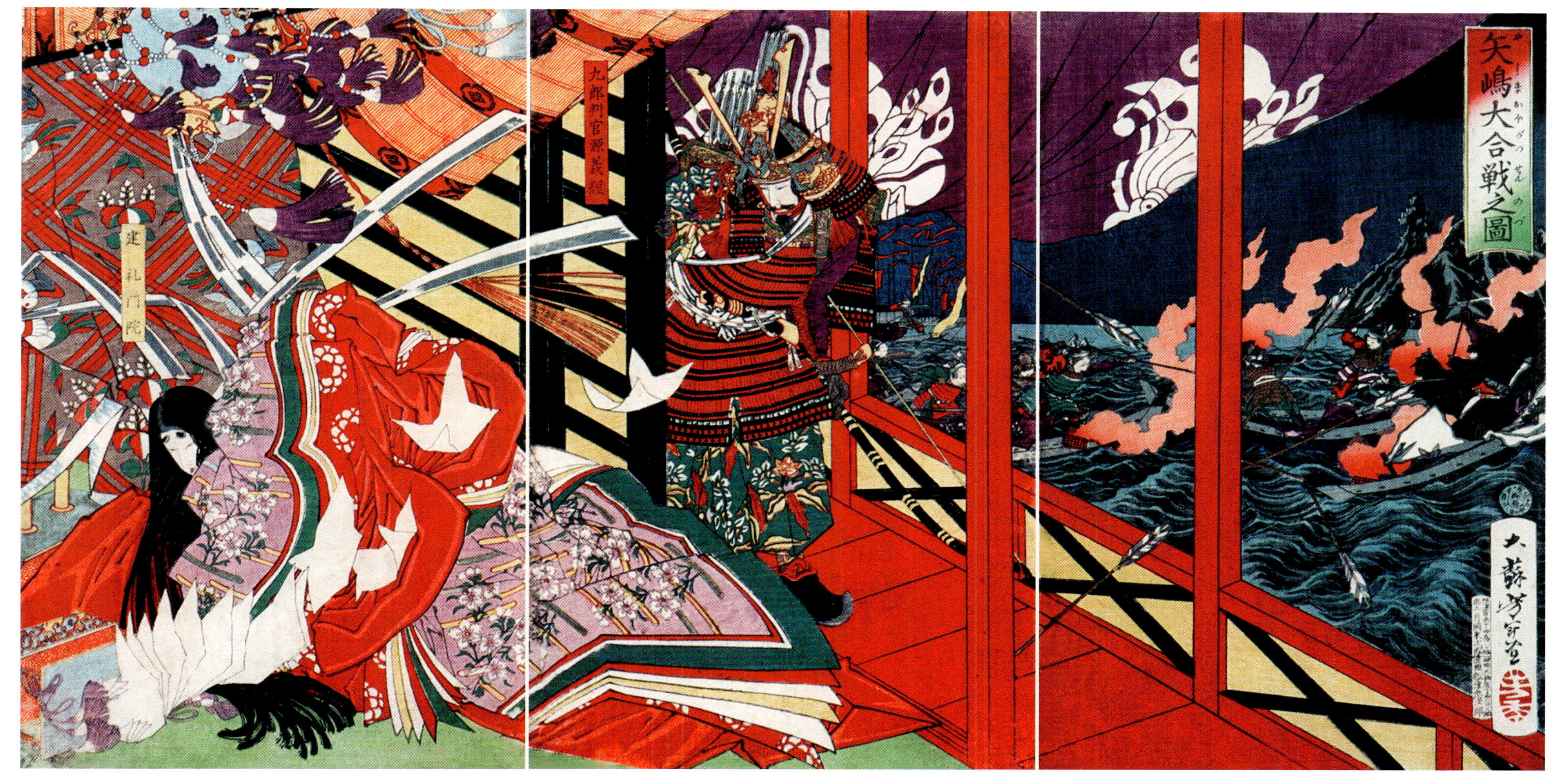

YASHIMA DAIKESSEN

"The Great Battle Of Yashima"; 1881

A different perspective on the battle of Yashima compared to Yoshitoshi's earlier illustrations, this triptych depicts Yoshitsune discovering Kenreimonin, daughter of Taira no Kiyomori and mother of the child emperor Antoku, aboard one of the Taira ships. Kenreimonin would be the only imperial survivor of the climactic Minamoto-Taira clash at Dan-no-Ura, reputedly being rescued after trying to drown herself.

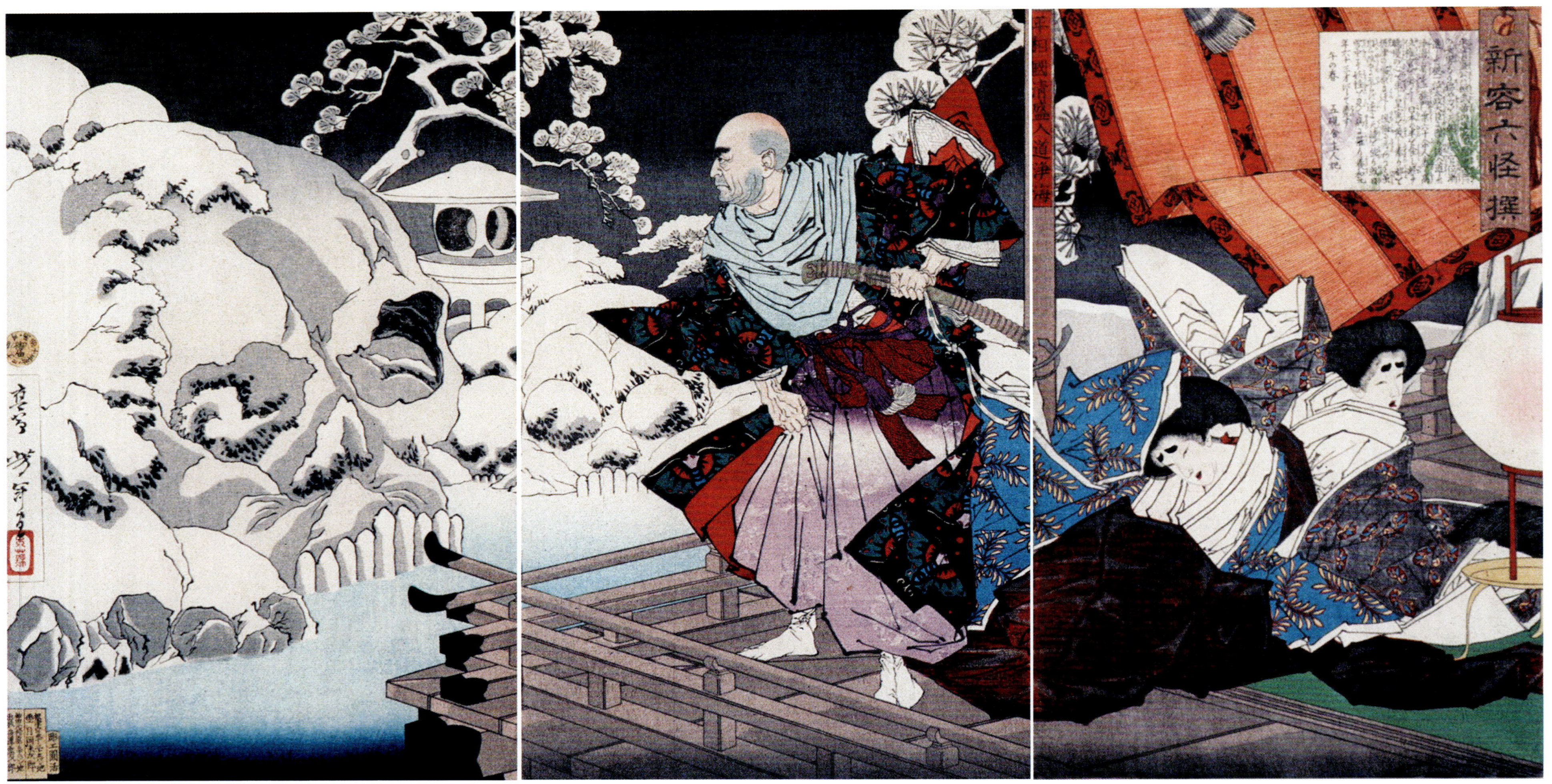

SHINYO ROKKAISEN
"Six Monsters With New Shapes"; 1882
The incipient madness of Taira-no-Kiyomori, haunted by guilt over his past crimes, who gazes out at his snow-covered garden and sees only skulls and bones, apparitions of his dead victims. A tribute to Hiroshige's classic design of 1845 and a classic example of the "double image". Seemingly the first of a projected six-triptych series, for which no other designs are known to exist.

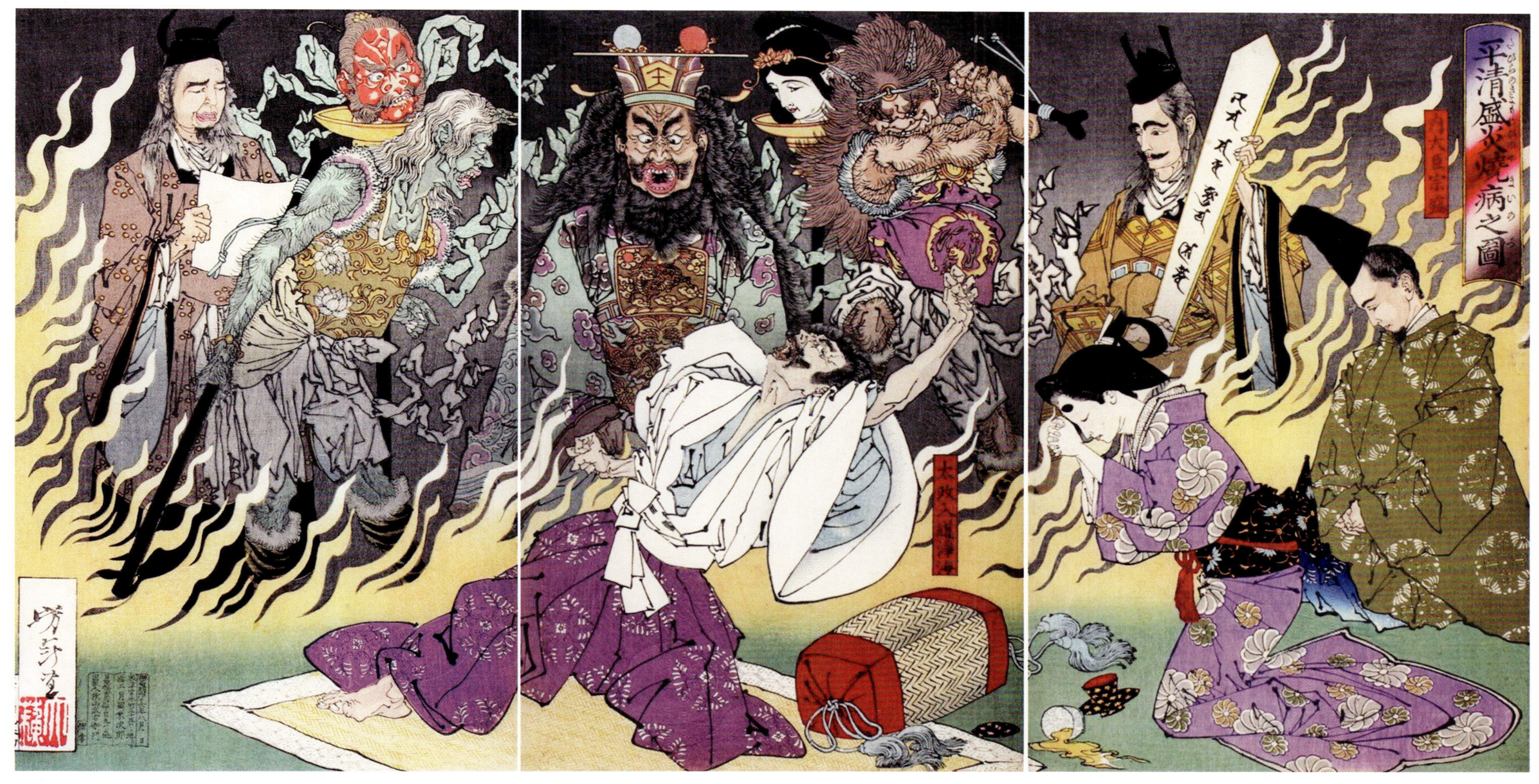

TAIRA NO KIYOMORI HINO YAMAI

"Taira-no-Kiyomori Burns With Fever"; 1883

Kiyomori, conqueror of the Minamoto clan in 1159, was finally struck by a boiling fever which tortured him with hallucinations of Enma, King of Hell, attended by demons and the ghosts of his victims. It is said that when he finally died, his corpse was too hot to touch for several hours.

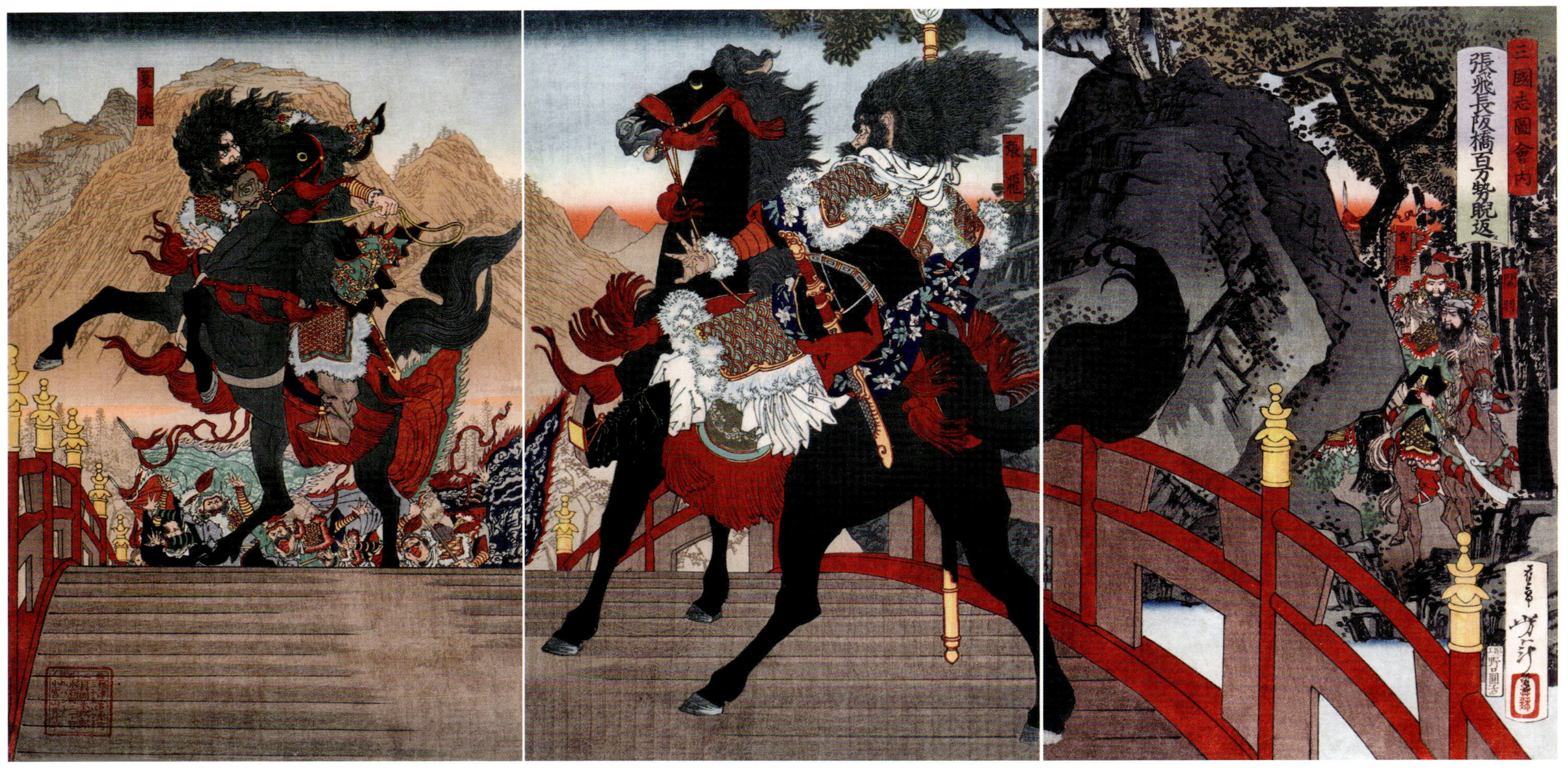

SANGOKUSHI ZUE NO UCHI CHOHI CHOHAN-KYO HYAKUMANZEI NIRAMIKAESU
"Scenes From *Sangokushi*: On Changban Bridge, Chohi Glares Back At One Million Foe"; 1884
Like Kuniyoshi before him, Yoshitoshi elected to illustrate scenes from the vast 5th century Chinese text *Sanguózhi* ("Records Of The Three Kingdoms"), known in Japanese as *Sangokushi*. This triptych depicts a famous episode in the year 208 when the warrior Zhang Fei (Chohi) deployed his few horsemen to hide in woods and make a massive commotion, fooling pursuers who believed a deadly ambush awaited them should they dare follow Zhang Fei across the bridge.

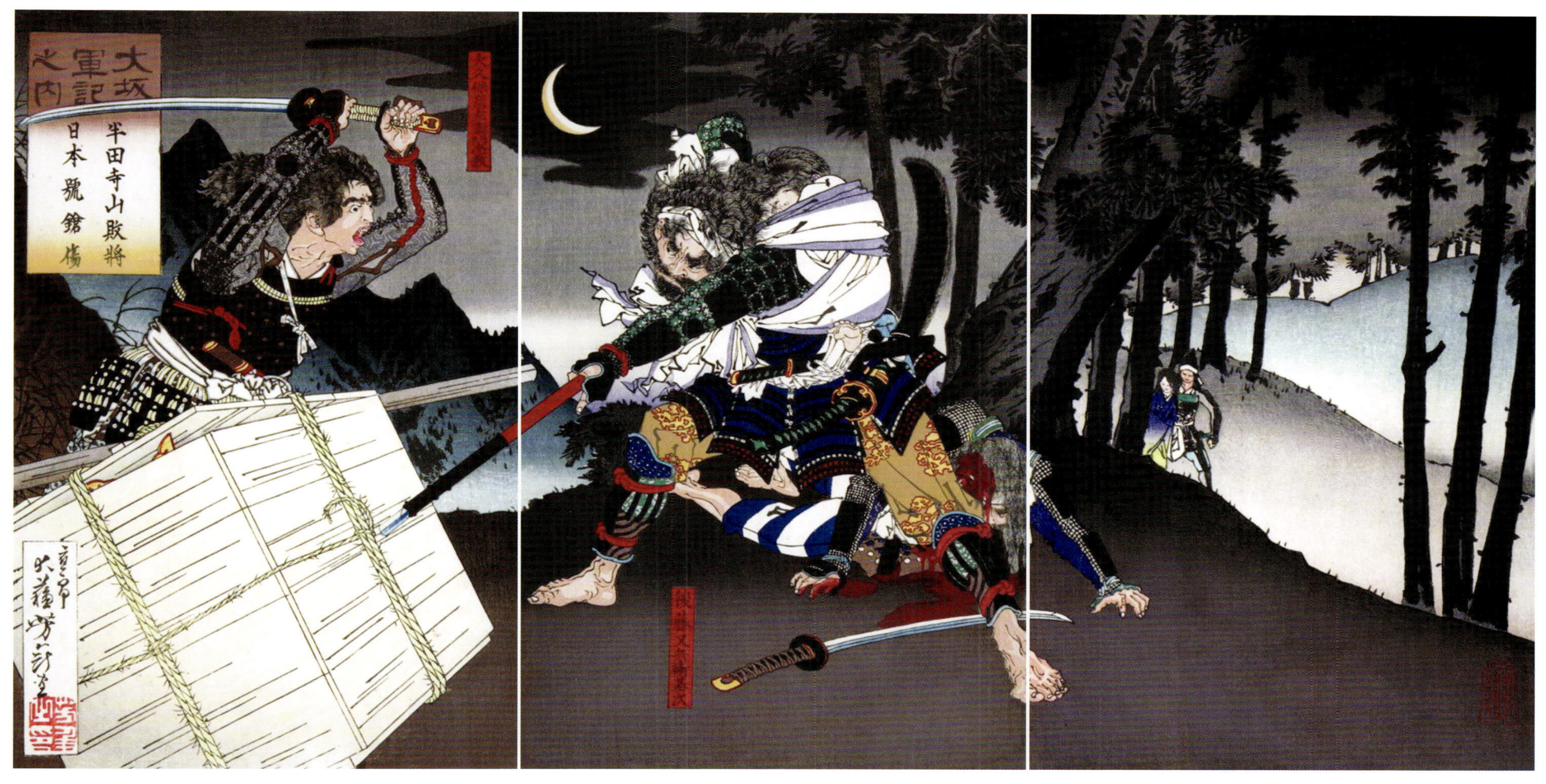

OSAKA GUNKI NO UCHI

"Osaka War Chronicle"; 1884

An illustration depicting events during the siege of Osaka of 1614-15, in which the Tokugawa shogunate waged a war of total destruction against the Toyotomi clan. The image shows a *samurai* follower of Tokugawa Ieyasu protecting a fallen general with a spear-wound from an attack by a follower of Toyotomi Hideyori.

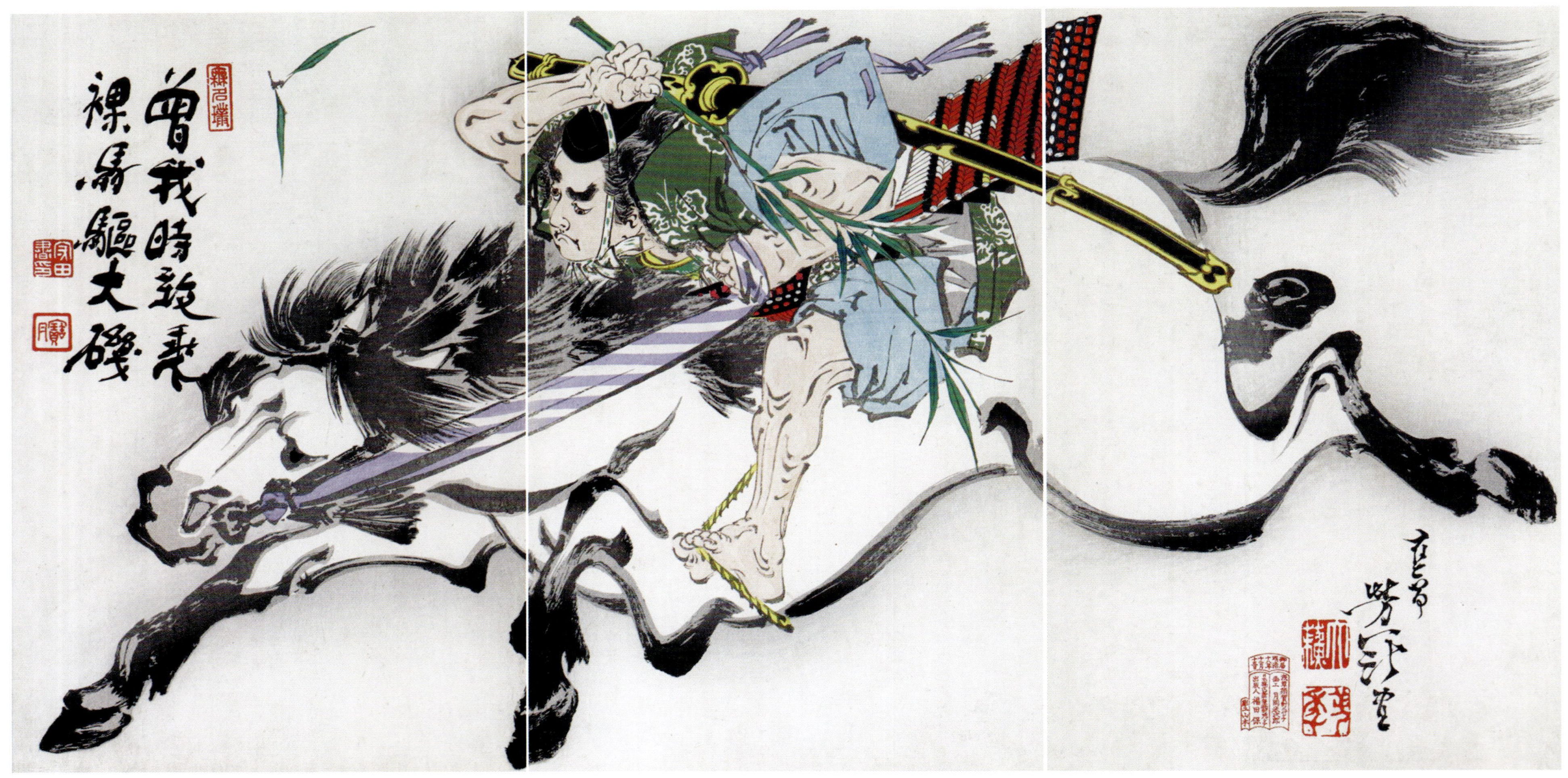

SOGA TOKIMUNE NORI HADAKAUMA KAKERU OISO

"Soga Tokimune Galloping Bareback To Oiso"; 1885

In this image derived from *Soga Monogatari*, Soga Goro Tokimune is depicted on a crazed ride to Oiso to join his brother before embarking on their infamous revenge rampage. In a significant change of style Yoshitoshi drafted this illustration using impressionistic brush-strokes, calligraphy and an empty background space, liberating his subject to convey unfettered velocity.

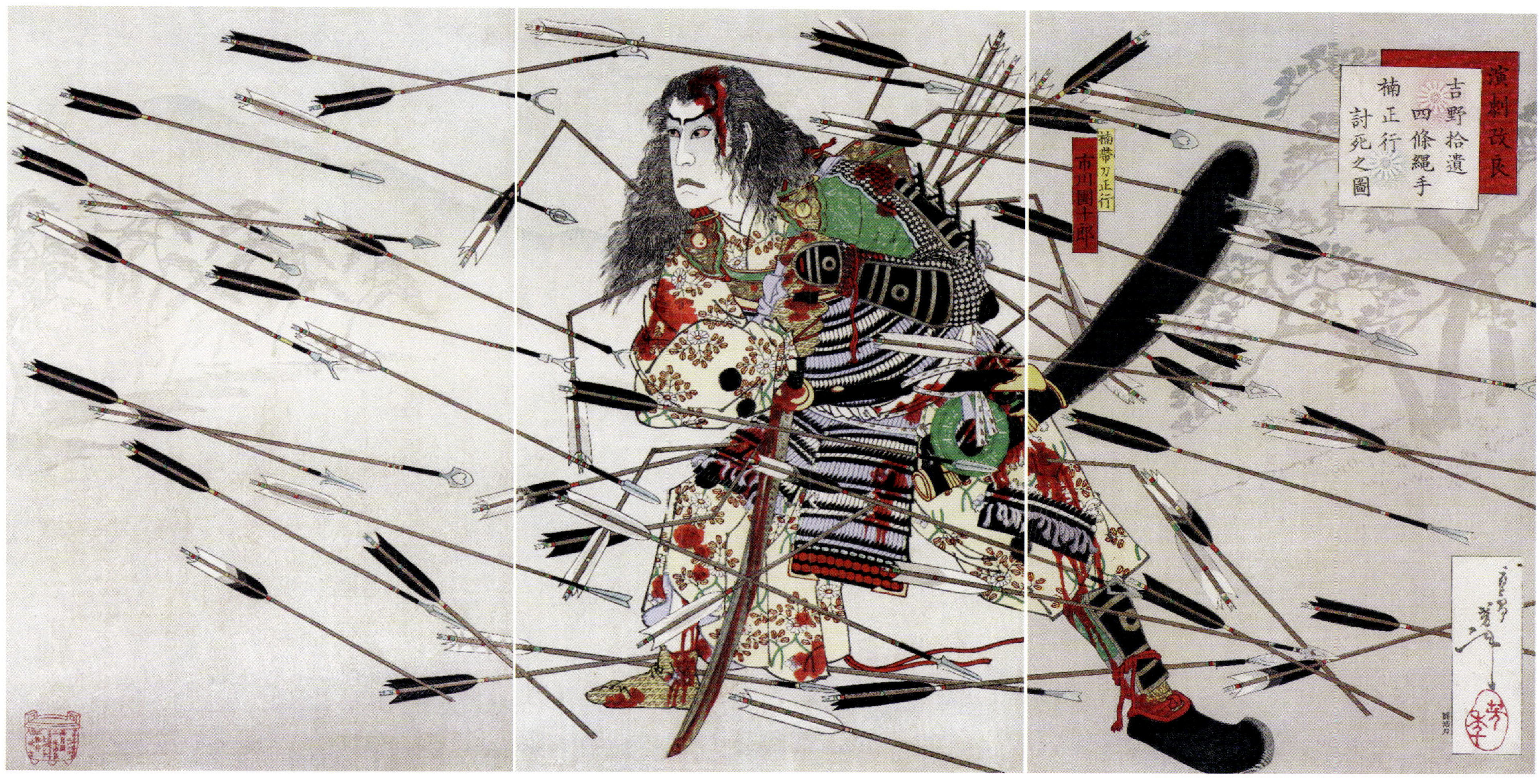

ENGEKI KAIRYO YOSHINO SHU KUSUNOKI MASATSURA UCHIJINI

"Reformed Theatre: The Battle-Death Of Kusunoki Masatsura From *Yoshino Shui*"; 1886

A different kind of warrior triptych from Yoshitoshi, this *yakusha-e* (actor print) is a *mitate* (imaginary portrait) of the famous *kabuki* actor Ichikawa Danjuro IX in the role of Kusunoki Masatsura from the play *Yoshino Shui Meika No Homare* ("Gleaning Praise For A Famous Poem At Yoshino"), which in reality was never produced for the stage. The play was the first offering from the Engeki Kairyokai, a society which in the mid-1880s demanded a shift towards a more modernized form of theatre; the script was presented at a gathering attended by Danjuro and other luminaries, but none were inclined to validate it. The play was based upon the life and death of the *samurai* Kusunoki, a supporter of the Southern Imperial Court during Japan's Nanbokucho Wars of the 14th century who was killed at the battle of Shijonawate in 1348, but not before composing a famous death poem on the Nyoirin temple door in Yoshino.